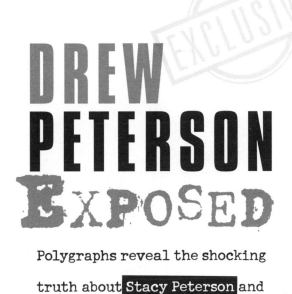

DREW PETERSON EXPOSED

Polygraphs reveal the shocking

truth about Stacy Peterson and

Kathleen Savio.

DREW PETERSON
EXPOSED

Polygraphs reveal the shocking
truth about Stacy Peterson and
Kathleen Savio.

BY DEREK ARMSTRONG

KÜNATI

LARGO, USA

DREW PETERSON EXPOSED

For information, contact Kunati Inc., Book Publishers in Canada. USA: 6901 Bryan Dairy Road, Suite 150, Largo, FL 33777 USA Canada: 75 First Street, Suite 128, Orangeville, ON L9W 5B6 CANADA. E-mail: info@kunati.com.

FIRST EDITION

Designed by Kam Wai Yu
Persona Corp. | www.personaco.com

ISBN-13: 978-1-60164-187-8   EAN 9781601641878
Non-Fiction / Current Affairs / Investigative News

Published by Kunati Inc. (USA) and Kunati Inc. (Canada).
Provocative. Bold. Controversial.™

http://www.kunati.com

TM—Kunati and Kunati Trailer are trademarks owned by Kunati Inc.
Persona is a trademark owned by Persona Corp.
All other trademarks are the property of their respective owners.

IMPORTANT NOTE

Where a proper name or brand is spelled incorrectly, this is generally the way the quoted person or media source spelled the word. We have not corrected quoted spellings. Materials such as timelines or statements provided by outside sources are reproduced as received. We have not edited these materials.

An Important Note On Sources and Content

This is a book-length news story containing never before disclosed information about Drew Peterson, suspected in the disappearance of Stacy Peterson and the death of Kathleen Savio. The results of two long-awaited polygraphs administered to Drew Peterson, directly questioning him about the disappearance of wife Stacy Peterson and the death of third wife Kathleen Savio, are "breaking news" in this book, closely guarded results that I report on for the first time. In addition, the majority of this work discloses and "exposes" never-before-published materials from exclusive interviews with Drew Peterson.

IMPORTANT: To avoid slowing down the story and prose to the point of tedium, the author has chosen to omit the word ALLEGEDLY as a qualifier of any current event, comment, action, quotation, opinion, characterization or pending legal matter. In reading this book, you agree that the word "allegedly" or "alleged" is understood to be present in any apparently conclusive statement by any party (including those quoted), and its absence is strictly a style choice to prevent pace bog. The author believes all persons are "innocent until proven guilty in a court of law" and readers agree and understand the author's statements herein are meant to be read in this context. "He is guilty" should be read, "He is allegedly guilty."

Since this is a current news "crime" story, focused on very public events, the author has written it to be informational and educational. I am a Canadian Association of Journalists member and professional writer. For this book, I interviewed many people for hundreds of hours, and conducted an inquiry using common investigative journalism techniques, including interrogation, fact-checking, background checks of publicly available criminal, financial, court, and personal records, and many other legal means. Quotes from other media sources are short and used with permission or under FAIR USE provisions of copyright, in the same way other journalists use these provisions. My purposes for quoting other sources are those specifically addressed by the fair use provision: (1) criticism and comment, (2) scholarship and research, (3)

news reporting and (4) teaching (particularly relevant to current affairs and historical topics). Fair use quotes are sometimes (but not always) in quotation marks, indented or otherwise set off, and fully credited, unless in the form of a summary or commentary, in which case sources are usually provided in the endnotes and bibliography.

Other quotes and summaries of events are derived from exclusive interviews with people featured in this book, including exclusive and extensive taped interviews with Drew Peterson, and others which are strictly protected by the copyright on this work. Every effort was made to verify background information where possible. In most cases, quoted comments are the opinions of those interviewed, not of the author. Some chapters and sections are written in a narrative story-telling style. These are retellings or dramatizations of stories originally delivered in interviews or researched from other sources. In the interests of impartial and credible reporting, as many sources as possible are quoted to produce a balanced report. The author generally has not changed the names of people mentioned in this book if they've been previously characterized in published media reports. The author accepts no liability or responsibility for the opinions of others, generally quoting them for the purposes of full disclosure, commentary, criticism, news or education. The author accepts no liability for information quoted or summarized from interviews. These are the opinions of other people.

Photographs are normally credited. If not credited, they were shot by the author. Other photos are of historical interest and were provided by other parties with permission. Several were provided by Drew Peterson during interviews with the assurance he had the permission of those portrayed. Photographs of people in Drew Peterson's world are used only if the people shown have been publicly featured in high-profile media, thereby deemed "public figures" or people in the news. Again, all photographs are used for the purposes of news, commentary and education. As news and current affairs photos, model releases are not required. Photo credits are provided where known.

Table of Contents

A tired Drew Peterson, once a watch commander with Bolingbrook Police, now a "person of interest" or "suspect" in the disappearance of his fourth wife Stacy Peterson and pursued by the media as a person of interest in the death of his third wife Kathleen Savio. This photo was taken on day three of round-the-clock interviews, probably the reason he appears tired.

Author's photo

Photo courtesy of Brodsky & Odeh

Top: Drew Peterson in the author's hotel room in Chicago during a grueling interview session. Here he sorts through family pictures and shares anecdotes with the author.

Below: Drew Peterson's legal team, from left-to-right Andrew Abood, center Joel Brodsky, the legal team leader, and right a friend recently graduated from law school.

Author's photo

Satellite image on author's computer screen with Drew Peterson's Bolingbrook house circled.

Drew Peterson and his fourth wife Stacy.

Introduction

There can be no doubt Drew Peterson is guilty in the homicides of wives Stacy Peterson and Kathleen Savio. What other conclusion can we draw from the national media who have largely tried and convicted him, with spicy headlines such as: *"Is he a killer?"*[1] and *"Sgt. Drew Peterson Free Despite Two Murders"*?[2] or hip sound bites from Geraldo Rivera, proclaiming, "The media has convicted him with good reason."[3]

Any reasonable person must conclude his *alleged*[4] guilt from the ex-FBI profiler[5] who pointed out his lying body language on *Today*, and the newspaper columnists who wonder why he hasn't already been arrested. Caravans of media trucks flock to Peterson's quaint house at 6 Pheasant Chase Court in the bedroom community of Bolingbrook, Illinois, whenever a new rumor surfaces that "an arrest is imminent."[6] In an August 2008 public survey, 96 percent of Americans answered yes to the question "Did Drew Peterson have anything to do with Stacy's disappearance?"[7]

"Either I'm presumed guilty or I'm presumed innocent"

"Either I'm presumed guilty or I'm presumed innocent," suspect Drew Peterson said, in the first of several exclusive interviews for this book. "The media and most people seem to presume guilt— although people still ask for autographs."[8]

Popularity polls tend to support "presumed guilty" over "presumed innocent" among the general public.

The popular position
He's guilty of homicide in the cases of two of his wives as suggested by most mainstream media and the police, who automatically suspect "intimates" in any suspicious death.

The unpopular position
He's innocent and Stacy Peterson ran away, Kathleen died accidentally and most of America got it wrong.

Who can we believe? The experts, analysts, journalists and police? Or a cradle-robbing ex-cop and his hired-gun lawyer Joel Brodsky?

Neither the "guilty" side nor the "innocent" side is particularly convincing from the point of view of a court of law at this time, beyond the notion of "presumed innocent until proven guilty," but in the court of public opinion, the "guilty" scenario plays well. After all, how could FBI profilers, ex-detective Mark Fuhrman,[9] Illinois State Police detectives, FOX and CNN all be wrong? Everyone knows Geraldo's never wrong. Nancy Grace is sometimes wrong, but she speaks from the heart for victims everywhere. Not to mention neighbors, bloggers, family members of the alleged victims, a church pastor and most reasonable people. All of these people versus the lonely and arrogant voice of Drew Peterson who said, "Expose me for what I am. I'm no angel, but I'm no devil either."

The case for a damning and evil portrayal of Drew Peterson: witnesses came forward with stories of baby-sitting confessions, police-sanctioned wiretaps and heavy blue barrels "warm to the touch" that might contain bodies. There are family members who say both of Peterson's wives felt threatened, citing stories of a briefcase "full of letters"[10] from third wife Kathleen Savio in which she is said to have written, "his next step is to take my children away or to kill me." There's hearsay from Pastor Neil Schori, who claims Stacy confessed, "He killed Kathleen," and we know pastors can't lie, so it's all pretty convincing,[11] even though she returned home to Peterson after this extraordinary revelation. Most damning of all, Peterson has no alibi for the time of Stacy's disappearance, refused to search for his missing wife, projects an arrogant public persona, hates the media, and "cracks wise" with anyone who takes him on.

The case for innocence is simple: Drew says, "I didn't do anything."

And nearly everyone tells Peterson there's only one way to prove it.

"Drew, take a polygraph"

Since there seems to be no forensic or eyewitness evidence yet a veritable mountain of damning circumstances and hearsay, everyone hammers at Peterson, "Drew, take a polygraph."[12] On multiple occasions the police, journalists, the blogosphere, and various authors (myself included) have urged Peterson to strap himself in and get it over with. The "no" replies came so fast and furious from Drew Peterson, you'd think we were inviting him to strap in for a roasting in "ol' sparky." He even turned down an offer to take a test on the popular game show *The Moment of Truth* on FOX TV.[13]

On advice of his lawyer, the always exuberant Joel Brodsky, Peterson repeatedly said no.

To Jamie Colby of FOX TV, who asked, "why not take a lie detector test if, in fact, you had nothing to do with Stacy's disappearance?" Drew replied, "I will if my lawyer says it's okay."

It wasn't okay.[14]

On *Larry King Live* a viewer asked: "Are you willing to take a polygraph test concerning Stacy's disappearance?"[15]

Peterson referred the decision to his lawyer. "If he tells me to take one, I'll take one."

But his lawyer, Joel Brodsky, said no.

Two Extremes of Drew-mania—"Fry him!" or "Drew for President!"

Not to stand on something as inconvenient as the Bill of Rights and Miranda rights, two of Peterson's past friends allegedly wore a wiretap at the behest of Illinois State Police to record Peterson's conversations. Since Peterson had already invoked his right to counsel and silence, the rousing headlines "He's done" and "He's going away"[16] might mislead readers that such a tap was proper, legal or even likely. The soap opera took another bizarre twist later when one of these "wiretap friends," Lenny Wawczak, was arrested for assaulting Peterson. Then Wawczak's checkered criminal and financial past was disclosed on FOX TV. This is the succulent stuff of legend and talk shows, soap operas and tabloids, and frenetic blogosphere speculation.

The blog hype is uncensored fun, running from "Drew's a f**king murderer. Fry him,"[17] to "Drew for President!"[18] I'm sure even Peterson would not endorse either extreme, although he would probably get a chuckle out of this post on You Tube: "Even if he didn't do anything unlawful, that guy should be punished simply for being a colossal a**hole."[19]

A Drew and Stacy Peterson industry has arisen. Registered and not-so-registered charities raise funds for "Find Stacy Peterson" searches. Past friends' stories sell for tens of thousands of dollars to the *National Enquirer* and other media. Signed Drew baseball caps and tees sell on eBay. Some of the highest trafficked websites and blogs are exclusively dedicated to the Petersons, although the anti-Drew blogs outnumber pro-Drew blogs, by my count, 97 to 1. It's only a matter of time before a movie is announced, and can there be any doubt that "true crime" television broadcasts and other books are already on the production agendas?

Of course, Stacy Peterson is officially missing, and Kathleen Savio's death was pronounced accidental in the original coroner's inquest, but this doesn't add up to a very interesting story. After a spectacular exhumation of Savio, Peterson's third wife, the famous forensic "gun for hire" Doctor Michael Baden (of O.J. Simpson fame) declared the death "consistent with a homicide made to look like an accident."[20] Murder is the way to go if you want to sell newspapers or capture viewers—or sell books—the more sensational the better. Can there be any doubt that someone—and we all know who— murdered Stacy too? It only makes sense.

For myself, an author of crime books, it's hardly compelling to investigate yet another runaway mother and pursue nebulous sightings of Stacy Peterson in Florida, Asia and tropical islands. Homicide is a much steamier meal for writers, especially if the plate is heaped with such salty appetizers as a thirty-year age difference between spouses, infidelity, pedophilia, turncoat friends out for money, and an apparently remorseless ex-cop with "illegal" guns (see page 197). Sizzling hot scandal sells books, newspapers and air time. Connect the dots: custody battle, Stacy disappears, cradle-robbing husband, previous wife mysteriously dead—a soap opera of luscious scandal. It's pretty "consistent" with the prevailing theory that a notorious husband got rid of inconvenient wives.

My mind was long ago made up. Peterson looked guilty, sounded guilty, so he must be guilty. Allegedly guilty. (I tire of this word quickly, so indulge me by reading the word "allegedly" throughout this book wherever I sound conclusive, especially where my opinion is not supported by a court of law.)

By all accounts, I was about to meet someone as Satanic and notorious as the Night Stalker Richard Ramirez or Charles Manson.

"The moment you phoned Drew they knew about you."

In television interviews Peterson appeared big and imposing, an unflappable man impossible to intimidate. He remained inscrutable in the face of Larry King. He smiled through Matt Lauer's best cross-examination on *Today*. His team held their own when grilled by Nancy Grace of CNN, the famous on-screen lawyer who, according to a current lawsuit in Florida,[21] drove one guest to suicide after trademark "aggressive questioning." I am no Nancy Grace, so I hardly expected I could intimidate this veteran cop.

When I first met the bigger-than-life villain Drew Peterson, I was struck by how small he was. The man I met was hunched over with fatigue, making him appear at least two inches shorter than his

Top: View of Millennium Park from conference room of Brodsky and Odeh, where Drew Peterson took his first polygraph test. The blinds were closed for the test.

Bottom: Joel Brodsky explaining autopsy findings to the author. Joel is lead lawyer for the "Peterson team," a twenty-five-year criminal trial lawyer veteran who has appeared on numerous national television shows as an expert.

Author's photo

true height.

I was in conference with his lawyer Joel Brodsky, sitting in the law firm's lofty lake-view corner office in Chicago, arguing the merits of a polygraph—a lie-detector test—for Peterson.

In walked the "sinister man" himself.

"And here he is," Brodsky said, his animated, freckled face lighting up with a smile.

I turned in my chair, expecting cloven hooves and horns. Instead, I saw a tired-looking man in a sport shirt and jeans, noticeably greyer than on his last TV appearance. "There's a familiar face," I said, trying to sound light, but frankly crackling with tension.

"Sure," he answered simply, as if the very idea of notorious celebrity was exhausting.

I wondered if I would feel a cold chill as I shook hands with this man for the first time. After all, he was portrayed as a sociopath and psychopath in media coverage. Instead, I received a gentlemanly shake and nod that made me think of anyone's silver-haired father.

"How you doing?" Peterson asked in a low, friendly voice.

In place of the arrogant and flashy man I had seen on *Today* and *Larry King Live*, decked out in a suit and posturing with assertive spread legs and calm, folded hands, I met a man who hadn't shaved in days, with waxy bags under his eyes that betrayed stress and lack of sleep.

I wasn't able to reconcile months of media horror stories with a fairly typical middle-aged American father in jeans. The Drew Peterson I met crossed his legs, cupped his whiskered chin in his hands and looked entirely exhausted.

The tension wound up again a moment later when I asked about the ongoing Special Grand Jury. Peterson and Brodsky laid their cell phones on Brodsky's crowded desk and popped out their batteries.

"Drew's phone is tapped. They can listen with the batteries in, even if it's turned off," Brodsky explained with a self-assured grin. He requested I do the same. "The moment you called Drew, they knew about you."

Ooooo-kaaaaay. I hope I didn't roll my eyes, but I'm sure my eyebrows did lift visibly. I was pretty sure Illinois State Police had better things to do than tap my phone.

This had gone from an investigative story to 007 spoof in a heartbeat. Even though I doubted the far-fetched theory of cell batteries powering cell phone bugs (having made a mental note to use this in my next Alban Bane thriller),[22] this act of apparent paranoia did more to convince me I had to write this book. This would be an investigative writer's dream story.

I was prepared to write a stinging indictment of Mr. Peterson based on a steady diet of tabloid-style TV news coverage since October 2007, media stories which neatly lined up all the Peterson timelines into a most compelling series of damning circumstances, combined with my own belief, echoed in many newspaper columns, that Stacy Peterson would never have run away with another man and left two toddler children (mothers just don't do that, do they?)

I placed my digital voice recorder on the desk and spun it to make sure the twin microphones recorded every word.

"Why did you agree to do a polygraph now after declining so many requests from police and media before?"

"I think it's the thing to do," Drew answered simply, his voice at the same time sonorous and apparently genuine.

More pragmatic, lawyer Brodsky added, "I advised against it." His perpetually happy face became animated as he transformed into the advocate. He's a lot more personable and thoughtful than he appears on television, the kind of man who almost literally bounces out of his skin with excess energy and projects a sense of vitality that's oddly endearing. As with Drew, my impression of this man is almost entirely the opposite of the persona he projects on national TV. "But Drew always thought it was the thing to do from the beginning. Some day he may want to open a business, or go back to work. How can he do that with all this hanging over him?"

Over the next few weeks Peterson would be very forthright in answering my tough questions, revealing a dark side, especially in his weakness for women and gallows humor that has regularly plunged him into hot water with the media. I didn't sense arrogance so much as resignation. "Being presumed guilty in the media," he would later tell me in interviews, "just wears you out." I suppose my willingness to presume innocence allowed him to open up in interviews over the next few weeks. My style of interviewing is to listen. Eventually they say enough. Or too much.

I've spent a fair bit of time in the "dark and sinister" household of Peterson, met his children, investigated the investigators, and "exposed" Peterson's not entirely wholesome world.

We live in the age of instant TV and blogs

As an important personal sidebar, this book allowed me to pursue one of my favorite themes, often explored in my crime fiction, but described best by the *Daily Herald* of Chicago: "We live in an age of CourtTV, and MSNBC excess and Fox News hyperbole, and they all seem to take every other news organization down the same irresponsible path."[23] The *Daily Herald* went on to challenge the media about how fair it is to report suspects' names unless charges are imminent. They gave several examples of trial by media and the damage it can do, including Drew Peterson and JonBenet Ramsey, as reasons why they would not report on Drew Peterson:

"We don't identify crime suspects unless we know they are about to be charged, and there's no suggestion that Peterson is about to be charged with anything. Or that he ever will be. But look around at all the news media– locally and across the country—and goodness sakes, they're all over this thing. Every scandalous word and shred of gossip."

"The good and the bad."

In this first meeting I told Drew Peterson, "Understand that I'm going to report everything. The good and the bad. I won't hype or bash you, but I'm not going to hide the ugly. Can you live with that?"

Drew Peterson, always composed, nodded his head. "I have nothing to hide. I just want people to hear my side for a change."

I was prepared to let the investigation steer this book. *Drew Peterson Exposed* became the title before I began extensive interviews with this enigmatic, imperturbable, sometimes disturbing man. The mission was simple: expose and reveal whatever is discovered.

A few times during interviews, I would sit up, alarmed and surprised by a revelation, then he would laugh once more and we'd roll into another story of yet another past infidelity.

Tragedy, comedy of errors, tabloid sensation or *danse macabre*: regardless of classification, this is a story with no ending, and some might therefore argue, not a story at all.

Drew Peterson Exposed reveals new information, the results of sometimes too-candid interviews, the never-before-published polygraph results and, also for the first time, an "official" timeline of events from Drew Peterson. Maybe one day soon, we'll have an ending. Hopefully, at that time I can finish this story.

In the grand tradition of both real and literary detectives, my own Alban Bane included, it is always important to fully understand the "suspects," beginning with their history and ending with the circumstances, motivations, witness testimonies and, with luck, hard forensic evidence. In this book, I explore all of these elements as they currently stand, and reveal new evidence and information: exclusive interviews over hundreds of hours that include Peterson's life and history (the many infidelities and pranks that shaped the personality of our "suspect"), his motivations (the barely believable events that led up to October 28, 2007 when Stacy Peterson disappeared), the circumstances (a conflicted mess of timelines that I reverse-engineer), the "witnesses" (a true soap opera of discreditable conduct), the physical evidence (pretty hard to find in this case), and finally, most telling of all, the first-ever polygraphs administered to Sergeant Drew Peterson concerning the disappearance of Stacy Peterson and the death of Kathleen Savio.

Sociopath or Victim?

You must judge for yourself if ex-Sergeant Drew Peterson, suspected in the disappearance of fourth wife Stacy Peterson and the death of third wife Kathleen Savio, is monster or victim. Clearly, as depicted in the media, Drew Peterson can be nothing less than a sociopath with organized psychopathic qualities. He is attributed with:

- Coldly planning and executing the murder of two wives
- Meticulously removing all trace evidence from the crime scenes
- Committing these murders while having custody of his four children
- Placing a cooling corpse into a blue barrel and disposing of the body where no one, after months of searching, can find it
- Calling police to enter the home of his ex-wife, and maintaining his cool while investigators examine the scene of the crime.

Two days after the home visit, Peterson in the author's hotel room, continuing the interviews.

All of this is possible, providing Drew Peterson combines the qualities of a brilliant criminal mind with a sociopathic personality.

From my own research as a veteran crime writer, having created fictional psychopaths to inhabit my worlds, I felt compelled to investigate Drew Peterson—my chance to play the investigator. I knew that even if he wasn't as "bad" as portrayed in the media, to commit such crimes did require a sociopathic personality and the careful planning of an organized psychopath. Either that or he was innocent and extraordinarily unlucky.

The complexity of the timelines surrounding the alleged crimes, combined with the need for convoluted planning and Peterson's utterly cool persona under intense media and law-enforcement scrutiny point without doubt to a sociopath with a psychopathic disorder: only such a man could manage these nearly perfect crimes. Or they point to an innocent man who should never play the lottery. I was determined to discover the truth, starting with a complete history of Peterson, exploring with the best tools we have available—victimology histories (including families), polygraphs of the suspect, witness timeline analysis, examination of all publicly available evidence. If nothing else, this would provide excellent material for my next thriller. Or, more compellingly, something unprecedented in true crime.

Monster or victim? I hope, by the end of this book, we have an answer.

Top: Peterson in his "narc" days, with son Eric in his arms.

Right: All the Petersons in uniform, Drew as sergeant, Tommy as a Cub Scout, and Kris in his "Tigers" uniform.

Below: Drew Peterson with second wife Victoria. In front is Stephen (left) his stepdaughter (center) and his son Eric (right). Eric and Stephen are now adults.

The Many People in Drew Peterson's World

Important Note

"Double quotes" indicate verbatim words of Drew Peterson. 'Single quote' characterizations are media reported descriptions.

Principal Cast of Characters

Drew Peterson—'Cold-blooded monster' or "Mr. Mom"? Until the night of Stacy's disappearance, distinguished police veteran, night watch commander and SWAT team leader.

Stacy Peterson (missing person)—'Disappeared,' "runaway" or 'deceased'? Drew's fourth wife, mother of Lacy and Anthony. Stacy's mother Christie disappeared in strikingly similar circumstances in March, 1998, leaving behind her children. "Beloved" sister Jessica died in a house fire, sister Lacy died mysteriously as a baby, and "favorite" sister Tina died of cancer at thirty.

Kathleen (Kathy) Savio (deceased)—'Accidentally drowned' or 'homicide'? Drew's third wife, mother of Kris and Tommy.

Joel Brodsky—Drew Peterson's high-profile lead attorney, assigned after Peterson's first appearance on *Today* with Matt Lauer. He is portrayed in media as 'colorful, controversial and aggressive.' He is a senior partner in the law firm of Brodsky & Odeh with twenty-five years' experience practicing law. He graduated Drake University and DePaul University's College of Law. He has appeared on *Larry King Live*, *Today* and elsewhere in his high-profile role as lead attorney for Peterson. His brother is Judge David Brodsky of Lake County.

Reem Odeh—Joel Brodsky's partner in Brodsky & Odeh, a brilliant lawyer most adversaries underestimate because of her model good looks.

Sharon Bychowski—'Nosey neighbor' or 'dear friend' of Stacy? Depends on the media report. Bychowski helps run the findstacypeterson.com charity and organizes "Find Stacy" fund-raisers; she consistently claims Stacy told her, "If I disappear, it's not an accident … he (Peterson) killed me."[24]

Roy Taylor—"Unemployed full-time Stacy-searcher" or 'well-meaning' friend? According to Drew Peterson, he regularly threatens Peterson and family.

Lacy Peterson—The "little princess," three-year-old daughter of Drew and Stacy Peterson.

Anthony Peterson—"Budding athlete" five-year-old son of Drew and Stacy.

Kris Peterson—"Straight A" fourteen-year-old son of Drew Peterson and Kathleen Savio.

Tommy Peterson—"Top of his class" fifteen-year-old freshman high school student, son of Drew Peterson and Kathleen Savio.

Stephen Paul Peterson—Second son of Drew Peterson and first wife Carol. Stephen is now a police officer, married and expecting his first child, and remains very close to Drew, Lacy, Anthony, Kris and Tommy Peterson. Reports deny he was ever a "person of interest" in Stacy's disappearance.[25]

Eric Drew Peterson—Drew Peterson's first son with first wife Carol. Eric and Drew Peterson have been alienated since Peterson married Stacy, a woman younger than his son. Peterson says: "I love him and want him back in my life."

Cassandra Cales—"Out of the closet lesbian" sister of Stacy, and a champion of the Find Stacy campaigns.

Yelton Cales—'Paroled Pedophile' brother of Stacy.

Anthony McKenzie Cales—Father of Stacy, called an "alcoholic" by his own daughter and "abusive" by his last wife. Stacy's mother Christie, divorced from Anthony, seems to have "disappeared" in a manner strikingly similar to Stacy's disappearance.

Christie Marie Toutges (missing person)—Stacy's mom, 'missing at 40 years old', since March 11, 1998, who Stacy said "ran away from the family" six years before Drew met Stacy. She was carrying her Bible and her purse, went for a walk, and never returned. Her disappearance remains a mystery and "unsolved" although in circumstances not dissimilar to Stacy's disappearance. Christie is also known as Christina, Christy and Chris; she also goes by Cales as well as Toutges.

Candice Aiken—Christie's sister, Stacy's favorite aunt helped her find religion; she lives in El Monte, California. At one time, the Peterson family wanted to move to California to be near Aunt Candice.

(Christina) Tina (deceased)—Stacy's half-sister, who died of cancer at thirty, precipitating Stacy's depression and loss of spirituality.

Glenn Selig—Long-time broadcast journalist and publicist, principal of Selig Multimedia, and hired by Drew Peterson's lawyer Joel Brodsky to help mitigate the "trial by media" of Peterson in national newspapers, tabloids and broadcast news/talk shows.

Richard Mims—Friend of Peterson's who sold a story for a substantial fee to the *National Enquirer*. Prior to the story he was a supporter of Peterson. He works on fund-raising to "help cover the cost of having these people come down … for the search for Stacy." Some scandal on GretaWire (FOX News Blog) regarding the future "donation" of the *National Enquirer* money to the search for Stacy.[26]

Paula Stark and Len Wawczak—The "wiretap" buddies, Lenny Wawzcak and Paula Stark, who claim they recorded incriminating statements secretly for Illinois State Police. Their credibility is in doubt due to past arrests for assault (Wawzcak), theft (Stark), an unpaid judgment against Wawzcak for $350,000 after Wawzcak ran down a man in a vehicle (while driving without a license), and several bankruptcy filings that challenge their motivation.[27] Peterson claims they want to "sell" their story.

Thomas Morphey—Drew Peterson's stepbrother who tried to commit suicide after claiming publicly that he helped Peterson load a large blue barrel into Peterson's Yukon SUV the day Stacy disappeared. No forensic evidence of the barrel was found, and Morphey is one of four ex-friend discredited witnesses.[28]

For a secondary cast of characters, listed alphabetically, please see Appendix.

Stacy congratulating Tommy Peterson at a band concert.

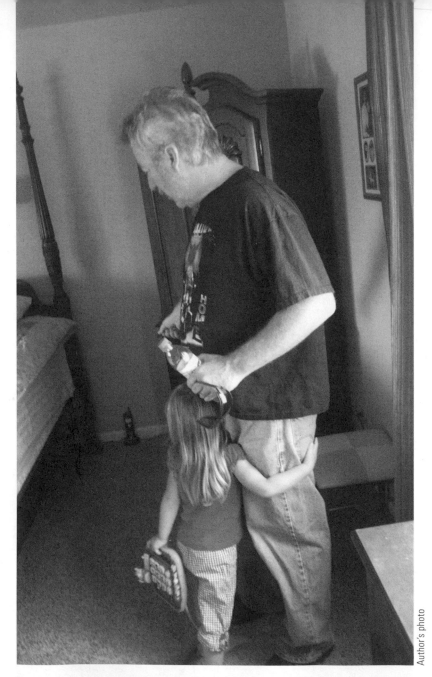

Drew Peterson is many things—jokester, ex-cop, "person of interest"—but towering over all his priorities is family. His daughter, three-year-old Lacy, loves Dad and she's his "little princess." Peterson points to an area of stained carpet the police investigated "thinking it was blood." It turned out to be a beverage.

The Peterson family in better times, just before Christmas. Rear, left to right, Stacy Peterson holding baby Lacy, Sergeant Drew Peterson; front left to right Anthony, Kris and Tommy. Lacy and Anthony are the children of Drew and Stacy. Anthony and Kris are adopted formally by Stacy and natural children of Drew Peterson and Kathy Savio.

"Isn't Mommy ever coming back?"

Three-year-old Lacy Peterson clings to her father's hairy arm. "Isn't Mommy ever coming back? I don't think she's ever coming back."

"I dunno, baby." Drew Peterson strokes daughter Lacy's long, blond hair. He notices she's not crying, and she's staring up at him with sleepy brown eyes.

Lacy has clambered into bed with her father, a high climb onto the towering four-poster. Lacy finds refuge in Dad's arms whenever the media trucks show up on the street with their cameras and satellite dishes. At these times, blinds are pulled against the harsh glare of lights and television volumes are cranked louder, tuned to movie and cartoon programming rather than news. The basement

Drew Peterson at his home on the first day of the author's interviews. Peterson's tour included visits with the kids, tour of the house and all of Stacy's decor touches and the neighbors' "Stacy garden." The house and garden are exceptionally well kept.

recreation room is their only refuge.

It's ten o'clock, and Peterson pushes a pillow under Lacy's dainty head. Even for a three-year-old she's tiny in her pajamas and yellow lion's-head slippers, clutching her favorite pink and yellow blanket. Five-year-old Anthony is also in the king-sized bed, but he doesn't say anything. He's had a busy day throwing perfect hoops with his kid-sized basketball, riding his bike on neighborhood sidewalks and playing with Dad and the neighborhood kids. He's a normal, active kid, who usually sleeps in his own cool-kid's room. Both Lacy and Anthony feel safer with Dad in the master bedroom at the end of the hall when the reporters arrive and the light stands re-appear on the front lawn, a stark metal forest held together with duct tape and fed by snaking power cables.

Mr. Mom watches as his two youngest fall asleep, his own mind numb with the challenges of his peculiar life. Today, an ex-friend assaulted Peterson in front of Hydroglyphics Barber Shop. Two days ago, the same man went public with a story that he wore wiretaps for the state police. He tells everyone who'll listen: "Peterson's going away." Now Peterson can hear the distant thrum of the media truck generators that jam the street in front of their not-so-quiet home at 6 Pheasant Chase Court. Media are hot for sound bites on this latest twist in the ten months of tribulation since Stacy Peterson disappeared.

The ordeal is written on his face. He looks haggard, with exaggerated bags in puffy, reddened cheeks. His handsome face appears aged and sports a gray, trimmed beard that mirrors arched salt-and-pepper eyebrows. He barely resembles the laughing, dark-haired police sergeant of a year ago.

Peterson, in his own words, "went from being a Watch Commander at the Bolingbrook police to being a mom. Mother of four." Life is pretty busy for a full-time stay-at-home mom, even without the media camping out on his lawn. In the lulls between media drop-ins, life has become a reassuring routine, his home a place of peaceful refuge for the under-siege suspect Drew Peterson.

"The kids get me up. I make them breakfast. I get them dressed. Take them to school. If there's no school, I play with them. I make them lunch. I clean up after lunch. I do the house cleaning, laundry, chores. Pick up the kids from school. We play some more. I make dinner. We have dinner. We give baths after dinner, watch a little

Lacy and Anthony in airplanes bought for them by Stacy when they were two and three, on the sidewalk in front of the house.

Above: Stacy on her second birthday, looking very much like Lacy as a child of the same age (left).

Top: A "shrine to Stacy" next door to the Peterson house is a frightening area for the children who stay away as much as they can. Notice the "Find Stacy" posters on the boat and twenty-four-hour camera mounted on the house aimed at the Peterson house.

Bottom: The one remaining sanctuary at the Peterson house is the backyard pool.

TV, play some more, then go to bed. You know, there's playing and kidding around and kids' activities in between. That starts one morning, it's over at night, starts over again the next morning."[29]

By any measure, this is an extraordinary household, nestled on a rarely quiet cul-de-sac in the "bedroom" suburb of Bolingbrook, a short trip by I-55 from downtown Chicago. When not inundated by media trucks and camped-out cameramen, the neighborhood feels typical, in this summer of 2008, dozing under the drone of lawn mowers, the laughter of children who play on sidewalks or splash in Peterson's backyard pool, and the occasional fly-over by small planes from the nearby single-runway Clow Airport. The neighborhood is like any middle-class American suburb, rich with parks and greenways, each property sporting at least one mature tree. Cars park in wide driveways rather than on curbsides, and there are more kids than cars on the asphalt.

But it's a neighborhood divided. To one side of Peterson's quaint house is a semi-permanent memorial to missing wife Stacy, hosted by a neighbor who is terrified of Peterson—so much so she sought an "order of protection." This same outspoken neighbor set up twenty-four-hour spy cameras and hosted a street party that featured a piñata with Peterson's face and the penned message, "I killed Stacy." Another neighborhood house is home to the principal at Anthony's school, a nice man who always has time for Peterson's kids, but is stiff and formal with Peterson. The neighborhood seems to want this all to end. Every time the media trucks re-appear, the signs go up on lawns: No Media. People close blinds and lock doors.

The "sinister" house of Drew Peterson is an ordinary 1980s-style two-level brick-and-siding house with faux shutters decorating sparkling clean windows. In summer, the slightly raised front garden is colorful with yellow day lilies and blooming hostas, strategically highlighted with solar-powered garden lights. Well-watered baskets hang from the inviting front porch, made homey and quaint with cushioned lawn furniture meant for enjoying summer lemonade or foamy beer. The lawn is green and weed-free, well fertilized and trim.

On days when the media trucks are not parked on the street, the garage door is always open, a busy intersection for the kids. It overflows with toys, fat-wheeled tricycles, mountain bikes, adorable

Peterson's always on the look-out these days for media or the 50 percent of neighbors who are "anti-Drew." The garage is so full of children's toys and tools, all the vehicles are parked in the driveway, which became a focus of various "witness" timeflows. Seen in the driveway is Peterson's famous GMC Yukon and Stacy's car.

"airplane" vehicles for the toddlers, kites and ten-speed bicycles hanging from neatly placed hooks on the dry-walled ceiling. Stacked shelving holds almost immaculately organized paint, tools and carefully wound extension cords. In one corner, almost buried under the colorful debris of childhood, are impressively functional tools: an air compressor, stacked pails in multiple colors and a floor mop. The floor is concrete, lightly stained from gas and oil and windshield washer fluids.

Sparkling and perfectly waxed, parked neatly in the middle of the garage, in pride of place, is Stacy Peterson's gorgeous maroon-colored Harley Davidson Speedster, chrome glittering, seat gleaming, tires shining, as if polished by loving hands, ready for the return of its mistress. "I'm keeping it for her," Drew tells visitors. "That's Stacy's Harley. Keeps her off mine." And he rumbles with sad laughter, probably as he realizes she's not coming back.

After ten months he says he's given up hope she'll return to him. Police hint that she might be dead and point fingers at him.

Above: Peterson as "Mr. Mom," making Lacy's bed. Peterson is a single parent with no help, who does all the housework, yard work, plays with and raises his kids, and is an almost model parent, much loved by his four live-in children. He also raised two other sons who are now adults.

Right: The family dining area is the main center of activity in the Peterson household.

Author's photos

Broadcast media pretty much have tried and convicted him of her murder. Half the neighbors in the close-knit community seem to mirror the beliefs of the media, some vocally. The other half aren't so sure, and remain stiffly polite. Everyone, regardless of their beliefs, has a smile for Peterson's adorable kids. Peterson himself gave up on the private investigator he hired: "One minute Stacy's in Asia, the next she's in Mexico. I get letters from people who see her in a Kroger grocery store in Peoria." His voice sounds tired as he explains this, and he buffs out a smudge on the glittering gas tank of Stacy's Harley.

Peterson's own substantially larger Harley, metallic blue and equally showroom shiny, sits out in the driveway with the two other vehicles, a GMC Yukon, and maroon Grand Am, both recently searched by police forensic teams. Both vehicles are as polished as the motorcycles, right down to the mag wheels. The asphalt is dark grey, recently coated with topping, only slightly marred with the scrapes of motorcycle stands.

On a normal, non-media day, the kids are active in the yard, oblivious of the "sinister" nature of their house. Anthony and Lacy are usually on their small bicycles. When supervised, they swim in the giant above-ground pool in the backyard. They're allowed to play on the sidewalk of the safe, traffic-free cul-de-sac, although they're careful to stay clear of the only danger in the neighborhood, a peculiar garden of potted flowers at the neighboring house.

The kids seem to consciously stay clear of this neighbor's house with its two trailered boats—one trailer mounted with a "search boat" sign sporting large letters **www.findstacypeterson.com**, the other a flat-bottomed boat displaying "Where's Stacy?" posters along the rails. These are the two search boats funded by concerned Stacy-searchers, although they've remained in the driveway of the well-tended house of Sharon Bychowski for months. According to the website, land searches still happen each weekend, although few people show up. No water search has been reported since May, 2008.

The children avoid the "search" boats, and even the Bychowski house with its multiple posters in each window, posters that shout, "Where's Stacy?" It's confusing for Lacy, Anthony, Kris and Tommy to see this bizarre memorial on the front lawn next door. Nestled amongst stone angels and dozens of potted flowers decked out in ribbons and hand-made tributes to Stacy is a billboard-sized lawn sign, also screaming "Where is Stacy???" notably punctuated with three giant question marks.

Two cameras, permanently mounted on the neighbor's house, are pointed at Peterson's front and backyard, recording daily life at 6 Pheasant Chase Court. Every moment of the children's playtime is captured on Bychowski's cameras. The juxtaposition of a divided community, "Big Brother" cameras filming the street twenty-four/ seven, abandoned search boats, haunting memorials, media truck visits, regular suburban summer lawn chores, and children playing on the sidewalks, makes this neighborhood unique in America.

The dynamic changes on some weekends, when the memorial house transforms into a yard party. Friends of neighbor Bychowski show up to "tend the Stacy garden" and hurl insults at Peterson as he cuts his lawn, with variations on "Murderer!" sometimes accompanied by the theme song from the *COPS* TV show blaring from a speaker: "Bad boys, bad boys, What you goin' to do when they come for you?" The neighborhood children have learned to stay clear of the weekend parties. On a few occasions, Drew's children have been cornered by these well-meaning friends of Stacy, and are confronted with questions a child should never have to answer. If there's a crowd, Bychowski's adult son Roy will "call him out" and threaten to kill Peterson, often in front of his children. Sometimes the police are called.

Well-known private investigator Paul Huebl describes Sharon Bychowski as a neighbor "who never misses any opportunity to mug for cameras or show her hatred for Drew Peterson."[30]

This is life at 6 Pheasant Chase Court, Bolingbrook. On media days such as today, with the latest headline "Reports of wiretaps emerge in Peterson case,"[31] lawns bristle with light stands, booms, wheeled dollies with monitors, cameras and microphones.

No one wants to miss "the imminent arrest of Drew Peterson."[32]

And no one's asking if Peterson's guilty or innocent. Nearly everyone assumes he's guilty.

Stacy with Lacy in downtown Naperville at the River Works.

Guilty?

"Drew snapped Stacy's neck in their bed."

This account of Stacy's disappearance—here described as a homicide—is derived from accounts of neighbor and ex-friend witness timelines, ex-LAPD detective Mark Fuhrman's speculative timeline as reported on FOX TV, stories on CNN, and the December 17, 2007 National Enquirer story from Richard Mims. This is a dramatized hearsay account. There is no polygraph to verify this account, and most of the witnesses disagree on key events (see "Timeline October 28, 2007, According to Various Media Sources"). The National Enquirer reportedly paid $35,000 for Mims' story.

"My one mommy died, and my other mommy went away." Kris Peterson says. Thirteen-year-old Kris is mature for his age, more teenager than little boy, close-cropped hair revealing slightly

Photo courtesy of Drew Peterson

reddened ears. He's a champion wrestler at school and a good kid. He's normally a quiet teen, but today he says, "I don't know what to think about this."

Mims must have been surprised by the mature, even tone of Kris Peterson, so like his dad in the almost eerie calm: *I don't know what to think about this.* Did Kris say that? He tries to touch Kris's shoulder, to reassure him, but drops his hand in confusion. "Well, you just have to hope for the best," he says awkwardly. He tells Kris that Mom will be home.

Of course, Ric no longer believes these empty reassurances. He believed Stacy was missing, only days ago, when Drew Peterson told him, "Stacy ran off with another man. She found someone she wants to be with."

Mims is unshaven from the last few days at Peterson's house. For four days, since Stacy disappeared, he's stayed with Drew Peterson and the kids, babysitting at times, running errands, helping out. It's a terrible time. According to Peterson, his wife has run off, apparently taking $25,000 in cash and leaving her car at the Clow International Airport, never to return. Mims' grey-blond hair tumbles off in every direction, and he's sure his eyes show his fatigue. He hopes his anxiety doesn't show, because now he's very much afraid of his ex-friend Drew Peterson, a man who is an expert with guns and martial arts. In a lot of ways, Mims looks up to Peterson. Peterson has it all: a gorgeous twenty-three-year-old wife, four great kids, two adult sons, a nice house, two Harleys, a swimming pool, two cars. Mims struggles to makes ends meet. He can't help being a little jealous.

Now that the media have circled the wagons and it's pretty clear everyone suspects Drew had something to do with Stacy's disappearance, Mims doesn't know what to think. Mothers don't run off on their four young children. No way that could happen. Mims is starting to believe the rumors.

Kris's too cool stare and calm adult-like words unnerve Mims. Upstairs, they can hear four-year-old Anthony and two-year-old Lacy running around, screaming and laughing. They are dressed in their Spider-Man and Tinkerbell costumes, ready for trick-or-treating. But Mims focuses on Kris. Kris tells of how he heard his dad and adoptive mom argue a few nights ago. They shouted about divorces and affairs. Then there was a sudden silence. Mims knows Kris's bedroom is next door to his parents' room, and he also knows

Stacy yells loudly when she's mad. He has no doubt Kris would hear an argument. He wonders why Kris would tell Mims, a casual family associate, and why he would sound sympathetic to Stacy, after all just his step-mom.

Suddenly he feels a Halloween chill, a spectral cold that makes him shiver, as if the ghost of Stacy had passed through him. He is suddenly convinced that Drew snapped Stacy's neck in her bed. Kris never said this, but Mims has a sudden, vivid picture of it. He knows Drew is a karate expert. Just like in the movies, he could have snapped her neck. She wouldn't have a chance to scream. He visualizes Peterson as some kind of Steven Seagal super martial artist with Ninja powers. Suddenly, he wants to be anywhere but here in the Peterson house.

Later, he'll find out from ever-present neighbor Sharon Bychowski, who claims to be Stacy's best friend, that Kris told her, "I was in my bedroom and I heard mommy and daddy fighting." Kris, according to Sharon and Mims, heard Stacy yelling she wanted a divorce and she wanted his father to move out of the house. Then things were suddenly quiet. With Peterson's skill, surely he could snap her neck in total silence, unheard by Kris. It could happen that way. Chuck Norris or Seagal could do it. So could Drew Peterson.

Mims puts it all together in his head. He remembers how he asked Peterson on October 28, "Dude, what's going on?"

"Stacy ran off with another man," Peterson said that night, stone cold calm. "She called about nine PM, and said she found someone she wants to be with."

Mims played the detective and probed his old friend.

"Well I got up around eleven o'clock and Stacy was gone," Peterson said. "I didn't think much of it because she was supposed to see her grandfather."

"Dude, is she dating someone else?"

"I think she's dating four or five different guys from the intelligence I can gather." Drew told him how he got receipts from TGI Friday's that showed she had gone out with a guy.

"Are you serious? When did all this start?"

Peterson explained how it all began when he enrolled Stacy in school to take her nursing classes. "That's when Stacy started seeing the f—king street rats that she hung out with before I knew her."

So, this frightening Halloween night, with the monsters on the street trick-or-treating, and maybe a real, live monster hanging out in his lair at 6 Pheasant Chase Court, Mims is scared for his life. Their friendship has boiled down to a moment of terror. He spends the night in Kris's room with the door locked. He watches as Drew invites reporters into the house the next day, apparently only inviting the pretty ones in.

Finally, his nerve is completely shattered when Peterson stares him dead-cold in the face, and says coolly, "I'm going to have to ask you to be my hostage when the cops come for me. Maybe I'll have a standoff with them." Peterson laughs it off, but Mims is too shocked to laugh along.

He believes his "friend" Peterson might actually take him hostage. And he decides to do something. He decides to sell his story to the *National Enquirer*. Then, everyone would know what really happened.

Analysis: This hearsay-dramatized account substantially differs from the following dramatizations. For example, Kris Peterson denies the conversation reported by Mims. Credibility of witnesses and motivation must be considered.

Ric Mims Changes his Mind?

Ric Mims seems to have had a change of heart between his conversation with Kris Peterson on October 31, 2007 (as reported in the *National Enquirer* and dramatized in the scene "Drew snapped Stacy's neck in their bed") and November 7, 2007 when he did an extensive interview with Greta Van Susteren on FOX News. On November 7, a few days *after* his revealing conversation with Kris Peterson, he had a slightly different public story:

Greta: Now, Ric, you have been standing by your friend Sergeant Peterson since the very beginning. You thought that Stacy ran away. Do you still think that?
Mims: Yes, I do … I haven't got any type of intuition or anything from what he's said that he's—there's any foul play … I'm just—like you, I'm waiting for Stacy to be found.

"I'm scared for my life"

Cassandra Cales loves to play with nieces Lacy and Anthony, and spends much of Friday night, October 26, chasing the kids up and down the stairs, into their rooms, but she can see Stacy isn't in a good mood, even though she loves Halloween.[33] Lately, this has been fairly typical for Stacy. Cassandra worries about her, but typically, she doesn't show it.

Cassandra's hair is drawn back taut, revealing a high forehead and dark eyelashes, in stark contrast to Stacy's cascading hair. Cassandra is good at hiding her feelings, closing them behind the mask of a serene face, but Stacy's a lot more open, her face transforming with her mood. She can look happy and angelic one moment, dark and thunderous the next.

Stacy leans close to her sister. "How do you feel about the divorce?"

This isn't the first time Stacy's asked this. Everyone knows Stacy plans to divorce Drew, but now her face shows her tension, aging her young model-perfect features.

Cassandra is not one to hide her feelings, or whisper, especially regarding Drew. She's never really liked Stacy's much-too-old husband. In her typical husky tone, she says, "Well, I'm scared."

Stacy presses even closer. "Why are you scared?"

"Because of what happened to Kathy. His ex-wife. It's just kinda weird." The tension is nearly electric between them.

Stacy whispers, "I'm scared

Cassandra Cales (with the very gun involved in the Peterson gun charges) posing with a provocative sister Stacy.

for my life. That's why I'm telling you this. If I disappear, I want you to find me."

Cassandra feels sure something is wrong, and the feeling sticks with her through the weekend. Probably she shouldn't have left Stacy alone. But she did, and soon she'll regret it. Saturday night over dinner she feels the anxiety.

It gnaws at her even as she sleeps that night. When she wakes, she doesn't immediately remember her fears, not until later when she tries to phone Stacy. Throughout the day, she is unable to get her sister. She gets her nephew Kris at the Peterson house, and he says Stacy is at Grandpa's. She sighs. She isn't close to her grandpa, and he's in one of those "old-timer homes." She calls the number she has, but it is out of date. Finally, later in the day, she tries her Aunt Cassandra in California. What Cassandra says worries her even more. Cassandra says Grandpa doesn't remember making any plans with Stacy.

The worry gnaws at her all day and night. When she can't reach anyone at the Peterson house, she finally decides to drop in at eleven o'clock. The kids would be asleep, but she could at least confront Drew with "Where's my sister?" She has some "fund raiser money" for the kids, so she has a ready-made excuse to knock on the door unexpectedly so late on a Sunday.

She feels a flutter of panic when she sees no cars in the driveway, but she knocks on the door anyway.

But it's Kris who answers the door, not Drew, and her thirteen-year-old nephew looks sleepy. "What are you doing here?"

Trying to sound natural, she says, "I forgot to give you your fund-raiser money."

Kris laughs. "Okay."

Cassandra gives him the fund-raiser money. "Are you home alone?"

"Yeah. It's me, Tom, Anthony and Lacy."

"Oh, Mom didn't bring Anthony and Lacy to Grandpa's?"

He looks at the ground and says, "Mom and Dad got in a fight this morning. Mom left. Dad's out looking for her."

Cassandra feels the panic like a very real thing, and for some reason she just has to be anywhere but at this house. After she drives away, she realizes she should have stayed with the kids, but she continues. She stops at a Meijer's parking lot, and dials Drew's cell phone. She hears noises and shuffling and keys in the ignition and Drew sounds out of breath as he answers.

"Where's your sister?" he asks.

Angry, she snaps, "What do you mean? I'm calling you. Where's my sister?"

"She left me." There's a short pause. "I've been out looking for her all day."

She doesn't know what to say. "Okay. Well, what are you doing?"

"I'm at home. What are you doing?"

Cassandra's sure it must be a lie. She was just at his house. Unless he just got home, that moment, he was in his car somewhere.

She decides she needs to go to the police. She can't go to Bolingbrook Police, because he's a watch commander there, so she turns the key in her ignition and drives to Downers Grove Police Department, near where she lives.

Analysis: I present this dramatization based on the hearsay witnesses to highlight the discrepancies with Drew Peterson's account. Here, Cassandra indicates Peterson searched for Stacy all day, while Peterson claims he only searched after Stacy called him at 9 PM. Kris Peterson also denies he told Cassandra Mom and Dad had a fight. This comes down to credibility of the witness, and the validity of hearsay versus actual witness accounts.

A Hair of the Dog

Tom Morphey lay in the hospital bed, racked with pain. His hangovers usually passed unnoticed, nothing a hash pipe wouldn't fix. He had a vague recollection of the previous night, of disappointed faces, of Drew saying "Don't worry, man" of Bolingbrook cops—or were they state troopers?

Was I that wasted? Probably. There were just fragments of yesterday, or was it today? Last week? Time ran together in converging streams of fragmented details. He remembered things. Some things.

He knew he was in a hospital. Drew had been here. Or was that yesterday? The state troopers. His girlfriend? He struggled to remember. They had pumped him, cleaned him up. But now he wanted to be anywhere but the hospital. He couldn't eat. He just needed out. To get a hair of the dog.

The State Troopers had hammered him mercilessly about blue barrels and blue boxes and blue containers. Warm to the touch? I think so. Heavy? I think so. Or was it that movie that he saw last week. Or—he just needed a hair of the dog. Just a little something. Anything.

Analysis: It is difficult to analyze the credibility of this dramatized account due to issues with drug use and the following day's hospitalization.

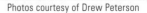

Photos courtesy of Drew Peterson

Tom Morphey, who gave a confusing account of blue barrels "warm to the touch" after Stacy Peterson disappeared. Morphey is "into drugs and booze" according to Peterson and "probably doesn't remember anything." Peterson was once his employer, and the night before Stacy Peterson disappeared helped take him to a job interview to help him out. "He was too drunk" according to Peterson and they canceled the interview.

Timeline October 28, 2007 According to Various Media Sources

Carefully constructed timeline from many media sources. This timeline illustrates the difficulty the Illinois State Police must face in building a coherent timeline, since key witnesses can't agree on times and events, as illustrated by my own detective work in the highlighted discrepancies. This doesn't mean some of these things didn't happen, but there are plenty of credibility issues with the accounts of various witnesses.

October 28, 2007:
5:00 AM
• *People Magazine*—"Peterson says he got off of work at 4 AM on Oct. 28 and got in bed beside his wife."[34]

6:00 to 9:00 AM
• *National Enquirer*—"Mims told the Enquirer, he (Kris Peterson) said: 'I was in my bedroom and I heard mommy and daddy fighting.' Kris told Sharon (Bychowski) that Stacy was yelling she wanted a divorce ... Mims said that suddenly things got quiet ..."[35]

Note: Discrepancy between this account and Zidarich's account on FOX below. Also, discrepancies in how Kris talks, one moment speaking like a toddler, the next like an adult. Cassandra Cales and Drew mention that Kris refers to his parents as Mom and Dad, while Mims says Kris called them "Mommy and Daddy."

9:40 AM
• Neighbor Sharon Bychowski very precisely reports both cars in the Peterson driveway

10:00 to 10:15 AM
• *On The Record with Greta Van Susteren*—"Bruce Zidarich shared back and forth text messages with Stacy. She then called him at 10:15. She said she had been just lounging in bed for a couple of hours and that she and her kids were going to the house to paint today."[36]

Note: Discrepancy between the Mims account, above describing an argument during this period, followed by a sudden silence, and this account by Zidarich.

• *On The Record with Greta Van Susteren*, speaking with ex-LAPD detective Mark Fuhrman (of O.J. Simpson fame)[37]—"About 10-10:15, the call that comes in that Stacy is last talked to—the call that Sharon, the neighbor puts in to talk to Stacy—she is not available. So, between that time, is either a time that she is incapacitated, she's not able to get to the phone because she's under the control of Drew Peterson or she is, by then, deceased."

Note: Discrepancies in most of Mark Fuhrman's accounts are fairly major. Here, he has Sharon calling but not getting an answer at 10-10:15 AM, while Bruce Zidarich had no trouble reaching Sharon.

Around 10 AM
• *Chicago Suburban News*—"Stacy's sister, Cassandra Cales, said the last telephone contact she had with her sister was about 10 AM Sunday. After that, all attempts to reach Stacy by cell phone were unsuccessful."[38]

Note: Incorrectly reported. Cassandra called in the afternoon and evening.

10:15 AM
• *On The Record with Greta Van Susteren* —CASSANDRA: "No, I guess Bruce talked to her at 10:15 and I was still sleeping and Bruce said that he would call her back when I woke up."

Note: Discrepancy between the Chicago Suburban News' account that Cassandra talked with her sister at 10 AM and this account that she was still sleeping after 10:15 AM the same day.[39]

11:00 AM to 1:30 PM
• *Nancy Grace CNN*—"When I asked him when was the last time he saw Stacy, he said, well, when he got up at 11 AM, she was already gone. But from 11 AM to 1:30 PM, both cars were in the driveway … Sharon, the neighbor, plus all the neighbors' reports from—all created a timeline."[40]

Note: Ignoring the strange sentence structure of his response, we assume Mims meant Sharon and the neighbors saw the two cars. Major discrepancy between Mims' account on CNN and report in the Bolingbrook Reporter and other sources. Bychowski saw only one car in the drive after 11:15 AM

11:15 AM
• *Bolingbrook Reporter*—"11:15 AM - Bychowski returns from the grocery store and says she saw only one of the vehicles in Peterson's driveway. Bychowski calls next door to see if the Peterson children want to come over for suckers. She asks for Stacy when one of the children answers and Drew Peterson tells her his wife went to visit her grandfather." [41]

Note: Discrepancy with Mims' account above.

12:00 PM
• *On The Record with Greta Van Susteren*, speaking with ex-LAPD detective Mark Fuhrman[42]—"Well, in this phone call, Sharon calls and, ah, one of the children, Kris, answers the phone ... Sharon says, 'Can I talk to your mom?' Long pause. Ah, and Sharon's described this to me as a very uneasy pause ... 'You don't know if your mom's there?' And at that time Drew takes the phone and tells Sharon that Stacy went to her grandfather's to run some errands. Well, we know that's not true. That's lie one. Drew Peterson's committed himself to a lie because he didn't expect Sharon to call ..."

Note: Discrepancy—Fuhrman seems to conclude that Peterson is lying, missing the obvious possibility that Stacy could be lying. She never went to Grandpa's, but it was Stacy who told Peterson she was going there in Peterson's account. There's no evidence either way.

1:00 PM
• *On The Record with Greta Van Susteren*, speaking with ex-LAPD detective Mark Fuhrman[43]— Greta: "At about 1 o'clock or 1:15 did Drew ask Sharon to babysit on that Sunday?"
MF: "No, I believe Sharon, when she was in that conversation at noon said, 'well if you need me to watch the younger kids or you want me to feed 'em, bring 'em over.' Now, when he brings the two

younger children over at 1 o'clock ..."

Note: Discrepancy—Kris and Tommy Peterson babysat Lacy and Anthony in their account. Fuhrman is mixing up his timeline with the following day when Peterson asked her to babysit so that he could visit Morphey in the hospital. This is verified by three people: Peterson, Kris and Tommy.

1:30 PM

• *On The Record with Greta Van Susteren*, interviewing Cassandra Cales, Stacy's sister—"When she (Stacy) didn't call, I called her like 1:30 and her phone was off and that's when I started getting suspicious and scared ... then I called the house and that's when Kris answered the phone and said she went to Grandpa's. So I called my uncle because my Grandpa's number wouldn't go through, he must have changed his number ... so I called my aunt in California and she spoke to my Grandpa three times that day, Sunday, and no intentions, he said nothing about Stacy coming out."

Note: Time doesn't quite match up with Sharon's (the neighbor's) claim that she babysat the kids at her house until 1:30 PM. Odd that Cassandra didn't know her Grandpa's number changed. "Cassandra wasn't very close to her grandfather or most of the family," Peterson said, in an interview.

2:00 PM

• FOX News—"Peterson called in sick for Sunday night," Teppel said. "The call was taken by a dispatcher in the afternoon."[44]

Note: Lieutenant Teppel, Bolingbrook police, indicating when Peterson took the day off on Sunday.

4:00 PM

• *On The Record with Greta Van Susteren* on FOX—"At 4 PM Bruce (Zidarich) sent Stacy a text message saying 'Let's paint tomorrow.' He received no reply."[45]

7:00 PM

- *Sun-Times*—"A source familiar with the investigation said that at about 7 PM Drew Peterson picked up his relative (Thomas Morphey, a stepbrother) from a park and the two went to a local coffee shop."

Note: According to Peterson, Thomas Morphey is a drug addict who claimed he recalled carrying a blue barrel/square container (depending on which report you read) out of Peterson's house with Peterson. His recollections are somewhat fuzzy and strikingly near-identical to a mystery movie on TV playing at the time (a kid watches a husband carry a wife's body out of the house in a blue barrel). Shortly after his claim, he attempted suicide. In Peterson's account of the timeline, Peterson was at home with his children, and they confirm that he was at home, mostly discrediting Morphey's account. Furthermore, Peterson claims that he took his children at this time to McDonald's for dinner, a very public place. The kids recall playing in the McDonald's playground.

7:00 PM

- *On The Record with Greta Van Susteren* on FOX—"Bruce said that Cassandra called him around 7 PM and said she had not been able to reach Stacy all day."[46]

Note: We must assume he meant since the morning, since he disclosed he spoke to her at 10:15 AM and text messaged back and forth with her.

8:00 PM to 9:00 PM

- *On The Record with Greta Van Susteren*, speaking with ex-LAPD detective Mark Fuhrman[47]—"The next two most important calls are the calls at 8 o'clock, that Drew Peterson says he puts in to Stacy's cell phone, which—I believe that Thomas Morphey is with him at that time, and he probably witnessed that, because that would fit in with Drew believing she's alive or just missing, or not at home. And then the 9 o'clock call that Thomas Morphey sees come up on the cell phone that he's told not to answer.

Note: At this time, Peterson's children recall Peterson at home, and remember Peterson's older teen Tom getting home from band practice.

9:21 PM

• *On The Record with Greta Van Susteren*, with the ex-O.J. Simpson detective Mark Fuhrman—"At 7:37 PM, two men entered a Krispy Kreme store, did not purchase anything, sat at a table until 9:21 and then left ... Mark Fuhrman reviewed them (surveillance videos) and saw two white males who came in at 7:37 PM ... the video is of poor quality, so it's difficult to tell ..."[48]

Note: This appears to be an effort to give credibility to Morphey's story that he helped Peterson with a blue container. Unfortunately, the two white men are unidentifiable and could have been anyone. And Peterson's teenager says he was at home.

11:00 PM

• FOX News "Where is Stacy Peterson? Missing woman's sister speaks to Greta"—CASSANDRA: "So I go to the Peterson house ... no cars are in the driveway ... It was about 11 o'clock at night ... I knocked on the door. Kris answered the door ... I says 'Are you home alone?' And he says 'Yeah, it's me, Tom, Anthony and Lacy'... and then he said something, but I'm not going to say it ... He looked at the ground and said, 'Mom and Dad got in a fight this morning. Mom left and Dad's out looking for her.' "

Note: After an author interview, Kris Peterson disclosed that yes, Cassandra dropped off the money that night, but no, he never mentioned a fight between "Mom and Dad."

11:26 PM

• FOX News "Where is Stacy Peterson? Missing woman's sister speaks to Greta"—CASSANDRA: "11:26 PM I call Drew's cell phone. I can hear noises and shuffling, keys going into ignition and stuff ... And he's saying 'Where's your sister?' 'I'm calling you, where's my sister?' "

Note: This account agrees with Peterson's timeline, where he arrives home after looking for his wife around 11 PM and recalls Cassandra calling him as he arrives at the driveway of the house.

The ceremony. Left to right: the presiding pastor, Cassandra Cales (Stacy's sister), Stacy Peterson, Anthony Peterson (in Drew's arms), Drew Peterson and Stephen Peterson, Drew's adult son by his first wife Carol.

Innocent?

"Do you know the whereabouts of your wife Stacy?"

This account of October 28, 2007, the night Stacy disappeared, is dramatized from interviews with Drew Peterson recorded in June, 2008. We'll call this the "Innocent" of the "Guilty and Innocent" presentations. Compare this to the "Guilty" account. Is this "Innocent" account of October 28, 2007 factual as Peterson remembers it? Peterson took two polygraphs to help verify his story. Refer to the chapter "Did You Physically Harm Your Wife?"

The weekend before Halloween in Bolingbrook was a festive time with the leaves in color and houses decorated with faux spider webs, grinning pumpkins and dancing skeletons. This October, 2007 would finish with an average temperature of 60.4 degrees, well above the normal of 54.1, the mildest Halloween in eighty years.[49] But this was still sweater-and-glove weather, especially at night in the windy suburbs.

Stacy Peterson, as always, had decorated the porch with Jack-o'-lanterns and worked on costumes for the kids. There wasn't much to signal this year would be different from any other. Like any other Halloween, now just days away, the kids would rush from house to house in homemade costumes—princesses and monsters and the living dead. That weekend, adults and older teenagers would hit the theatres to see the latest gruesome-fest, in the form of *Saw 4*, and televisions would show old *Halloween* and *Nightmare on Elm Street* reruns.

In stores, Christmas had started its early arrival. Bloomingdale's, Macy's and all the big stores in Chicago were already festive with lights and elaborate window displays for Christmas. Christmas was Stacy Peterson's favorite time of year, a time when her credit cards zoomed to the maximum. "Stacy overbought for everyone," Peterson would tell friends with weary humor. "She wanted everyone to have the things she never had."

But this year would be more tricks than treats in the Peterson household.

There were subtle signals, Peterson would tell friends afterwards, that things might change. "I was very much in love with Stacy. She made me very happy." But, more and more the in-laws drove a wedge between them. "We were practically feeding the in-laws. Stacy would make extra food and run it over to her family. She gave her father her older car, although he sold it for beer money. We talked about moving to California, or anywhere that was not within driving distance of her family. Her brother's a convicted pedophile. Her father's an alcoholic. Her half-sister always hated me. It was very, very difficult."

Yet nothing directly signaled an abrupt change that particular weekend. Shortly before Halloween 2007, the household at 6 Pheasant Chase Court would change forever. Before the kids could wear their creepy costumes, an entirely different sort of darkness would descend on the neighborhood.

Sunday, October 28, the day is alternately hazy and clear, although Drew Peterson, a Night Watch Commander at Bolingbrook Police Department, doesn't pay attention to weather at five in the morning, on his way home from a particularly draining Saturday night shift. Sunday mornings are for sleep, and he is bone-weary as he drags himself home. He drives a little too fast through the winding subdivision streets, since the streets are deserted this early in the morning. He flings his GMC Yukon onto the asphalt driveway, in a hurry to park and get to bed, although scanning for bicycles and toys. As always, he enters through the welcoming clutter of the garage, stepping over toys.

He yawns again as he drops his keys in the large kitchen, not bothering to turn on lights. The kids are asleep and if he wants to sleep it's best to keep it that way. He peeks in on three-year-old Lacy, asleep in her frilly pink four-poster. Lacy is on her side, sleeping under a pink sign with magnificent scrolling letters: "The Princess sleeps here." He smiles, lifted through the exhaustion as always by her highness's dainty face and button nose. He pulls the pink comforter a little higher, gives her a kiss, and heads across the hall to Anthony's *Cars* sanctum.

Anthony is asleep, lying on his back, wearing his favorite number 3 baseball shirt. He is surrounded by posters and cutouts of his favorite characters from the Disney Pixar movie *Cars*. His way-cool boy's room, as with every eclectic room in the cozy home, was designed by mom Stacy and lovingly decorated by both parents. The shelves by the bed sport a welcome clutter of toys: Spider-Man mask ready for Halloween tricking, packages of Energizer batteries for toys, toy cars, a Pooh Bear cartoon framed with a picture of Dad snuggling baby Anthony on his chest, another "Cutie Pie" frame featuring Anthony on his first crawl across the living room carpet, an all-American family snapshot of the entire family with Stacy kneeling by Anthony's carriage, a grinning Drew beside her with arm on Stacy, his smiling older brothers Tommy and Kris looking on. There are many books, including, of course, Disney's *Cars*, classics from E.B. White, *A Fish Out of Water*, *The First Day of School*, *Family Fun Boredom Busters*, *Bunny Stories*, and an unlikely children's book, *Drop Dead*. Depending on shifts, these are

Stacy and Drew Peterson in downton Naperville, Illinois.

Author's photos

Above: Stacy's lovingly kept Harley Davidson, a shining maroon-colored motorcylce parked in their garage amid kids' toys, bikes and storage shelves.

Left: Stacy and Drew Peterson in their first trip together to Puerto Vallarta, a trip she would always cherish.

the books Peterson and Stacy read to Anthony before bedtime.

Peterson smiles at his son, refreshed slightly, thinking how perfect this room is for five-year-old Anthony, a true blue boy's room with its basketball hoop on the double closet doors, the little desk. He knows he doesn't have to check on the older kids, teens Kris and Tommy, but he does check on Kris in his starry room, lovingly decorated with a tapestry of stars painted over his bed. Tommy is in his teen room in the basement, a room decorated with music scores and crowded with keyboards.

Stacy is asleep on the big four-poster in the master bedroom. He doesn't wake her, because he knows she will have had a long night with the boys, getting them all to bed. His night shifts aren't easy on the family, but it is the reality of being a Night Watch Commander. It means she'll wake up when he crawls his tired cop ass into bed.

He stares at her, smiling sadly, wondering where it all went wrong. They were so happy, the perfect family despite the difference in their ages. The only strife in the family, since he married Stacy, was really with adult son Eric, who resented having a "mother" younger than himself. Eric never got over it, and moved out, after Peterson took his wife's side. "Stacy's head of the family now," Peterson would try and tell him, but Eric never listened. Until this year, life had been good. The death of Stacy's favorite sister to cancer had torn his wife apart. She had gone from unrelentingly spiritual and religious—"a very, very kind person," her church counselor Pastor Schori described her—to being a woman hopelessly adrift, no longer sure of herself, her God, or even her role as a mother. Until Tina passed away, she was a rock as a mother and wife. The days of sitting in Tina's hospital room as she wasted away, surrounded by family who prayed to God to cure Tina—too young to have terminal cancer—changed Stacy.

Now, she went to bed later, got up earlier, as if trying to avoid him. She seemed moodier, angrier. She had gone from cheerfully dreaming about moving to California to be near Aunt Candice and to "put a little distance" between her and her father and direct family, to falling into deep depressions that actually required medication at times.

Peterson flings off his shoes, still thinking of how life had changed since Tina passed away. Stacy was a different person. A stranger. Cold.

Too exhausted to think about it any more, he gently wakes Stacy. "I'm home."

"Uh-huh." He notices she is wearing a red jogging suit, almost as if to shield herself from his touch, or perhaps to cover the small scar on her stomach—a reminder of her teenage tummy tuck.

He kisses her on the cheek, a tired, dutiful gesture.

"Going to my grandpa's later," she says, sounding tired, not even opening her eyes.

"'Kay. Go to sleep."

He feels like he has just closed his eyes when he is yanked back to consciousness. Anthony tugs on his arm, pulls on his blankets and complains he's hungry. Lacy runs down the hall, laughing. More out of habit than anything, he shouts, "Knock it off!" The running feet don't stop as Lacy bursts in to the room and holds her arms up to be lifted on to the bed.

"Morning Daddy!"

"Princess, I just got home. Can you get mommy?"

"Mommy's gone," Anthony says.

Peterson sits up, the fatigue dropping away. He feels the bed beside him. It is cold, the sheets tossed back. "Where's Tommy?" Tommy is the oldest, and if Stacy left, he'd be in charge of the kids.

"Downstairs, Dad. Having cereal."

"'Kay. Coming, princess. I'm coming."

Peterson dresses quickly, alert now, although remembering Stacy said she was going to visit her grandfather. He fixes the kids breakfast, which is, by popular request, peanut butter and jelly on white toast. He sits in their country-style dining room, open concept with the large kitchen and the view to the backyard. Stacy had painted the room in warm yellows, highlighted with wrought iron sconces and sculptures, decorating around the focal point, a brick fireplace that played such a prominent role in family Christmases. Lacy and Anthony race upstairs to try on their trick-or-treat costumes for Halloween. He smiles. They just couldn't wait for trick-or-treating.

Peterson sips milk—he doesn't like coffee—stares at the family portrait by the picture window. Stacy has gone to her grandfather's, and Peterson finds himself pursing his lips in subconscious disapproval. Normally she took the kids to her grandfather's, so he is not entirely sure if this was one of her made-up stories.

A happy day. Stacy and Drew Peterson were married in a lovely outdoor wedding ceremony. During the vows, Drew held their first son Anthony.

Lately, Stacy's been distant, and she's going out a lot. Stacy took advantage of his night shift to go out with old friends from her hotel-clerking days.

Today, he is on edge. He can tell by the way she avoids him, by her stiff body language, by their lack of even a decent family argument, that she is drifting away. Perhaps she's already gone. She shows less and less interest in family days on the weekends, and he is often alone with the kids. She spends more and more time at her father's place, or with her grandfather, or her sister, but the kids stay home.

Of course he knew when Stacy had changed. The near-overnight transformation began when her sister Tina passed away. Her family had drawn together in that time, especially her aunt and sisters, praying over Tina's bed in the hospital. Stacy slept less, shouted more, suddenly had less time for her own kids as she sat in the hospital holding her sister's withered hand. Tina wasted away externally, but it was Stacy who melted on the inside, her faith in God corroding. If Tina could die so young, there was no hope for anyone. At first she talked about Tina, and the prayer vigils and her hopes. Then she stopped. She came home, tired and angry and quiet.

Stacy became irritable, less likely to go to church, more likely to snap at Tommy or Kris, or even Lacy and Anthony. Peterson found himself intervening more and more. Instead of finding comfort in her children, they got in the way of her new-found hopelessness.

Tina's death drove Stacy back into the arms of the family she had tried so hard to escape. There were times in Peterson's married life when he felt sure she married him just to escape her father, brother and sisters. She rarely had nice things to say of them, calling her father abusive. She often talked of her dream, a time when the Peterson family, Drew, Stacy, Lacy, Anthony, Kris and Tommy, would move to California to be near her much-loved Aunt Candice. And to get away from the rest of the Cales clan.

. Peterson refills his milk and stands at the counter, staring at the brick fireplace. Happy memories still warm the now-empty hearth, but family Christmases aren't among them. Last Christmas, Stacy's grandfather brought his thirty-something girlfriend, sister Cassandra brought her "out of the closet" girlfriend, and the only upside was that brother Yelton was still in prison for sexual abuse of a minor. These were the family Christmases.

Peterson smiles as Anthony runs past in his Spider-Man costume. It isn't Halloween yet, but already they are superheroes and princesses. "Don't run, Spidey."

Peterson's older son Kris is on the couch, in front of the big-screen TV. Peterson almost reminds him of chores, but it is Sunday morning.

Peterson sighs and settles at his desk. He has a lot of paperwork to finish, reports for work. He rubs his eyes. He can't concentrate. He boots up his computer, checks his email, drinks some more milk, tunes in briefly to the sounds of his kids in different rooms of the house, tries to focus on work again, finally giving up.

Where is Stacy? He thinks about calling her, but he knows she will just snap at him.

Later, he makes the kids mac and cheese, wondering again what went wrong between Stacy and him.

"She had an affair."

"She had an affair," Peterson later told me in interviews. "I know that now."

She had always flirted with her "young men" from her hotel days, before she married. She had always been that way, even when he had met her. It was what attracted him to her. In those days, like other men, moths to her flame, he had fluttered around her, but unlike some of the younger men, he knew better than to actually fly into the fire. Peterson's infatuation became love within days, and their engagement was controversial, since his divorce with Kathleen was not settled, and he was much older. Much older, at more than double her age. Her vivacious charm, bright eyes, and sheer love of life attracted him. She told him that she was attracted to his masculine charm, a man's-man cop with a successful career and a ready sense of humor.

Their relationship never cooled off. There were trips to sunny destinations, cruises, endless fruity tequila-laced drinks on sandy beaches, fun times. She made him feel young. He probably made her feel secure and loved and she responded to his masculinity. Her vulnerability revealed itself early in her desires to improve on perfection. He argued against the "boob job" and the "tummy tuck" but they made her happy. In the end, he would always agree.

Through it all, she continued to flirt. Everywhere she went, she had to be the center of attention, but in a peculiar way this made him feel good too. When he bought her a car, the salesman gave him a thumbs-up and a wink—man-code for "way to rob the cradle." She was a gorgeous, sparkling nymph, who appealed to him as much as to any man she mesmerized.

And she was mostly loyal to him, he was sure. The kids came to love her, even though Kris and Tommy felt awkward that they were roughly half her age. Only the oldest son Eric, older than Stacy, never came around, distancing himself permanently from the new family unit.

Four years of happiness, and now this.

When sister Tina passed, it all changed. First the grief then the distance. Finally, Stacy had gone back to her old ways of aggressive flirting. She became more and more distant, and soon she was nearly a stranger. She had her temper tantrums too. He joked that her worst tempers came with her cycle, but the truth was she was cold much of the time since Tina passed away.

She had lost her hope. She lost her faith in God. Their prayers and laying on of hands at Tina's hospital bed had done nothing to save Tina. God had deserted Stacy. Nothing seemed right with the world for her anymore, and not even the kids were enough. More and more often he found his days spent with the kids instead of sleeping, as she went out for extended shopping sprees, returning with bags and bags of clothes.

Only yesterday, Stacy had brought home another armload of shopping bags full of clothes, still unpacked in the closet upstairs. Maxing out the credit cards was her way of dealing. It had all gone wrong. Perhaps it was his own fault for hoping he could be happy with a woman so young and vivacious. But he had been happy. She had been happy. She would get over it. Grief passed. She would see the children needed her. That he needed her.

Little stabs of guilt came on the heels of his fatigue-driven ponderings. He had never slept around—he'd always been loyal—but he did flirt. Paula Stark, wife of his new venture partner Lenny Wawczak, often threw herself at him in their nearby house. The flirting made Drew feel guilty. Lenny wasn't really a close friend, just a partner in their new scheme to renovate houses. Paula was sexy, and she knew it, an ex-stripper who still had the body that made her irresistible. But he had resisted.

Peterson sighs. He decides to dress, do some chores. If Stacy is away at grandpa's, he'll have to do the errands.

The bedroom seems empty. He reaches for the closet door. For the first time, he notices the shopping bags, full of new clothes she had bought only yesterday, are gone.

Peterson watched Lacy and Anthony on their bikes that afternoon, still simmering over the unfairness of another failing marriage. The leaves had turned on the tree on his lawn. He finished the errands, leaving the kids briefly with Tommy and Kris. They were old enough to baby-sit for a short time at least, and he was only gone a half hour.

He worked around the driveway without any enthusiasm, picking up a few toys.

Maybe a trip, just Stacy and him, might make a difference. Stacy loved to travel, drawn to hot beaches and tropical drinks decorated with little paper umbrellas. Or maybe just a weekend jaunt on their his-and-hers Harleys, just him and Stacy, to see the fall colors. It couldn't be over for them. The kids loved Stacy. A trip, a way to unwind, that would bring back the spark.

The kids were their joy. They were gorgeous kids, the flaming center of Peterson's life, his purpose. From dimpled and adorable Lacy to irrepressible Anthony, to the teenagers Kris and Tommy, both teens straight A students, one a wrestling champion, the other a talented musician. They were perfect children. Adult son Stephen was a Police Officer, and Peterson was particularly proud of him and his new family. And he still regretted Eric, alienated since Stacy moved in to the house.

"Button up your coat, princess," Peterson said, as Lacy raced down the driveway.

Analysis: Peterson's account of October 28th differs on key points from the hearsay accounts of Ric Mims and Cassandra Cales and witness testimony of Thomas Morphey previously presented. The stories of Mims, Cales and Morphey also differ on key points. Refer to the polygraph for some insight into the truthfulness—or lack thereof—of this dramatized account and also the breaking news last chapter "Postscript: Stacy's Plan?"

Exclusive Timeline from Drew Peterson
October 28, 2007

Between 5:30 and 6:00 AM
• Drew comes home from work at Bolingbrook Police Department • Talked to Stacy, she said she was going to visit her grandfather • Drew went to sleep

10:00 AM	11:00 AM	12:00 NOON	1:00 PM
Between 10:00 and 10:30 AM (maybe as late as 11:00 AM): • Drew awakened by children • Stacy gone, kids home		Drew at home with kids until 1:00 PM	

1:00 PM	1:30 PM	2:00 PM
• Children at home (Tom and Kris watching Anthony and Lacy) • Drew went out to run Sunday errands		• Drew calls work (Bolingbrook Police Dept) takes the night off. (He did this because he was retiring in December and had 1300 hours of accumulated sick time he needed to either use or loose {sic})

3:15 PM	6:00 PM
• Tom (14 year old son) is picked up for band concert by school friends	• Drew takes Kris, Anthony and Lacy to McDonald's. They have dinner and play at playground at McDonald's.

7:30 PM	8:00 PM
• Drew, Kris, Anthony and Lacy return home	• Tom gets home from band concert

9:00 PM	9:15 PM
• Drew at home, receives call from Stacy that she found someone and is leaving	• Drew leaves home to go and look for Stacy

Between 11:00 and 11:30 PM	11:45 PM
• Drew returns home • Cassandra Cales (Stacy's sister) called Drew after returned home (while he still was in the driveway of the home), Drew tells her Stacy called him and said she found someone else and left with another man, and she took her passport, money and her clothes	• Drew walked and got Stacy's car and drove it home

12:00 midnight	Around 2:30 AM
• Drew gets home and goes to bed	• Drew gets call from Bolingbrook PD telling him that Cassandra is making a missing persons report regarding Stacy • Drew vaguely recalls getting another call, it may have been from Cassandra's friend Bruce Zidrach. (Drew very tired and does not have a clear recollection of this call)

Peterson continues answering questions from the author as we drive to pick up son Tommy from the high school. Peterson is fiercely proud of all his children. Tommy and Kris are "straight A's" in school and Tommy's in the band. He is driving in the GMC Yukon that was siezed by State Police during the investigation.

"These timelines are messed up."

Timelines are testimonial-based as a rule, so when Joel Brodsky, lawyer for Drew Peterson, says, "These timelines are messed up," he's probably happy about it.

He is, in fact, smiling as he says this, pacing around his desk, necktie tossed aside, shirt unbuttoned, his hands dancing with boundless energy. His office is a large corner office, overlooking the "Magnificent Mile" and the lake in one of Chicago's pristine architectural gems, but size doesn't seem to matter, because every inch of the desk, sideboards, even much of the floor, is piled high with pending files, documents and pictures. For all the clutter, he knows instantly where everything is, diving into a pile and yanking out a document to demonstrate the point. His computer must be equally crowded with documents, because often when I pose a question, he prints off a new document for me: autopsy reports, witness statements, phone records—it all seems to reside in his desktop computer. Even as he paces, he stands over his keyboard and squints at his flat-screen monitor.

This is a different man than the one portrayed in tailor-made suits on *Larry King Live* or *Today*. He appears distinguished and youngish in person, in spite of a graying beard and a receding hairline that somehow suits him. His sleeves are rolled up, his glasses are perched halfway down his nose, his eyes sparkle with a teenager's enthusiasm, and his hands never stop moving. Earlier, as we talked autopsies, he demonstrated with his own body, revealing where a contusion might be, and showing me the specific size of a bruise. I can't help but think that the blog critics of Joel Brodsky—the one's I've come to know in my early research of the case—are in for a big surprise. Brodsky's a very sharp lawyer, and there's a lot going on in that freckled dome. On live TV he may pause and think, then correct himself, but any adversary in a courtroom would be wise to expect devastating surprises and savvy lawyering. As a crime fiction writer, I've already stored away Brodsky as a future template for a lawyer character in my next Alban Bane thriller.

"No one agrees on what happened," Brodsky continued. "Mims has a completely different story from Sharon. Cassandra doesn't agree with Bruce. We won't even talk about Morphey, because his timeline's a train wreck."

All this in response to my request for a timeline from Drew. I pushed: "Then an official timeline will settle it, won't it? I know you're holding your cards close, as any good attorney would, but if Drew's willing to take a polygraph, why not tie it to a timeline, too?"

I've prepared my logical arguments for this meeting. I know I don't want to leave without a timeline. The police probably don't have one from Peterson. No members of the media do. I could be exclusive on both the polygraphs and a timeline of the day Stacy "ran off"[50] and the day Kathleen died in her bathtub. I was prepared to camp out in Joel's office until I got it.

"Eyewitness … is the single greatest cause of wrongful convictions"

Key elements of the timelines rely on eyewitness testimony, for example the presence (or lack thereof) of cars in the driveway, and Thomas Morphey's astonishing account of the blue barrel on the night of October 28, 2007.

Some of my analysis is anchored in current research on the unreliability of eyewitnesses. I'm at best one of those much-despised armchair lawyers, although I know something about these things from my crime novels. Many wrongfully convicted persons were found guilty based solely on eyewitness accounts and other non-empirical evidence.

In "A Survey of Judges' Knowledge and Beliefs About Eyewitness Testimony," Richard A. Wise and Martin Safer reveal some important data that questions the whole notion of eyewitness testimony as admissible at all (not their words, my own conclusion), most pointedly their extrapolated statistic: "5,000 wrongful felony convictions in 1998."[51]

According to The Innocence Project, founded in 1992 by Barry C. Scheck and Peter J. Neufeld to assist prisoners who could be proven innocent through DNA testing, "Eyewitness misidentification is the single greatest cause of wrongful convictions nationwide, playing a role in more than 75% of convictions overturned through DNA testing."[52]

Based on these two pieces of data, incorrect eyewitness testimony could result in as many as 3750 wrongful convictions. Even assuming some part of this equation is wrong, we're still speaking of thousands of wrongful convictions each year, based on incorrect eyewitness testimony.

"Speaking Out"

More and more, prosecutors, stung by wrongful conviction statistics and the ensuing compensation or lawsuits, use eyewitnesses only to set a light appetizer course before juries, backing their cases up with hard forensic evidence. While the courts may have shifted from frequent reliance on eyewitnesses, including timelines, identifications and descriptions, the media tear into eyewitnesses as the main dish in their version of a public trial. Nothing is as compelling on the television reports, as an eyewitness speaking, preferably with some emotion. DNA and forensic evidence is just dry matter.

In the case of Drew Peterson, it hardly matters that the ex friends and neighbors conflict on nearly every point in their time flows. The individual sound bites are delicious, compelling, aromatic and emotional.

The FOX News coverage on *On The Record with Greta Van Susteren* illustrates this in the very titles of the regular reports on Drew Peterson:

- Kyle Opens Up
- Stacy Peterson's friend and neighbor describes vandalism at home
- Drew Peterson's friend goes 'On the Record' about domestic calls
- Speaking Out: Stacy Peterson's pastor reveals what she knew
- Trucker who claimed Drew Peterson approached him was lying
- Sgt. Drew Peterson's attorney responds to largest accusations against his client
- Stacy Peterson's stepsisters respond to Drew Peterson's decision to stay in the limelight
- Lisa, daughter of Drew Peterson's second wife, speaks out
- What sort of policeman was Sgt. Drew Peterson? Bolingbrook Police Chief Raymond McGury goes 'On the Record'
- Family of Drew Peterson's third wife speak out
- Missing woman's sister speaks to Greta

And many more. Of course, television is a visual medium, but a quick search of newspapers reveals, by my count, 211,672 words written about Drew Peterson based on interviewing potential, and often contradictory, witnesses, neighbors and ex-friends.

Since the media reporters don't stand as judge and jury, it hardly matters if the evidence is conclusive, leading, or even misleading. As long as it's interesting. Ratings are the rule, not judgments.

Of course, freedom of speech and the Constitution protects journalists as much as victims and criminals, so litigation against media, reporters and correspondents, book authors and publishers is quite rare, and hardly ever successful, as it should be. To hamper a free press, from mainstream press to book publishers and authors to bloggers, is inexcusable, in the same way it is inexcusable to convict an innocent for lack of evidence. A free society must have a

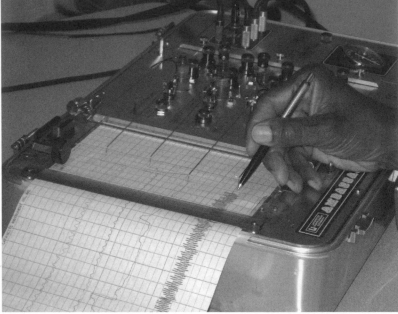

free press and the notion of "innocent until proven guilty." And in a free society, of course, there's a cliché for every occasion, including my favorite: "better to let ten guilty men go free than one innocent be punished."

"A polygraph would make a difference"

My quick search of various public reports on Drew and Stacy Peterson revealed sixteen requests, on the record, for polygraphs, from police, national media and me. Add to these literally hundreds of suggestions in the blog world; a quick search of "Drew Peterson" combined with "polygraph" produces many hits on Technorati and Google.

The problem with a polygraph for defense lawyers is that once it's "on the record" it stays there. If the polygraph is favorable to the "suspect," the police and media will point out that it's not admissible in many courts. If it's favorable to the prevailing theories of law enforcement or the media, it will be triumphantly held up as conclusive proof.

The very idea of submitting to a polygraph, for any suspect, is usually quite terrifying. To Drew Peterson, it merited no more than a confident shrug of the shoulders and a casual Chicago-style, "Sure."

"Did you physically harm your wife?"

The first of Drew Peterson's polygraph examinations took place in a thirty-second-floor boardroom of Chicago's historic Willoughby Towers, on a cool and clear Sunday, May 18, 2008. The elevators rattle and wheeze alarmingly as visitors climb some four hundred feet from the street, a grim reminder of two brave firefighters who died in this very elevator shaft in the 1980s, fighting a fire in a burning elevator car.

The view from lawyer Joel Brodsky's conference room, high atop one of the buildings that made Chicago famous as a living museum of architecture, is of unobstructed park and waterfront. Though this was cool sweatshirt weather in Chicago, the heat in the lofty boardroom was about to shoot up a few degrees as Peterson, a suspect in the disappearance of wife Stacy Peterson and in the death of third wife Kathleen Savio, was "wired up" by examiner Lee McCord, a thirty-four-year expert in the polygraph.[53]

After nearly ninety minutes of control questions, designed to test physiological responses to known true and false questions, McCord got right down to business.

"Did you have any involvement in the physical removal of your wife Stacy from your home on Sunday, October 28, 2007?"

Perspiration-free and unflappable, Peterson says, "No."

Showing no emotion at all, pen poised over the chart, McCord asked, "Did you in any way physically harm your wife Stacy during the time that she disappeared?"

Without hesitation, Drew Peterson answers, "No."

Lee McCord turns up the heat as the examination continues, the results of which are potentially explosive.

Polygraphs a Dream Tool?

The polygraph is an investigator's dream tool. Depending on which side of a "case" you land on, you'll either condemn it as a

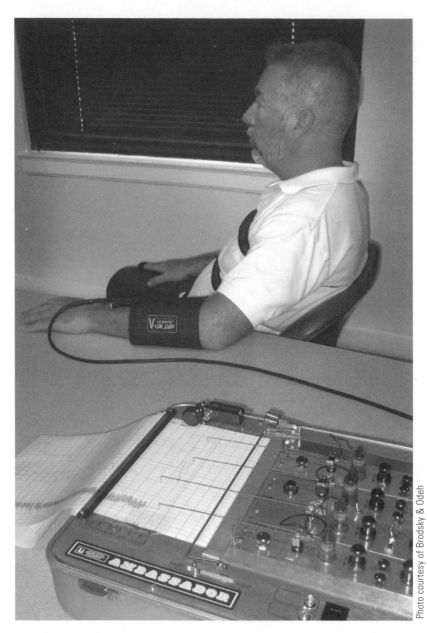

Drew Peterson, reluctantly "strapped in" to polygraph equipment, being examined by Lee McCord in the conference room of Brodsky & Odeh.

"toss of the coin"[54] or laud it as absolute proof of your claim. Fail a test, your defense lawyer can claim the venerable lie-detector is at best a fifty-fifty proposition. Pass a test, the same lawyer waves it in front of the media to dismiss sensationalized claims and defuse the modern-day "trial by media" tabloidization of the justice system.

Defense attorneys routinely advise their clients against taking polygraphs, calling them unreliable, unless, of course—after the fact—the results favor their client. Police just as routinely use polygraphs to create sufficient tension to encourage confession. A nicely placed "Are you sure of your answer?" in the middle of a polygraph examination can cause even a cool-headed perpetrator to change a story. In the absence of hard DNA evidence or eyewitness testimony, the lie-detector bluff may be a shortcut to a confession.

The infamous Mark Fuhrman[55] claimed O.J. Simpson failed a polygraph arranged by his defense team on the question of murdering his ex-wife: "One of the first things Shapiro (Simpson's defense attorney) did was arrange for Simpson to take a polygraph test. But he failed the test so completely that the results were kept secret ..."[56]

This was later denied by Simpson's lawyer F. Lee Bailey. In 2000, O.J. Simpson offered to take a polygraph to clear his name after the civil trial awarded damages against him.[57] Responding to Larry King on *Larry King Live* regarding renowned attorney Alan Dershowitz's claim that polygraphs are unreliable, the famous F. Lee Bailey said, "Well, I've been at it for better than forty-five years. I've been an expert witness in more than a dozen cases. I know it like the back of my hand. I can read the charts, and it's something that Alan Dershowitz doesn't know about. Between Alan and I, we know everything, but this is one of the things I know. So Alan can distrust it all he wants, but if Alan were charged with a murder he didn't commit and I told him to take a polygraph, I bet he'd do it."[58]

The disagreement between these two legendary lawyers reflects the general disagreement in various research studies. The American Polygraph Association attempts to clarify the dispute: "If 10 polygraph examinations are administered and the examiner is correct in 7 decisions, wrong in 1 and has 2 inconclusive test results, we calculate the accuracy rate as 87.5% (8 definitive results, 7 of which were correct.) Critics of the polygraph technique would calculate the accuracy rate in this example as 70%, (10 examinations with 7 correct decisions)."[59]

Regardless of interpretation, polygraphs are at least 70 percent accurate, and by some accounts as reliable as 98 percent (See "Average accuracy of 98 percent"). Many federal courts, at the discretion of judges, will accept polygraphs.

Polygraphs are widely used by all law enforcement agencies, from federal to local, the legal community from US Attorney Offices to Parole and Probation Departments, and are admissible in some states in courts of law.[60] Specifically, polygraphs are widely used [61]by:

- Law Enforcement Agencies: Federal Law Enforcement Agencies, State Law Enforcement Agencies, and Local Law Enforcement Agencies such as Police and Sheriff's Departments.[62]
- Legal Community: US Attorney Offices, District Attorney Offices, Public Defender Offices, Defense Attorneys, Parole & Probation Departments.[63]
- Private Sector: Companies and Corporations under the restrictions and limitations of the Employee Polygraph Protection Act of 1988 (EPPA).[64]
- Private citizens in matters not involving the legal or criminal justice system.[65]
- Attorneys in civil litigation.[66]

"Very revealing questions"

To which I would add, if it's good enough for FOX TV, it's good enough for most people.

FOX TV's *The Moment of Truth*, a show with "23 million viewers,"[67] asks contestants very revealing questions, verified by a polygraph. There's no talk of accuracy. Contestants faced with the polygraph either tell the truth or leave the show before the heat gets turned too high. So far, according to *TV Guide*, "no player has been fired ... at least not yet" but "*Truth* has torn lovebirds apart."[68] There can be no doubt that most viewers, and all of the contestants, accept the absolute veracity of the polygraph.

According to Mike Darnell, FOX's president of alternative entertainment, "In the vast majority of contestants, 99% don't say the machine is wrong ... I don't think we ever got in wrong in the 24 contestants we've had. And they never protested."[69]

TV Week's feature on *The Moment of Truth*, adds, "The American Polygraph Association, from compiling hundreds of research studies on the matter, says field examinations produced an accuracy rate between 92% and 98%. Laboratory-based examinations were less accurate at 80% to 81%."[70]

Interestingly, Drew Peterson's team downplayed rumors that Peterson was asked to appear on *The Moment of Truth*. At first, my queries about this rumor were deflected, but finally I obtained an admission from Peterson in one of my interviews: "I was willing to take a polygraph on national TV. I've got nothing to hide. But we never got too far with it."

"Average accuracy of 98 percent"

The American Polygraph Association leads in compiling research into the validity of polygraphs:

Researchers conducted 12 studies of the validity of field examinations, following 2,174 field examinations, providing an average accuracy of 98 percent. Researchers conducted 11 studies involving the reliability of independent analyses of 1,609 sets of charts from field examinations confirmed by independent evidence, providing an average accuracy of 92 percent. Researchers conducted 41 studies involving the accuracy of 1,787 laboratory simulations of polygraph examinations, producing an average accuracy of 80 percent.[71]

"Most Americans Suspect Drew Peterson"

In a MediaCurves survey[72] designed to measure changes in viewer responses to a fixed question over the course of TV coverage, 56 percent of Americans thought Drew Peterson was "guilty" in the disappearance of Stacy at the beginning of the famous first appearance on *Today* with Matt Lauer. By the end of the show, this increased to 68 percent believing he was guilty.

This only proves he's not his best advocate—or not very convincing—when suited up and confronted with an experienced national talk show host. Interestingly, in the comments area of this survey, one sharp viewer wrote: "I wish they would quit fooling around and make him take a lie detector test. That alone would show just how guilty he is. Lock him up and throw away the key!"

"I have nothing to hide."

So what do we make of Drew Peterson's willingness to take a polygraph? During one of my hours-long interview sessions, I asked if he'd retake the polygraph. His smile never faltered for a moment. "Sure. Why not?" Even when I asked if he'd do it publicly, perhaps on national TV, he said, "I have nothing to hide."

"Why do you think you are a suspect in the death of Kathleen Savio?" I asked, making sure my recorder was taping.

"I was a cop for thirty years. We always suspect the intimates," ex-Sergeant Peterson said. "Me, personally, I still believe it was an accident." Again, he didn't seem agitated or angry. It seemed to be nearly impossible to get a rise out of Drew Peterson.

Peterson leaned closer, eyes unwavering. "I can look you in the eye and tell you I had nothing to do with Stacy's disappearance or Kathleen's death."

"The primary purpose of a polygraph … truthful or untruthful."

The American Association of Police Polygraphists state as the primary purpose of a polygraph:

"The primary purpose of a polygraph examination is to determine if the person being examined is being truthful or untruthful to the issue under investigation." They go on to state that the polygraph may be used to test the veracity of suspects, victims and informants.

Important to the test, are the polygraphist's credentials and the instrument, which *"must be capable of recording visually, permanently and simultaneously, indications of a person's:*

1. *Cardiovascular pattern and changes therein.,*
2. *Respiratory pattern and changes therein.*
3. *Changes in skin resistance (Electrodermal Responses)."*

The polygraph instrument should be calibrated as per manufacturer's instructions.[73]

Assuming Drew's Guilt

Since I was as influenced by media reporting as anyone else, I began my extensive interviews with Drew Peterson assuming his guilt, even taking an investigator's method of interview by changing the subject frequently in an effort to throw my "suspect" off guard. Peterson remained remarkably consistent and calm, even after days of interviews, often without a break for food. Of course I'm no detective, and I'm not intimidating at all—I work my interviews by building confidence, not by bullying. I recorded every moment of our interviews. By coming back to the same question, unexpectedly, over and over, I've found that most interview subjects slip up a time or two. It's a time-honored method.

What can I take from his willingness to retake polygraphs, even on TV, his consistency in my interviews, and my research into homicide rates among "intimates"? Nothing, at this point. I hammered away with my questions, assuming guilt, simply because the police, the public and the media had already tried and convicted him. A quick visit to almost any Peterson blog reveals spicy comments by the thousands, variations on these un-edited posts to FOX TV's Greta Van Susteren blog:[74]

* He's a nut ... the media is doing their job.
* Get this lying SOB off the street ...
* Yes I think Drew killed her ... the media did not make up my mind in any way!
* The jerk has EVERYTHING TO DO WITH HER DISAPPEARANCE!! ... the media is doing their job... the guy's a circus sideshow ...
* Why doesn't someone just assassinate him?

«Back to Browse

FOX NEWS.com

We Report.
You Decide.

SEARC

HOME | U.S. | WORLD | POLITICS | BUSINESS | HEALTH | SCITECH | ENTER

RADIO | MOBILE | FOX & Friends | Live Desk | Studio B | Your World | Special Report | FOX Re

ON THE RECORD / Greta Van Susteren

December 7th, 2007 6:44 AM Eastern

FRIDAY: Ric Mims Sold Story to National Enquirer????

by Greta Van Susteren

At least one newspaper is reporting that Ric Mims - former friend of Sgt. Drew Peterson I ass
not current friend - sold his story to the National Enquirer. How much? And what is his rea
find out, click here

So...POST YO

Ric Mims, a so-called ex-friend of Peterson,
sold his story to the *National Enquirer* for
$35,000. The story is somewhat incredible,
recounting a "snapped neck" and other
sensational details.

Author's photo

- He is evil.
- Now if for some small chance (like a billion to one) that he is innocent, then we, the media, etc will owe this man a lifelong never ending apology. However I do believe that he's guilty. If someone accused me, the VERY FIRST thing I would do is to tell them to give me a lie detector test.
- Come on Greta, Dr. Baden, MARK FURMAN. When did your show become judge and jury for this case? Mark Furman is making it up as he goes and you seem to be swallowing the whole bit. Mark Furman has no legal right to be investigating this case. What a joke. Get real unless you want to lose all credibility.

What Exactly is the Case?

What exactly is the "case" against Peterson in the disappearance of wife Stacy? According to ex-FBI profiler Clint Van Zandt, who analyzed Peterson's performance on the now infamous *Today* interviews with Matt Laucr, the case is built on these "facts":

- Peterson was thirty years his wife's senior
- Peterson was deceptive with his wives, particularly relating to his infidelities
- Peterson allegedly beat his third wife
- Peterson was paying child support
- Stacy Peterson told her neighbor she was afraid of Peterson.[75]

I must admit I was as ready as anyone to assume the worst of Peterson, but none of this seemed particularly compelling to me, especially if Peterson was willing to subject himself to a polygraph, and assuming he passed. The age difference doesn't seem relevant in today's world. Peterson admits his infidelities, and deception with wives is pretty common. Peterson wasn't charged with beating his third wife, and "paying child support" seems a weak motive for murder given he's now supporting all of his children alone.

So the case against Peterson seems mostly related to his moral character, and nearly every blog on the Internet condemns the ex-police officer for that.

Since Van Zandt's rather subjective analysis, somewhat more concrete elements have materialized in media stories, including ex-friends turned witnesses, a crusading neighbor, and a conflicted timeline that doesn't hold up to scrutiny:

- Neighbor Sharon Bychowski saw cars in the driveway at certain times (an account that contradicts other witnesses), and presented some hearsay recollections from Peterson's son Kris, which Kris denies.
- Ex-friend Richard Mims sold a highly exaggerated story to the *National Enquirer* for $35,000.
- Stepbrother and ex-employee Thomas Morphey gave a fuzzy account of blue barrels (some say containers) warm to the touch, which are somewhat less than credible given his drug history, various experiments with barrel surfaces (testing the warmth theory), and the corroborated timeline of Peterson.

Which leaves us with the most entertaining installment in the soap opera to date.

"He's goin' away."

In yet another bizarre, barely credible incident, this one reminiscent of an episode of *Trailer Park Boys*,[76] "potty-mouthed"[77] Lenny Wawczak, who claims to be an ex-friend of Drew Peterson, cheerfully told Chicago-area media that he and his wife Paula Stark wore wiretaps on behalf of the Illinois State Police and "He's goin' away … He's done."

Described on FOX News as "two of Peterson's oldest and closest friends" by Greta Van Susteren, it turns out (in Wawczak's own account) that he is actually only a business acquaintance who first got to know Peterson after various run-ins with the law, later reported on FOX News in a follow-up.

In a July 24, 2008 interview on FOX, Van Susteren interviewed Wawczak and Paula Stark:

Greta: You taped Drew Peterson?
Wawczak: Yes Ma'am (looking uncomfortable, sitting on a couch in front of an empty aquarium).
Greta: Why?
Wawczak: Ah, we were asked to do it from the Illinois State Police. (Looks even less comfortable, chewing his lip.)

o Mall – News Story – WMAQ | Chicago

itness Evidence...   Help and How–To fo...   Veromi.net | People ...   stacy_peterson_chri...   Database Ac

Media Influences the Legal Syst... ⊗   Tom Morphey – News, photos, t... ⊗   Amazon.com: Objec

NBC5.com – Image

830/detail.html

69   I: **394000**   Rank: **34107**   Age: **May 24, 1998**   I: **0**   whois   source   Robo: **no**   Sitemap: **no**   Density   Links:

Author's photo

Breaking story in the *Sun-Times*, so-called ex friends of Drew Peterson, Lenny Wawczak and Paula Stark, either sell story or go for media face time. They claim to have worn a "wire" for the Illinois State Police. Most analysts find the story hard to believe, doubting the police would allow the release of information and questioning the technology demonstrated.

Greta: Paula, about how many hours of taping did you do of Drew Peterson?

Paula: (looking at her knee). Honestly, I don't think I could begin to guess. I would say (shakes head) over a thousand.

Greta: How is that, I mean I'm a little bit curious Len, that, why are you speaking out on this? Why is it all over the newspapers, and then you can't talk about it?

Wawczak: (licks lips, frowning) Yeah, exactly, um, we can—we can say various things, but naturally, I mean, you know, they don't wan' us sayin' exactly what went on ...

Greta: How long have you known Drew Peterson?

Wawczak: About sixteen, seventeen years ... no, honestly Greta, we only started talking on a regular basis shortly before Stacy went missing ... we were going to start rehabbing houses and stuff.

Paula: My relationship with him (Peterson) was just the homes and things. As soon as Stacy went missing is when he started ... telling me that he needed a woman like ... he could show me the world, and telling me he loves me ...

Greta: Did you actually wear a wire on your body or was it a tape device in the room?

Paula: No, it was on the body. It was on the body. Ah-ah Lenn was wearing it, I was wearing it.

Wawczak: You know what, him and Joel saying that, you know, we tried to borrow money off him and we stormed up out of there. You know what, it's just not true. It's not true.

Wawczak also vigorously denied that he met Peterson when he was arrested. Carefully choosing his words, he did not deny that he was arrested, only that Peterson arrested him.

Wawczak and Paula Stark had planned to go into business renovating homes in Bolingbrook and flipping them for a profit, just before Stacy disappeared. At this point they were casual acquaintances. After October 28, 2007, Lenny Wawczak and Paula Stark insinuated themselves into Peterson's life, babysitting and befriending the kids, and then not too subtly baiting Peterson. "Paula was the funniest," Peterson said. "She was so obvious when she tried to pry me for information. Wawczak wasn't quite as smart. He'd say things like 'We should burn that Stacy search boat' then try to imply I said it. He's not the smartest guy."

Peterson, who was licensed for electronic surveillance as a police officer, figured out a few months previously that they were likely "bait" for the wiretaps already planted in his home. "In wiretaps, we sometimes used to plant people in the room to encourage a conversation, to record a suspect's responses. Wawczak wasn't very good at it though. He did most of the talking. If there were tapes, you'd just hear me laughing at what he's saying."

Lenny Wawczak and Paula Stark couldn't resist breaking the story in a Chicago-area newspaper about the wiretaps. "Normally," Peterson said, "you'd never reveal the taps. That's just stupid. So, if the state police did allow them to talk to the media, I guess they're trying to 'rattle me.' Otherwise, they made a mistake." .

I can personally vouch for Peterson's paranoia about wiretaps. Several weeks before the Wawczak story broke about the wiretapping, Peterson told me, as we sat in the recreation room in his home, "My entire house is bugged. My phones and cell phone are tapped. Even my car and plane have GPS." He went so far as to suggest that because I had called his cell phone, my cell phone might be tapped too. "You can turn any phone into a bug if you want," he said. "If I want privacy, I'd have to go take the battery out of my cell phone and go somewhere public."

Peterson had continued with our lengthy interviews, knowing that—from his point of view—the Illinois State Police were likely listening.

It seems improbable that he didn't know he was being recorded when speaking with Wawczak and Stark, since most of their conversations were in Peterson's house, a place he "knows" is bugged. He also suspected his own cell phone—which he carries everywhere—has been turned into a listening device. "I used to supervise surveillance ops. We could hear everything clearer than you heard things on your own cell phone."

Peterson's attorney Joel Brodsky agreed: "I doubt they wore a wire. Their description in the newspaper's all wrong. State police use solid-state equipment. Their description was like something out of an old movie. But we do know that Wawczak and Stark's conversations with Drew were recorded. The home bugs we've known about since last year."

When I asked why they came forward with the story in the media, Brodsky theorized, "Either for money, or the state police sanctioned it as a way to shake up Peterson." Richard Mims' lucrative sale of his Drew story to the *National Enquirer* is an example of the kind of money to be made.

Having now spent a lot of time with Peterson, and given his thirty years as a police officer, including his undercover work, I doubted anything the state police could do would ever "shake up" Peterson. Brodsky agreed. "It's just all tactics. They don't have anything else they can do."

. For the record, Illinois State Police will not confirm or deny the "tapes" and, as of this writing, the state's attorney evaded the defense's proper demand for discovery.

Having Fun with Lenny-isms

Lenny-isms are almost as much fun to read on his blogs and media interviews as Rickyisms on the hit TV show *Trailer Park Boys*: "Why don't you f**k off. Go get some hyposuction," or "You make my words, I'm goin' to get my grade ten and everyone else can catch a boat to f**koffny land."[78]

Not quite as witty as Ricky, but just as profane, there are plenty of four-letter words on the "Justice Now For Kathleen and Stacy"[79] blog, one of Lenny Wawczak's sites (under the pseudonym of Ashley):

- …looking dumb as s**t as usual…
- Are you sweating yet A**holes?
- You 2 stupid f**kers
- Drew never arrested me once … another lie by them two f**kheads.
- Here's a hint for you, STUPID F**K…

"The noblest of motivations"

Lenny Wawczak and Paula Stark claim they wore a wiretap for the Illinois State Police for "the noblest of motivations." However, according to Peterson they "needed money" and an investigation by FOX Chicago, supports this suggestion: "They both have a checkered criminal and financial past and may need an influx of cash now more than ever."[80]

Wawczak and Stark, who claim to be Peterson's friends, met Stacy Peterson only once. In the FOX coverage, Paula Stark claimed she wore a wire to tape Drew Peterson at her husband's insistence because his father was shot to death. Lenny's father's killer, she says, was caught because a citizen did the right thing. "Don't tell that to the man Wawczak left bleeding in the street," FOX reports. Wawczak ran down a man on a Bolingbrook street in 2001, was charged with hit-and-run, and later sued successfully by the victim for $350,000. Wawczak never paid. "Wawczak has never had a driver's license. He was found guilty of leaving the scene of an accident. Bonner (the victim) told me he has never collected a dime, and probably never will."

Wawczak filed for bankruptcy in 2004. Stark has filed for bankruptcy six times since 1998. FOX reports, "But they claim they had enough money to buy fixer-upper homes with Peterson." Stark in the interview said, "We decided we were going to go into business with him." When challenged on Peterson's claim that they made up the wiretap story to sell it for money, Stark said, "We don't need money. If I ever needed money, it would be my mother."

In a recent FOX TV poll, 41.22 percent of Americans agreed that "Drew Peterson is right when he says his former friends are telling a story motivated by money."[81]

Either adding to Wawczak's credibility, or damaging it, the ex-friend also admitted to having an "online romance" with Peterson in the guise of the now-famous "Ashley," and in this guise he apparently tried to sell his story to the *National Enquirer*. The news of Wawczak's female alter ego broke one day after he claimed publicly to have done the wiretap. In the *Reporter*, Peterson was quoted as saying "I've been playing practical jokes for most of my life and for someone to get me like that, I'm impressed."

Wiretaps real?

Drew Peterson himself believes his house, cell phone and probably his cars are "bugged" and this is possible. On a discovery motion from the defense team of Brodsky & Odeh, a five-hundred-page discovery was eventually delivered from the state's attorney, relating to the "guns charges" and some revealing facts have come to light. (In particular see the last chapter "Postscript: Stacy's Plan?") However, on the specific requirement of disclosure on surveillance, the state's attorney evaded the request. "This is not proper," lawyer Joel Brodsky indicated, "especially given the extraordinary revelations in the affidavit so far."

"Drew. take a lie detector test"

This often repeated demand—"Drew, take a lie detector test"[82]—is no doubt driven by the frustrating lack of real evidence. There is plenty of reason to suspect, but nothing hard to land a case on.

The way to convince Peterson is to either make it worth his while—"Hey, you could put all this behind you"—or to show that it's the popular thing to do with the broader American public. Peterson is the first to admit he loves the limelight, the "class clown" who never outgrew the center-stage addiction.

The solution? Send Peterson to Jamie Colby's FOX News report "To Take or Not to Take: Drew Peterson and the Lie Detector Question." The long string of responses to the question in her blog is almost like a challenge. Comment after comment, with variations on:

- I would LOVE to see Drew take the test ... I DON'T think he will.
- He likes control and he would lose some taking the test.
- Drew impresses me as the kind of guy that might think he could beat a lie detector. I doubt he will ...
- He's a pathological liar. No he will never take the test.
- He's afraid of the truth.
- Yes he should but NO he will not!!! He is a coward!!

The last comment, and the long string of others, is like a gauntlet, a challenge. Of course Drew Peterson will take a polygraph.

For the first time, Peterson has agreed to these polygraphs, revealed in this book.

Before revealing those results, and because media and public sentiment against the notorious ex-cop Peterson seems to be almost entirely based on his presumed moral character, I decided to interview Peterson extensively on his past, reminding him, almost holding it over him like a threat, that the polygraph would reveal all.

He promised to be honest, even where his moral character was in question.

There can be no doubt that Peterson's a colorful character. My interviews revealed a man who is very much "in love with himself"

and he's proud of it. He boasts about infidelities. His escapades through his very dramatic career as an MP, protecting the president of the United States and the emperor of Japan, and as a narcotics undercover officer—where he was fired (then reinstated) for going too deep undercover—are the stuff of movie legend, and they reveal a not entirely appetizing character. Since, in investigations, a key plank in any case is always the "suspect's" character—and before revealing the results of the polygraph (oh, go ahead, if you can't wait, flip ahead!)—I present here, exclusively, for the first time, the real story of Peterson's colorful past, full of unedited dark moments, hilarious situations, and some very revealing history.

The story spans his early "girl-crazy" teen years to his later "girl-crazy" adult life as cop and cradle-robbing husband, including how he met Kathleen and Stacy, how their marriages fell apart and what came after.

I'll begin with a recent incident that illustrates his irrepressible character, and his out-of-control libido (arguably, the characteristic that continues to get him in trouble), then move on to a quick fly-by on his earlier life and bring us back to the present. Then, dear readers, I promise to reveal the results of the polygraphs and show whether they support or demolish his stories of not-always-scrupled innocence.

Photo courtesy of Drew Peterson

Stacy and Drew Peterson during trip to St. Thomas.

"The dating game"

This Thursday pre-dawn is like any other on Pheasant Chase Court. Children are sleeping, the streetlights are on, but at the end of each driveway in the cul-de-sac are big double-wheeled media trucks, vibrating and noisy. Generators drone, a sound that carries to suburban bedrooms. The neighbors who are used to the invasive sound can sleep. Instead of pleasant dreams, the neighbors endure a living nightmare.

As dawn approaches, a dusky grey giving way to a warm sunrise, this dead-end street is revealed as a neighborhood under siege. The sun glitters off dozens of satellites, then glances off asphalt rooftops and warms the snow.

Most houses have variations on "Keep Out" signs, some hand-

88 ■ DEREK ARMSTRONG

made, some hastily bought at Wal-Mart and stapled to stakes every two or three strides, sometimes strung with yellow tape to keep nosy journalists from sniffing too close to doors. Porch columns sport "No Interviews" signs, boldly slanting across cut up cardboard box lids in black magic marker.

The neighborhood might be divided on opinions of Drew Peterson's innocence or guilt, but no one on Pheasant Chase Court loves the media. Most houses wilt under the hot lights if Peterson steps outside.

With double-wheeled satellite trailers and trucks on both sides of the street, there's barely room for neighborhood cars to squeeze by on their way to drop off kids at school, commute to work or run errands. Some driveways are half-blocked. Children rarely play on the sidewalks, their laughing voices missing now, even though they spend afternoons outside in backyards. Garage doors, normally wide open, revealing the jumble of tools and toys that characterize suburban life, are firmly closed. Curtains and blinds shade windows, but waiting journalists often see the inhabitants peek out.

Inside number 6 Pheasant Chase Court, Drew Peterson makes breakfast for all four of his kids, even squeezing orange juice. He kisses Lacy. "Every bite, baby," he says, lightly, his voice slightly fluttery as he thinks about the interview to come.

Lacy rubs her cheek. "I don't like your hairy face," she complains.

"It's yucky," Peterson agrees.

He scoops up the dishes. "Be good while I'm outside. Tommy, you look after the kids."

"I want to come, too."

"I'll only be fifteen minutes. Right outside the house."

Tommy starts helping with the dishes. "'Kay."

As soon as Peterson leaves the house, Anthony and Lacy Peterson are first to peer out the windows, waving at the journalists. Some of the camera crews wave back.

"There's Dad!" Anthony Peterson yells.

"I can't see." Lacy tugs on his kid-sized football jersey.

Anthony helps Lacy get a better view and they watch Dad stride out through new snow.

They watch as Dad, sporting a gray beard and brown leather bomber jacket heads out of the garage to greet the waiting FOX TV camera team. Dad looks more jovial than usual.

Drew Peterson crunches through snow as he heads towards the FOX News crew set up on the sidewalk at the end of his driveway. As always, he banters with the camera crew, has them laughing, and then stands steady as they mike him. He's a veteran of the wire-up procedure. After a sound test, they're ready to go.

Peterson has long ago reconciled himself to his strange notoriety. The news media call at all hours and leave messages on his old-style answering machine. At first, he ignored the media. Later, as they camped out, he tried snubbing them, insulting them, even once or twice chasing them off his property. He has learned that none of this works. Now, he brings them coffee, or cracks wise with them. He accepts interviews from time to time to answer the latest soap opera-ish scandal, like today's interview about his joking offer to participate in a local talk show set up for a Drew Peterson dating game. He's careful never to answer questions his lawyer has put on the "no" list.

"I can't not deal with these people," he said in an early interview for this book. "They camp out. They harass. They make life impossible. My family are virtual prisoners. If I don't have fun with them, I'll go crazy."

Today is a fun day. He's responding on national TV to the much publicized call-in to the popular Chicago-area radio talk show on JACK FM WJMK 104.3.[83] Peterson, backed by his lawyer Brodsky, called in to defuse talk show host Steve Dahl's ongoing satirical "attacks" on Peterson in the form of songs about him. They joked for a while about the time Dahl was brought in on a parking ticket warrant in Bolingbrook, "back in the day when Bolingbrook was four cops," and Peterson was one of them. A hilarious head-to-head between Dahl and Peterson on the air drew a wide audience and national attention:

Dahl: I do believe in innocent until proven guilty.
Peterson: Well, thank you. I wish the rest of the country did.
Dahl: Well, we love a missing wife. We can't help ourselves … So, can I ask you a question?
Peterson: Sure.
Dahl: If she ran off with another guy … no guy has turned up missing. I'm just thinking this might be an avenue to pursue.

Peterson: You think? (sounding sarcastic)
Dahl: Guys aren't missed as much as girls. Cause guys are jerks. As we know.

The interview fell into a repartee over Peterson's love life, the stalkers on the Internet, the girls blowing kisses on the street, then Brodsky suggested a "Win a Date with Drew Contest" as a joke:

Dahl: I'll line up the bachelorettes. And Drew gets to pick from the three girls.
Peterson: Okay. Sounds good. Only three?
Dahl: I think we're probably going to send a chaperone on the date, just to be on the safe—
Peterson: Wait, wait, wait, wait! Steve Dahl has to be the chaperone. I like that.
Dahl: I'll go on the date? Oh, all right, I'll do that too. What the hell.
Peterson: But no three-way stuff.
Dahl: No, no three-way stuff, no. (Everyone laughs)

After Peterson hung up, Dahl, on the air, shouted: "Yikes! … that was pretty awesome. Tomorrow, Drew Peterson Dating Game, eight o'clock."

The whole thing amused Peterson, a rare moment of lightness in his under-siege life. Now FOX wants to know more about the event, and why it was canceled. The truth is, the cancellation was disappointing to Peterson, who had lined up questions sure to inflame the fury of women everywhere, with jabs at widely known facts about Stacy's past. His questions included:

- "Do you need a boob job?" Stacy had asked Peterson to pay for cosmetic surgery in their first year together.
- "Do you get PMS?" Peterson has been demolished in the media for his statement on *Today* that Stacy and he fought whenever she had her premenstrual syndrome.
- "Do you have any tattoos and are they spelled correctly?"

Peterson thought his questions hilarious. If they had aired, the results would have been explosive. His sense of humor doesn't always mix well with news media types. "It's a cop thing," he'd tell everyone. "We always joke, no matter how dark everything seems.

It's our defense mechanism."

Now, Peterson listens to Shepard Smith's preamble on FOX News,[84] talking about the case to date and the Drew Peterson Dating Game. "Drew Peterson, former cop, and a suspect in the disappearance of his wife, live on studio B ..."

Shepard runs through the old crib-notes version of circumstances that make Peterson the handy suspect. Stacy Peterson disappeared in suspicious circumstances. His fourth wife, police say, "may have been murdered." Four searches of Peterson's property; "they've scoured his vehicles and taken his guns." Neighbors reported seeing Drew Peterson and another man hauling a barrel "large enough to hold a person" shortly after Stacy's disappearance.

Shepard then explains how the case has been the focus of radio talk shows in the area, and "two days ago Drew Peterson called into a local talk show, along with his lawyer, and the talk turned to a dating game-type show, in which Drew Peterson could find another woman."

Peterson tries not to roll his eyes at this intro, something he's very accustomed to. The inky black portrayal sticks to him everywhere he goes, not helped by his on-screen humor and apparent lack of sensitivity.

"Drew, is the dating game going to happen?" Shepard begins.

"No. Hi, Shepard, how you doing? No, it looks like it's not going to happen. The radio station chickened out."

"What was the thinking behind that? The dating game."

"Well, for the last three months we've been getting a lot of criticism from this particular personality, Steve Dahl, and he's been imitating my voice and making up several songs about my situation, so we decided to call in and maybe let some air out of him ... When we called, we joked a bit on the air ... they were a little frazzled that we called." He laughs. "But it was all in good fun ... My attorney says, 'Oh, why don't you get Drew a date, Mr. Dahl,' and he came up with the idea of a dating game."

"Are you—Are you going to do it?"

Peterson heard the voice in his ear, just barely making out the question. "No. It was just a comedy bit we were going to do. And I guess the next thing, they were setting up contestants, but I guess they got such heat over it, they chickened out."

Shepard begins the anticipated segue into other topics, asking him how he manages to stay so upbeat given "the fact your wife's been missing for three months."

Peterson knows where this is going, but he says, "Oh, you do what you can. I'm not going to go hide in the corner and cry about it."

Then Shepard hits a subject that is absolutely taboo: Peterson's children. "How has this affected your children?"

Peterson tries not to show his impatience with the forbidden question. By now, most journalists know he won't talk about his children. Bad enough he has to bundle Lacy in her pink blanket just to take her to school so the cameras won't film her, but there is no way Peterson will allow his children to be exploited. He tries a neutral answer. "Oh, they're pretty upset, but I guess that's not what we're going to talk about today." He laughs, missing most of what Shepard is saying.

"No, I meant about the dating. How has this idea of Daddy dating affected them? It's my understanding from you that their mom is on a ski vacation? Is that right?"

Peterson, a veteran of aggressive and sometimes clumsy segues, tries not to sigh. He politely answers a few more non-related questions. "The little ones are missing their mom. We went through her birthday and the Holidays and that was rough for everybody."

"And the fact that you're a suspect in her disappearance, how difficult has that been and how have you handled that with your family?"

Peterson knows he has to cut this short. The interview was clearly a thinly disguised subterfuge to drill down to topics of a more scandalous nature, but questions he's answered many times before. He tries a generic approach. "Well, every day's a new day."

"The neighbors said they saw you carrying out a big blue barrel—"

Peterson expected the attack, but he just says, "Again, Shepard, that's not what we agreed to talk about."

"I didn't agree to any restrictions on our conversation. I would never do that. Well, I wondered—"

Peterson decides he must cut it off now. As usual, the media are determined to portray him in the worst light, and he can only shut down the interview before they make him look goofy. He pulls

Picture # 1

Message Archive for [ ] ashley

Message   Edit   View

Date ▽	Contact	Your Profile
4/4/2008	bpd95969	ashley
4/2/2008	bpd95969	ashley
3/30/2008	bpd95969	ashley
3/29/2008	bpd95969	ashley
3/21/2008	bpd95969	ashley
3/20/2008	bpd95969	ashley
3/18/2008	bpd95969	ashley

- Messages
  - bpd95969
- Conferences
- SMS Messages

ashley (3/21/2008 2:19:23 AM): i would love to be a kid again ... man th

ashley (3/21/2008 2:20:11 AM): had * not has —this keyboard i am using stick alot on here

bpd95969 (3/21/2008 2:20:53 AM): id like to start again in jr high i was the most wearing out keyboard

ashley (3/21/2008 2:21:38 AM): i go thru so many keyboards a year ...

ashley (3/21/2008 2:22:14 AM): so do you talk to anyone else on yahoo

bpd95969 (3/21/2008 2:23:23 AM): actually i was gonna try on line dating but i chance. told u i was a virgin

ashley (3/21/2008 2:24:04 AM): online dating where ? on yahoo ?

bpd95969 (3/21/2008 2:25:18 AM): ya something like that but im afraid of the n someone for the first time

ashley (3/21/2008 2:25:41 AM): why because your Drew Peterson ?

bpd95969 (3/21/2008 2:26:06 AM): i cant even post a photo on my profile

ashley (3/21/2008 2:26:52 AM): yea i understand that part

ashley (3/21/2008 2:26:59 AM): hmmm

bpd95969 (3/21/2008 2:28:11 AM): i think if i dont have an american girl by ne bride you can spec one out like a car just cant talk to them

ashley (3/21/2008 2:28:27 AM): and let me tell you most bitches are no Drew or see Drew thier gonna be running

One of the less appetizing soap opera incidents in the whole Peterson affair involved Len Wawczak, who claimed to be a friend of Peterson's (Peterson says he was only a business acquaintance). Wawczak posed as Drew's online mistress, Ashley. Their online conversations were legendary among the anti-Drew audiences. Right, inset, the story that Wawczak was Ashley. Photo by author.

UPDATED: Peterson amused by former friend's online impersonation

By Danya Hooker, dhooker@mysuburbanlife.com
GateHouse News Service
Fri Jul 25, 2008, 02:40 AM CDT

Story Tools: 📧 Email This | 🖨 Print This

Bolingbrook, IL -

Drew Peterson said Thursday he was impressed by former friend Len Wawczak's online impersonation of a woman for two months and called the stunt "comical."

Earlier Thursday, Wawczak admitted he had posed as a woman named Ashley and began an online romance with Peterson in order to gather information on the former Bolingbrook police sergeant suspected in the Oct. 28 disappearance of his wife, Stacy.

"I was very taken," Peterson said. "I've been playing practical jokes for most of my life and for someone to get me like that, I'm impressed."

The revelation came just one day after news broke that Wawczak and his wife, Paula Stark, at the alleged behest of state police, had been secretly recording their conversations with Peterson for nearly seven months.

"My idea was to show people that he really is what they think he is," Wawczak said of the online affair. "He's a liar."

The idea for the online spoof came when Peterson showed Wawczak chats he was having with other women online. Wawczak said he memorized Peterson's username, went home to set up his own account and began creating his alter ego, Ashley, a 29-year-old Web designer from southern Illinois.

Ashley's last name, Gabrys, was really the name of someone he used to know. He picked Granite City as Ashley's hometown because he knows someone who lives there who could provide local information if needed.

Lenny Wawczak sits at the computer where he posed as Ashley, a 29-year-old Web site designer from southern Illinois who flirted with Drew Peterson online.
By Danya Hooker

"I had everything covered," Wawczak said.

Within days, Peterson started opening up to Ashley. The chats, which Wawczak has posted clips of on a blog he created, show Peterson expressing his love for Ashley, asking to meet her and making several racy comments.

"One day I went over to his house and he said 'Hey, look at this, look at this chick I'm talking to.' And he pulls out the picture of Ashley," Wawczak said. "I found it hard to keep a straight face then."

The online romance ended in May when Ashley told Peterson that she had driven by his house and saw him sitting with another woman on his porch. Wawczak said he had heard that Peterson was with this woman and that he decided to make Ashley seem jealous.

Wawczak said police have seen the chats and that he published them online after receiving approval from state police. He said they also asked permission to go public about the wiretapping operation, which ended in June.

Illinois State Police Sgt. Tom Burek declined to comment Wednesday.

Peterson would have found out about it shortly anyway, Wawczak said, because authorities are required to notify the subject of such investigations after the recording ceased. Although the notification would not identify Wawczak and Stark, he said they were the only ones around Peterson enough to make the operation useful.

the earphone out of his ear "Well, then, I guess I gotta walk away. Have a good day, Mr. Shepard. It was nice talking to you." He turns from the camera. "Unhook me guys." He laughs. "Unhook me." Once unhooked, he smiles at the camera crew. "Have a good day, guys." And he heads back to the refuge of his family.

"You really do chat with this Ashley?"

Ashley, a romantic online interest of Peterson's, was never popular, even when she "turned on Drew," a popular sport amongst Peterson's friends. Even among Drew-haters, especially after rumors "she" was trying to sell her story to the *National Enquirer*, Ashley was never embraced by the Anti-Drewpie crowd (as they sometimes call themselves). Drewpies, a very small crowd, are the niche of Drew groupies, who pursue him for autographs and defend him in blogs.

This particular episode in the soap opera of Peterson's life is particularly revealing of the practical jokester side of his personality, an attitude that consistently gets him into trouble with neighbors and online bloggers who believe his time would be best spent searching for Stacy.

"I'm trapped in my house by media and suspicion, and I'm a stay-at-home mom," Drew told me in June interviews. "So I have fun chatting online."

"You really do chat with this Ashley?" My own voice on my recorded tapes sounds somewhat incredulous. "Don't you think it's damaging to be portrayed this way?"

"I don't care. I'm not trying to say I'm the sweetest guy on earth. I'm honest about everything."

"This Ashley could be a truck driver whiling away the hours in a motel somewhere," I said. I had this picture in my head of some twenty-hour-a-day blog addict playing a prank. I had read some of the posts, and they were somewhat lewd. "Or the police."

Drew laughs. "I know. Fun, isn't it?"

As it turns out, Ashley is none other than neighbor Len Wawczak, a man who later claims they've been recording conversations with Drew Peterson on behalf of the Illinois State Police.

Peterson's the first to admit Len pulled a good one.

Peterson can't be accused of not having a sense of humor. While in narcotics, he was fired for misconduct (later exonerated). As a joke at this time, he posed for a double-exposure with himself both as the arresting officer and perp.

"I'm no angel."

"I always had to be funny," Peterson told me in our second face-to-face meeting, this meeting at his house.

I had already met his family: his adorable kids, Lacy three and Anthony five, his talented teens, aspiring musician Tommy and wrestler-champ Kris, and even his grown-up son Steve, now a police officer like Dad.

We sat, now, in the cool recreation room, in too-plush leather sofa and loveseat, alongside the red pool table. The room is decorated with airplane themes, "because Stacy knows I'm nuts about my planes."

Here we would sit for twelve hours, without eating or breaking

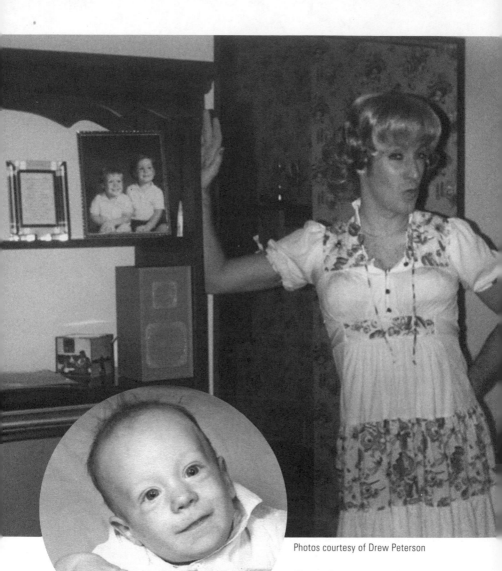

Photos courtesy of Drew Peterson

Above: Peterson has always been known as the "class clown" from his school days through his entire thirty years in the Bolingbrook police. Here, Peterson dresses in drag for Halloween, stepping away from the tough-guy look.

Inset: Drew Peterson as a baby.

(except once to pick up his teenager Tommy from school). I was so absorbed by Peterson's amazing ability to recall names and details of his life, I forgot to break for food or the bathroom. He definitely has a cop-oriented mind, a head for details that spans decades.

My goal for the day's session, to learn what made Peterson the man he is. The sex-capades, the pranks, the undercover work, the close calls where lives were almost lost—all of it. These are the things that made Peterson what he is today, either sociopathic killer or innocent victim of the modern-day equivalent of a lynch mob.

"Expose me for what I am. I'm no angel, but I'm no devil either. But I have to be funny. Always." Ask him about his youth, he'd answer, "I was always working or chasing girls. Work hard, play hard, that was me."

Peterson admits he was always involved in shenanigans, ever since kindergarten. He was never a malicious prankster, but he had a genuine need to be the "funny guy."

The oldest of three siblings, he came from a good family. He loved his father, a man who proudly smoked stogies and was never shy about discipline. "He raised us like marines," Drew Peterson says, pointing

Drew Peterson (left) with younger brother Paul and their Dad at Paul's wedding.

proudly at a picture of his father in the backyard of the family home, smoking his inevitable cigar. If any of the Peterson kids objected, Dad's response was predictable.

"Be home at six o'clock."
"But Dad."
"Five o'clock."
"But Dad."
"Four o'clock."
"Yes, sir."

Mom complemented Peterson's dad, always loyal and loving and known for her immaculately clean house. No one made a mess

Photos courtesy of Drew Peterson

Two pictures of Drew with his brother and sister. They remain a close family.
Opposite: Drew as a child at back with younger brother Paul on left and Laura on right.
Above: a later family photo with oldest sibling Drew, sister Laura and brother Paul on
his knee.

in the Peterson house. Unlike in the next generation of Petersons, there were no infidelities, few marital issues, although the love of the children connects the different generations.

In those days, in the early fifties and later in the sixties, family time was almost a cliché of the perfect American life: no television, friends over every weekend for dinner, cards and drinks, family moments and neighborly socializing. Drew Peterson would remember it as a good, disciplined, loving home, and he genuinely loved his father, mother, sister and brother, and especially his uncles.

"I was not one of the pretty people."

Drew Peterson was a pretty normal all-American kid. He went to every school dance, hung out with his friends in typical fifties style, not quite *American Graffiti* but close enough. He was always the worker. At fifteen his first job was at the nearby Burger King as counter help, a sometimes pimply teen who eventually became manager.

As a teenager/young man, his favorite memories were of his Al Bundy-like experience as a women's shoes salesperson. Customers were attracted to his wild sense of humor and he would always remember it as a "crazy time" and really fun. "I was at a mall, selling shoes, but that job was a lot of fun." Like the time they locked the assistant manager in the front window for most of the day, bringing in record traffic to the store as people came to report the wild man in the show window.

Peterson always had a job, all the way through high school, working part time after school, learning to crack the irreverent jokes, making people laugh and like him, attracting a crowd of good friends, but above all, having fun. Later, he'd become a clinical intern at the Heinz Veterans Hospital, working with patients on alcoholism and drug abuse.

He worked and saved his money for flying lessons. "You can work," his dad told him, "but you save half your money for your education." Later he convinced his dad that his obtaining his pilot's license was "education," and in the end he saved enough to get his license by the age of seventeen.

In school he was known as the "class clown," the guy everyone laughed at or with. You either liked him a lot or didn't, but he'd barely notice. He ran the mile in high school, always into sports, tried out for football his freshman year, then broke his hip, but mostly he was remembered as the guy who was always in trouble for "goofing around." He was a popular kid more because he was always participating, horsing around and hanging out with the cool kids, "although I was not one of the pretty people."

High school was for high jinks. He had this insatiable desire to make people laugh. Everyone—fellow teachers, students, the principal.

He was a "regular" at the principal's office. "The principal would call me Mr. Peterson, by my last name, and I'd always call him by his first name, and even though I was in trouble, I'd get the principal laughing." He'd goof around in class. He'd goof around in sports. He'd goof around after school.

"I was so obnoxious the party stopped."

Peterson might have been a hard worker, but that didn't stop him from being the king of partiers, known especially for his practical jokes.

Peterson's early experiences with alcohol at a young age probably steered him clear of alcoholism, but his parties were memorable. His first drinking experience, at a friend's place—with the parents conveniently away—led to his first vomit-fest. He neatly threw up into the outstretched hands of his buddy Dave Dunning. His friend stood there astonished, unable to speak, with a handful of puke. "I was so obnoxious the party stopped."

The classical "Drew-style" gag is still somewhat famous today. A friend had a party at his house when the parents were out for the evening. When his friend went out for more beer, Drew had everyone carry the "front room" furniture out of the house. They set up all the furniture, exactly as it had been in the living room, but on the front lawn, complete with lights run from extension cords.

Peterson laughs. "Then the parents came home, and we're all sitting in the furniture on the front lawn drinking beer. We were all under age."

Every weekend in high school boasted of similar instances, usually with Peterson as the "ring leader" of any practical jokes or party gags. He had an *"American Graffiti-like"*[85] crew of buddies who ran with all his jokes, and they became somewhat famous in the school and neighborhood for their elaborately harmless pranks. Even at his part-time job as counter help at a burger joint he couldn't stop the jokes. "We used to have food fights, then when the customers'd come in we'd reassemble all the burgers. It's just something you do as kids in these places." There was one employee, Dale, not too popular, and whenever he'd have a burger, the rest of the crew would slip crickets into it. "I don't think he'd know what a burger was supposed to taste like without the crickets," Peterson said, again laughing.

Life was no different during his stint selling women's shoes at the Yorktown mall. He was seventeen. "We were so obnoxious there that the counter girls were afraid to come into the back room with us." The manager of the store loved Peterson, and his friend Dave, because they sold more shoes "with their shenanigans" than the full-timers did, charming customers. The assistant manager hated Peterson because he was the butt of the incessant jokes. The time they locked the assistant manager in the display window, he banged on the window, turning red, and Peterson and his buddy Dave just stared and laughed. Another time they "stuffed a stock boy" in a garbage bin and sent him up the elevator. Fortunately, the stock boy laughed, more or less used to Peterson by this time. There was also an elaborate initiation ritual devised by Peterson for new salespeople. "Every store in the mall was in on it. We'd send them out for a wall stretcher, but every store they went to they'd be sent to another store. They'd spend their whole first day pursuing the non-existent wall stretcher."

"I had to get my mom to sign so I could get married."

He would go on to marry his high school sweetheart, Carol Hamilton. "She was a freshman, I was a senior."

Aha! I leaned forward in the too-comfortable leather chair, about to crack wise about his "cradle robbing" even in high school. "How old were you when you married?"

"She was seventeen. I was twenty." He probably saw what I was getting at. Stacy was also seventeen when he married her. But he nodded and moved on with his story. "I was friends with her brother.

I originally took her out to aggravate her brother. He always said the joke was on me, because I ended up marrying her."

The time Peterson remembers most fondly was his assignment later, as an MP, to guard the president of the United States. "It was funny at the time. Here I was guarding the president of the United States, but I had to get my mom to sign so I could get married."

Carol finished her last year of high school out in Virginia where Peterson was stationed after he joined the military police.

In junior college Peterson studied law enforcement, always his dream. He had it all carefully planned. He would join the army and become a military policeman. Two years in service qualified him for an education, and if he could get into the military police, he would have an important direct route into civilian police work. He always knew he would be a police officer.

Through high school, and later into Military Police School and basic training, he was seeing his soon-to-be wife Carol. "She caught me fooling around once," Peterson said, with his customary rumbling laugh. "Big drama on both sides, she finally forgave me, we ended up getting engaged, and shortly after, we married."

The shenanigans continued in the army, though, and Peterson joked that, because he was married, he lived off-post, so he could get in "half as much trouble."

"Military Police is a great qualifier," Peterson told me. "I knew I wanted to get onto a civilian police force, but getting on a police department anywhere is really competitive. There'd be as many as five hundred people showing up for two jobs. For me, my history with the Military Police helped."

Peterson went into the army for two years at the tail end of Viet Nam. "Being an MP gave me the experience. I did presidential security, dignitary security. I guarded Alexander Haig. I even guarded the emperor of Japan. Whenever there was a laying of a wreath at the Tomb of the Unknown Soldier, we were involved."

"My first experience with corruption"

Drew Peterson had "top secret" security clearance at the 561st MP company. The 561st is known as a "spit and polish" outfit, and everyone was issued dress blues and dress whites for dignitary

Photos courtesy of Drew Peterson

Author photo of a somewhat haggard Drew Peterson during interviews for this book, proudly holding a picture of the 561st MP unit. He is pointing at himself as a Military Police officer.

Above:
Peterson on patrol as a Miltary Police officer in the US Army.

Left:
A young Drew Peterson in dress blues, the type of uniform he would wear on VIP duty guarding President Ford or the emperor of Japan.

guard duty. His enthusiasm and drive—and a bevy of screenings, interviews, tests and polygraphs—had landed him in a very high-profile area of the military police, in spite of his youth at only nineteen years of age.

During his term, from the age of nineteen to twenty-one, "I had my first experience with corruption" in the police. His supervisors in the Military Police were "dealing marijuana." These MP supervisors were "some of the biggest dealers in the D.C. area."

While at Fort Myer, Drew Peterson was involved with the CID people, exposing the corruption. "It's not that I'm proud of exposing them, but I thought it was wrong. Here are these guys, supposed to be enforcing the law, and instead they're breaking the law. Me and another guy named Peterson also were involved in bringing them down."

Less glamorous, Peterson also had to take stints on gate duty, patrol work, and breaking up the inevitable bar fights. And, married or not, he still found he couldn't resist the girls.

Aside from corruption and more girls, his tour in the Military Police was notable for more Drew-like crazy stuff. Every day brought something new. One of his buddies, a guy named Bohanan, was known for clumsiness. One day, he broke a window in the guardhouse with a stone. Bohanan wanted to make up a story that someone had done a "drive-by shooting" and fired at the gatehouse. Peterson, never one to back down from a prank, talked him out of it: "You do that, the FBI'll be here. You'll be investigated. You'll be charged with filing a false report. It'll be a big deal." He ended up talking Bohanan into making up a story about tripping and falling into the glass. "It's appear clumsy, or get involved in a big investigation." After that, any time someone was clumsy on the base, it was known as "pulling a Bohanan."

"Quick draw" Peterson

Another Drew-like stunt involved a goofy game of "quick draw" with the guns. When on duty, MPs typically carry their sidearm with the magazine in, but no bullet in the chamber. On quiet nights, Peterson and a buddy pulled the magazine out and whiled away the hours playing "quick draw" with the guns. One night, a car came to the gatehouse, so they quickly put the magazines back in. Later, when they went back to the draw-game, his buddy forgot to remove the magazine. BOOM! His friend shot a hole right through the stop sign. Fortunately, they weren't quick-drawing on each other.

So, what do Drew and friend do? Report the accident? Make up a story? No! They spend the rest of the night searching for a replacement stop sign and switched the signs.

"Then we had to find another bullet," Peterson said, unable to restrain another laugh, "because we were issued ten at the beginning of the night." Ten bullets had to be turned in at the end of duty.

Peterson also loves to tell stories of the co-ed barracks. "Really, my pranks were nothing next to these guys. I wasn't living on post, because I was married. But one day I walked into the barracks and six of the guys were having sex with the same girl—not at the same time, of course." Later, this girl disappeared for two months, only to return to the base pregnant. All of a sudden, the six guys who were "bragging" of the "shagging" denied they even knew her. "On the base, they were a lot wilder than I was."

The stories of sex-capades are pretty much endless. Two fellow officers Peterson knew well, male and female MPs, were partners on shift. When they didn't show up at the end of duty, everyone went out looking for them. They were found a couple hours later—in the back of their squad car, "totally naked." In their excitement, and because of the cold, they shut the door, forgetting the back doors lock against prisoner escapes. They couldn't get out, and had to wait for rescue. Their clothes were in the front seat. Totally naked, they emerged to a gale of laughter from their troop mates.

VIP Duty

Peterson fondly remembers the VIP duty. He tells these stories with that child-like glint in his eye, but his voice firms up into a proud rumble as he tells of how he once guarded Alexander Haig, when he was the supreme allied commander of the NATO troops. "We had received death threats against him," Drew explained.

He helped protect Gerald Ford, honored to serve as the MP in dress blues who opened the limo door for the president. The president laid a wreath at the Tomb of the Unknown Soldier. President Ford tripped on the step and Peterson, true to type, let out a suppressed chuckle. Everyone looked at Peterson rather than at President Ford, and their glares said it all: "Don't laugh at the president."

Not long after, he was on gate duty when Omar Bradley, the last living five-star general, visited the base. The distinguished general got out of the car and shook his hand. He was on his way to the officers' club.

"It was a very exciting time, a lot of fun for a twenty-year-old kid," Peterson said, almost launching out of his seat. He truly came alive in the interviews when he spoke of his army days. "The VIPs, police duty, the pranks, the sex, the bar room brawls we had to break up. I got my teeth knocked out breaking up a bar room fight. All this is plastic here." He points at his teeth.

"All of it?" I ask.

"No just this here. I got hit with a bottle that came out of nowhere. I was spitting teeth. This brawl was so big, they were giving guys MP bands and sticks—just guys out of the barracks—just to go in and help break it up."

"Girls were my weakness"

Through it all—school and jobs, army and a wife—he always found time for girls. He was a self-admitted girl-crazy boy with hormones wildly out of control. "I was always chasing the girls. And always working. Girls were my weakness."

"Still are," I said, dryly.

"Still are," he agreed. "When I got out of the army, Carol had stuck with me through it all. We moved in with Carol's parents for a while."

Now the real search began for a civilian police force to build his career. Peterson tested everywhere, test after test, polygraph after polygraph. For any given position, he'd be competing with up to five hundred people. "Bolingbrook picked me first and I ended up going to work on the Bolingbrook police department for nearly three decades."

Bolingbrook police started Peterson back in basic police training at the Cook County Police Academy. The basic training began all over again, complete with push-ups, sit-ups, hand-to-hand, PT, riot training, target practice, running; the "goofing around" began all over again too. Peterson was in high form, out-pranking the best of them.

Training was so intense he'd drag himself home each night and head straight for the bathroom. His hands and feet would be black and blue from the sticks and the hand-to-hand combat, but somehow Peterson found time to goof around with fellow trainees. He rose to the top of the shooting class, winning the top award for marksmanship.

When Peterson graduated, he returned to the Bolingbrook Police under a new chief, Bill Charninsky. During his initial probation, Peterson was assigned patrol duty for seven months, but his potential was immediately exploited when he was accepted into the elite Narcotics Squad, an undercover unit made up of officers from multiple jurisdictions. Peterson was "dying" to get on the squad, an elite posting, even though he was fairly junior in experience. Competition for MANS (Metro Area Narcotics Squad), as it was known, was fierce, but he was accepted quickly.

To fit in as an undercover investigator, he grew a scruffy beard and hair to his shoulders: he could pass for any thug on the street. He traded in his dress blues from the MP days, and his crisp patrol uniform from Bolingbrook for un-tucked plaid shirts, denim vests and denim pants with big seventies-style belts, then-stylish tinted glasses and bangs that hung down past his bushy eyebrows. With a hidden holster and a big Browning High Power, he easily passed for a guy even the Hell's Angels would stay clear of in a rumble.

Undercover narcotics, if possible, was even more challenging and stimulating—and fun—than the riotous years in the army as an MP. The duty was dangerous, and this brought out the old "Quick Draw Peterson" again, practical jokes and all. And, of course, the girl-chasing remained a regular part of his life, wife number one notwithstanding.

"I had to lie to my girlfriend to go home and see my wife"

MANS was the top-of-the-top elite undercover squad in Illinois, made up of officers from many forces and jurisdictions. Peterson, "this little guy from Bolingbrook," found himself competing in a unit filled with ex-Seals, ex-Marine security forces (KAGs), officers who had done everything, been everywhere. The entire team were undercovers, sent to work in towns and cities where they wouldn't be known.

Peterson and the MANS team in 1980. Mans was a multi-jurisdictional—and highly effective—narcotics undercover team and stands for Metro Area Narcotics Squad. L to R back: Charles Milonoski (Ski), Drew Peterson, Robert Flowers, Keith Kostalny. Front L to R: Steve Stahl, Gary Kramer, Reginald Lashley (who was shot in the face in one raid—(see chapter "I was covered in blood")—and Tom Quillman.

Where the ex-Seals and KAGs became the bust-down-the-door search warrant guys, Peterson used his "smart mouth" to make himself indispensible to the hand-to-hand buys on the street. His easygoing humor and street smarts made him "feel right" even among strangers who were drug dealers. He would get to know a junior person and work his way up to the more important people. "I'd buy dope," Peterson said. "I worked literally hundreds of cases, and we made hundreds of arrests."

Peterson excelled at undercover, fitting in naturally with the dealers, using the tools he had honed in his high school and army days—good humor, party skills, the gift of the gab, and even his practical-joker persona. He would go on to win awards for his undercover work in narcotics.

"But being a married man, I didn't belong in that unit. We were a wild bunch. Everyone else had girlfriends. I had a wife. We spent so much time on the job, so much time in character, that when it was over, everyone would scatter, everyone would go off chasing women. Including me."

He shakes his head. "It got so nuts one time that I had to lie to my girlfriend to go home and see my wife. It's not something I'm proud of, but it's basically what happened."

For an entire year on MANS, Peterson steadily saw one girl, while still married to an unsuspecting Carol, not-too-unwillingly dragged out to bars and clubs by his fellow "narcs," all sporting long seventies-style hair and beards. The relationship was so serious, he spent as much time with his girlfriend as he did with his wife.

Not to be outdone by the fates, Peterson ended up divorced from Carol, only to find out his serious girlfriend was cheating on him with her ex-husband. He threw her out of the house.

I'm sure I couldn't help but roll my eyes a little. I think I can hear my own sigh on the tape. "A little double standard there?"

"A big double standard," Peterson agreed, nodding his head and shrugging at the same time.

"A live-for-today sort of outfit."

MANS was a dangerous unit, a "live-for-today sort of outfit." On any given day you could end up with a bullet between the eyes from a big 357 Magnum. Even if the bullet missed, in a small bedroom of a raided house, the roar of a big-caliber handgun could deafen an officer. Every raid was exciting, and afterwards the sense of relief—of having survived another night—was so high, that the party, the drinking and the girls were inevitable releases. Peterson's now famous horseplay was in demand with the squad, especially after a successful operation.

MANS operations relied on "shock and awe" long before George Bush's presidency. "We'd hit the house so hard they wouldn't have time to do anything," Peterson said, scratching his new beard, a silvery reflection of the longer black beard he sported in MANS. "We'd have guns on them, and handcuffs on them, and pull them out of bed, all before they woke up. Within eight to fifteen seconds we'd be able to secure a house. Most times."

A few times, when the MANS team couldn't secure probable cause or a warrant, they'd have "fun" with the dealers. "We'd load up the RAID van and charge up to the house, sirens blazing, shouting. Next thing you know you'd hear the toilets flushing. We'd walk away laughing. We couldn't bust them, but we hurt their business." He smiles, sounding truly proud. "We got the dope off the street, even when we couldn't make a bust. That happened a few times. It was funny stuff."

The funny stuff could turn dark too. In one incident that lives on in the MANS hall of fame, one obnoxious perp was so difficult, one of Peterson's friends, a Will County Deputy, took a picture off the wall, and smashed it over the guy's head. He yelled, "Look, this guy's been framed!" The man wasn't hurt, and even the perp ended up laughing. Long after the MANS team stopped laughing, the man, still sporting the broken frame, continued to laugh.

Downtime meant girlfriend time. Between operations and raids, everyone would take precious time with the girlfriends. Girls were never a problem in those days for narcotics officers. The danger drew them, the mystique attracted them, and the cops—in this team, all guys—were rough and ready for some fun. Including Drew Peterson.

"They'd find out you were a cop, and that was exciting," Peterson said, holding a well-crinkled eight-by-ten photo of his ex-MANS team in one hand. "The long hair and the beard—you were dangerous. Undercover cop, thrilling."

Peterson (left) as a narc undercover officer, goofing around after a major "bust." They are posing in the actual house after a successful raid, celebrating after a large operation. The "perp" posing here is actually fellow narc Paul Kupas who was then a Will County Deputy on assignment with MANS, (Metro Area Narcotics Squad) a multi-jurisdiction drugs task force.

Photos courtesy of Drew Peterson

Peterson as narc, in beard, shoulder-length hair and flannel shirt. Peterson was one of the top "buyers" who would trap dealers. In his narc career he received many commendations and made hundreds of busts with his fellow team members. In his second term as a narc, he got into trouble as a "loose cannon" for pursuing an investigation on his own and for implicating a state's attorney. He was fired and later re-hired after he was exonerated.

Peterson seems lost in this past world, as we go through boxes of old photos. Today's interviews take place in the 23rd floor hotel room on Michigan Avenue. My room is literally filled with boxes of Peterson photos, now scattered everywhere on the desk, the floor, the chairs, the bar. These are photos I've brought along as prompts to Peterson's memory, although he doesn't seem to need any memory prods. He remembers every name, every incident, like it was yesterday. He speaks with urgency, an excitement and pace that makes it clear this was the best time of his life, a wild time of girls, danger, more girls, excitement, more girls, and lots of horsing around. There may be fatigue lines around his eyes, from the sleepless nights under siege in today's Bolingbrook, but as he relives his not-totally-wholesome past, his eyes sparkle with a twenty-five-year-old's vigor.

He seems to speak more openly here, in my suite, than he did at his house. Perhaps it was the delighted play and thump-thump-thump of little feet on the living room floor upstairs that kept him somewhat staid and quiet at his home, but here, as we go through box after box of photos, a totally uninhibited, laughing Drew Peterson chats on for hour after hour, missing lunch, then dinner, and still going on well into the late hours.

"Another seventeen-year-old girl?"

The beards, long hair, big guns and loose life-style were more than just the affectations of live-for-today cops. "Narc cops have to live a nearly biker life," Peterson said. "I fit in, not just because of my beard, but because I don't judge people. I can get along with anyone." On paper, these words carry some conceit, but in person, he delivers this line with sincerity.

MANS officers could rarely leave their jobs behind entirely, even socially. Even in their off hours they wore their beards, long hair and flannels, probably drawing sideways glances from street cops, definitely getting the dirty looks when they went out on dates with pretty, well-dressed women.

Even the "good cop, bad cop" routine was played out in the dating game. One of Peterson's buddies, "Wild Bill," a burly macho kind of a guy, would go up to women in a bar, sometimes so overpowering he'd have the women calling for bouncers. Peterson would play the good cop and march up and "rescue" the girl from his Wild Bill. "Is this guy bothering you?" It worked like a charm for Peterson, although it annoyed his buddy.

In those days, "the more obnoxious I was with women, the more attracted they were," Peterson said, looking serious. "And the more I'd treat them like gold and jewels, the faster I'd lose them."

The best "hunting ground" for casual dating, as it turned out, was the state's attorney's office. The MANS team would go there often, working cases, but would spend a lot of their off-time going from desk to desk to desk, chatting up the women.

One girl in particular, another seventeen-year-old—again, I'm sure I showed my dismay on my normally emotionless features— became a major target of undercover officer Drew Peterson. She was already being pursued by half the assistant state's attorneys, but she wouldn't have anything to do with them.

"Another seventeen-year-old?" I couldn't help it.

"Guess so. I was only twenty-three. She wanted to go out with me. We started going out. The assistant state's attorneys were all bad-mouthing me to her face, with things like 'Drew got some girl pregnant.' But she didn't care. She just looked at 'em and laughed and said, 'I'll be sure to take my pill then.' It drove them all crazy."

"She threw the divorce papers at me."

"My first divorce cost sixty-seven dollars," Peterson said. "It was a mutual thing, and we worked out everything ourselves." Carol hardly ever saw Peterson, as an undercover agent, and she likely was tired of his rumored infidelity.

"Fine, I'll give you a divorce," she said instantly. "No problem."

A lawyer friend drew up the papers, and Peterson's first sergeant Chuck Dennis, acted as a notary public. They found Carol at The Jewel. She signed the papers, but then, suddenly, "she threw the divorce papers at me."

Not to miss the odd humor of the moment, Peterson and Chuck snatched the papers out of the air and notarized them.

Carol and Peterson went their separate ways and Carol married a high school friend of Peterson's. She's been happy ever since.

And Peterson, now a Narc without a wife, would move into a truly frenzied phase of his "womanizing" career.

"I was covered in blood."

The humor was partially a defense mechanism. Being in MANS was a bloody business. One of MANS' top buying agents, aside from Peterson himself, was tough-guy Tommy Silvas, a Joliet city copper. On one bloody night, he was in buying the drugs.

"After the buy comes the raid. As the buying agent you should always be the last guy back into the house. On this night, after a good buy, Tommy came out of the house, signaled, and the MANS team charged the house, running in as always with the objective of securing in seconds. The house was in turmoil. Cops yelled, 'Police! Get down! Don't move!' and when thug dealers didn't cooperate, they threw them into walls. It all happened in seconds to the music of breaking furniture and glass, shouts and curses. What you don't want to hear is the percussion instrument—the guns, more like cannons than guns in crowded rooms."

Whenever a gun does discharge, an extra spurt of adrenalin stimulates already rapidly firing synapses, and both good guys and bad guys are ready to shoot to kill. Knives, guns, any shiny weapon does it.

This night, the explosion deafens everyone, freezing them in comical moments of struggle, like a violent Saturday-morning cartoon. Peterson rushes for the kitchen, where the perps have fled.

A searing bright muzzle flash, a huge explosion, and Peterson's crouching with his own gun ready. Peterson lunges for the light switch.

On the worn linoleum floor, once a dirty gray and black, is a bright splash of red gore. Peterson registers it's none of his buddies. A man lies in a growing pool of blood, already so much blood that the other cops are leaving trails of red boot prints.

The acrid smell of the discharge hangs sharp in the air, also pungent with the tang of sweat and the newer, sweeter smell of spilled blood.

Tommy's gun is hot and still smoking. He had shot the perp. His face registers a fierce shock.

Peterson kneels quickly, turns the perp, thinking he had a gun. In the man's hand is a long blade. Peterson doesn't hesitate. His army training kicks in and he starts CPR, his bloody hands pressing down on the blasted heart. From what he can see, it's a perfect shot, straight to the heart, but Peterson doesn't stop. He keeps pumping until it's clear it's useless.

He stands up, covered in the man's spent life force. It was a clean kill. The man had a weapon in a crowded room, ignoring the police's commands to drop it. But Peterson knows how Tommy must feel. How he feels, too, unable to save the man's life.

The next day, they would discover that Tommy's bullet took out half the man's heart, an explosive Glaser round that instantly killed the man. No one will cry over this drug dealer, a man who himself had killed. But Peterson will never forget how he spent long minutes trying to resuscitate a heart that would never again pump life. Especially later, when it is discovered that the dead perpetrator had hepatitis.

Tommy was exonerated by a grand jury, everyone knew it was a good shoot, but it takes time to get past these moments when a man's life is taken.

"This is the reason we play hard," Peterson said. "This was one of those weird moments in your life. There really are slow-motion moments when things like this happen. We had a lot of them back then."

Another of those moments was a raid gone slightly off-course. Officer Lashley was on the porch of a subject house. Close behind him were Peterson and the MANS crew.

Lashley knocks on the door to announce the police. Instead, his voice roars out, "Put down the gun!" A handgun discharges and Lashley goes down. Peterson runs for Lashley. He sees blood in the corner of Lashley's eye.

In that moment, the house is assailed under a barrage of police bullets. Every single bullet in every single gun seems to be firing at the same time, entire clips emptied. The door is riddled with bullet holes. A cop is down and no one's waiting for the next shot from inside the house. The firing continues as Peterson kneels by Lashley and starts to pull him off the porch.

Somehow, impossibly it seems, the perpetrator had hit the floor and crawled away against a hail of bullets, all without a scratch. The police had to literally dig him out of his refuge in the basement.

Fortunately for Lashley—and probably the perpetrator—the bullet only lightly grazed Lashley's cheek, drawing a trail of blood. It's a minor scratch.

"A crazy, crazy week"

After this, Tommy Silvas and Peterson went to Drug Enforcement Administration (DEA) school in Saint Louis. Tommy would go on to be Peterson's partner for a while. Tommy was "this little southern fella, a Joliet copper, stood about five foot something tall." Every other phrase, ended with "Y'all" in classic southern style.

DEA school is a big deal for anyone in narcotics. It's a two-week course, as much about the party as the priceless chance to learn. This would be the womanizer week to end all womanizing weeks, even though Peterson and Tommy are forced to share a hotel room. The one sour note on the party-hearty week is that Tommy's a smoker, and they fight constantly over his cigarettes. Peterson can't stand being around anyone who smokes.

Tommy, not one to waste time, was fast to pick up the hotel desk clerk, a pretty young girl. They came into the room, where Peterson lay on the bed. Tommy was smoking as he entered.

Peterson, with typical cop-buddy humor, drew his unloaded piece and "drew down" on his partner. "I told you mother, no smoking in this room." Tommy dove behind a chair. The desk clerk screamed. Peterson followed Tommy with his gun as his friend rolled behind the other bed. Peterson tracked his partner perfectly, and the girl cowered against the wall, terrified, even though Tommy and Peterson were both laughing.

Needless to say, she fled the room, and Tommy lost his first date.

But the flight attendants were on strike, and Peterson and Tommy found themselves working their way through the grounded attendants with the gusto of horny bulls. Even by Peterson's standards, it was a "crazy, crazy week." Peterson ended up with a different lady every night of the week.

Some would say it was a form of poetic justice, but the second week down in St. Louis, Peterson caught mono.

The craziness spilled over into class time as well. Peterson, never one to be shown up by the DEA teachers, was assigned to work a buy-bust in a phony hotel room. They had to establish a buy, perform the raid, find the drugs then write it up. The perps were played by experienced DEA agents. Peterson's team scored great points in the critique for their routine, in which they posed as Gideon's Bible distributors delivering Bibles to the hotel room, but after the bust, a key part of the grading was "getting the perp to talk."

Naturally, the experienced DEA agent wasn't about to make it easy for them. Peterson, always the rough-and-tumble joker, said, "Let me show you how they do it in Joliet." He grabbed the actor-perp by the head, took him to the window, and rolled up the window on his neck.

"You can't do that!" the DEA agent shouted.

"Sure I can," Peterson said. "Now tell me where you stashed the dope."

"Okay, okay!"

Moments later, everyone laughing, the DEA agent gave him a thumbs-up critique for originality, even though he commented, "I assume you wouldn't do that in a real bust." Naturally, Peterson agreed he would not.

"My first run in with the Illinois State Police"

Another hilarious week, at least from the point of view of a working cop, was the Drug School at the Illinois State Police Academy. "They expected us to behave like recruited state troopers," Peterson recalls with a laugh. "That wasn't going to happen. We were experienced narcotics, all scruffy and bearded. We decided from the beginning we were going to break every rule of the school."

On the first night there the MANS crew filled up one of the bathtubs with beer and ice. The next day the men streaked the ladies' dormitory.

The highlight of the week was a brilliant example of cop-meets-bad-guy comic timing. Near the last day of the school, a crowd of narcs—who looked like anything but cops—sat at a table in a restaurant, toasting the week.

"The biggest loser of all time came up to our table, a table of grungy, bearded guys, and tried to sell us dope." Peterson really belly laughs as he recalls this. Of course, off duty or not, they weren't about to pass up the chance. One of them does the buy, then they surround him in an unbroken ring of narcotics officers. "Talk about bad luck. Loser of the year."

That same week was memorable for one of Peterson's famous "dating" escapades. He made the mistake of dating a Springfield sergeant's daughter. His second big mistake was getting intimate with her in the basement of the sergeant's house.

"Next thing you know, this door crashes open in the basement," Peterson said. "And, there was the biggest man I've ever seen in my life, standing in the doorway, standing there with a big hat and a black coat, and he was a Springfield sergeant."

"Oh shit," Peterson said.

The sergeant's daughter is fixing herself up, straightening her clothes.

"Oh shit," Peterson said again. He stood up. "Hey, man, I'm the police. It's okay."

"Young man, I think you better leave," the giant sergeant says, but he doesn't move aside.

Peterson agrees—good idea. But the sergeant continues to stand in the doorway. Peterson remembers the scene as something like a very painful Saturday morning cartoon, Wile E. Coyote against the sheepdog. He doesn't escape the room without a good cartoon-style battering. The sergeant's elbows fly and fists pound, and Peterson finds himself running for his life. Strangely, Peterson is laughing as the blows fall, and it will remain one of his fondest memories.

Of course, his life will change dramatically in a few years, as the run-ins with the Illinois State Police become more serious, hardly comical, and certainly not comic book.

"Failure to report a bribe"

Peterson met Victoria O'Neil, wife number two, in these wilder days. Peterson wasn't really marrying-material in those mad days. Victoria was a svelte, half-Irish, half-American-Indian girl, beautiful and exotic and slight. Victoria was a partier too, always "slugging back the Jack Daniel's." Victoria was in the middle of a nasty divorce from an abusive alcoholic husband who ended up tangling with Peterson more than once. Peterson became "Vickie's" refuge. Together, they shared a common interest, and she was a woman who understood his wacky sense of humor. They opened a modest bar business together. The bar was both fun and profitable, and it was, in many ways, the glue of their marriage. The main issue in their early relationship was Peterson's new stepdaughter, Lisa Marie, who "hated" him from the beginning with a "you're not my father" attitude.

Vickie's daughter was eight, but instantly blamed Peterson for everything. She ignored his rules and discipline, lied every chance she got, and probably viewed him as an invader in the family unit. "She wasn't a bad kid," Peterson said, "but she was hell to grow up with."

This was his real "bad boys" period, with nights spent partying, literally "biting barmaids' asses," out with fellow cops, getting home around 6 AM, just in time for a quick nap, a shower, and back for roll call at 7:30.

As a narcotics officer, Peterson excelled, bringing down big drug dealers, worked on the first Class X drug case in Will County's history, continued to bring down the awards, including "police officer of the year" in 1979. As a cop, he was tops. As a husband, a flop by his own admission.

The hardest time for Peterson, professionally, was when his three-year tour was over in MANS. He had learned to thrive in the sweatshop boiler room of undercover narcotics, one of the best buyers, participating in all the raids, working street snitches and contacts. Occasionally he got in trouble for his independent streak, but mostly he pulled in the commendations for his high clearance rates.

Peterson went from being a high-level undercover narcotics

officer on a multi-jurisdiction team, to a patrol officer overnight. Off came the beard and long hair, out went the flannel shirts and denims, and he was back in uniform. But after two years on patrol, Peterson "couldn't take it" and they allowed him to re-enroll in narcotics.

"I had no business being in narcotics, now that I was married again, but it was my life," Peterson explained. "I loved being in narcotics. But the same routine started up. The women. The craziness. The parties."

The only difference on this two-year tour was that Peterson was now considered senior. He had more time supervising narcotics operations than most of the new crew of officers had in narcotics. The younger team members were officially Peterson's supervisors, because he was newly recruited. A whole set of new practices and procedures were completely alien to the go-get-'em Peterson philosophy, who lived by more of the six-shooter cowboy philosophy. The new team leader was a state agent, according to Peterson, "an inept leader." Peterson's opinion likely developed over the course of several run-ins over investigations.

One deal really stands out in Peterson's mind, because he nearly died over it. He was doing a drug buy behind a Dunkin' Donuts in Joliet. "The perp had a gun on me," Peterson said. Prematurely, the supervisor signaled for the arrest, but Peterson not only didn't get the signal, he had no chance to get out of harm's way with the dealer's gun still aimed at his chest. Peterson grabbed the gun while the perp was distracted. He wasn't hurt, but he never forgot the dangerous fumble.

This all came to a climax when a fed-up Peterson, using old tried-and-true methods from his first tour in MANS, pursued a case behind his supervisor's back. "Frankly, they would have blown the whole case," Peterson said, not meaning to sound arrogant. He tells these stories very matter-of-factly, with a dry wit and no sense of holding back or shame. "In MANS, my first three-year stint, we closed hundreds of cases. Under this new style of supervision, we were letting more people get off than we were nailing."

Not only would Peterson get into real trouble for going behind his supervisor's back, but it would come back to haunt him. He would be disciplined and fired, then portrayed in the national media as a "bad cop."

"I wanted this perp," Peterson explained. "The state was after the guy. The feds were after the guy. I got the guy." The perpetrator sold Peterson 10,000 hits of amphetamines. The dealer got out on appeal. This infuriated Peterson, who went after the criminal yet again, again going behind his supervisor's back.

"This was the way we did it in narcotics," Peterson said. "The first Class X bust we did came about in spite of department leaks to the perpetrators. Well, we learned to not tell too many people."

While Peterson was putting together his case against the perp, "this guy implicated a state's attorney for taking kickbacks. Well, I wrote that in my report." He shook his head. My director got me fired, I ended up getting criminally indicted for 'official misconduct' and 'failure to report an offer of a bribe' and nine counts of bullshit. And they fired me from the police department with no evidence I did anything wrong."

Astonished at what he viewed as corruption, Peterson took his case to the courts, and after six months he was fully vindicated and reinstated on the police department. The state's attorney later went on to become a state representative and later a judge.

Peterson's return did cause "a big upheaval in the police department" and Peterson was returned to humble patrol duty. He would miss undercover narcotics, but not the new rules and regulations.

"I was ballsy and obnoxious"

Peterson, still angered by the corruption, sued the then-police chief and the state's attorney. "I was ballsy and obnoxious, like any angry young cop would be," Peterson said.

The state's attorney and police chief hid behind the state's attorney's executive immunity and the lawsuit failed. The legal costs and loss of wages in the meanwhile, would take a toll on his shaky marriage with Victoria. They lost their house in these bad times. The financial woes, the stress of the termination, subsequent special prosecutor action and follow-on lawsuit were too much for a marriage also somewhat eroded by Peterson's famous infidelities.

Marriage over, just like that. House gone. And now Peterson "was hated" by the chief of police at the time. The public humiliation of the police chief made Peterson a target in the small police force.

Above: Drew Peterson being sworn in as sergeant at ceremony with Mayor Claar of Bolingbrook, photographed in 1999.

Right: Peterson sworn in as a Bolingbrook Police officer, June 1, 1977, by Grace Kohler, village clerk.

Photos courtesy of Drew Peterson

Left: Peterson as member of the R.E.A.C.T. Team, the Bolingbrook equivalent of SWAT.

Bottom: Peterson playing golf with friends. From left to right: Kenneth Each, John Moraveck, Drew Peterson, Michael Calcagno.

The police chief had minimal credibility after the investigation showed he lied under oath. He moved on to become the village administrator, and later moved to another state.

Still simmering, Peterson vented his anger in a new direction. He managed to get himself elected the head of the Will County Democratic Party. He was party chairman for the township. He ran a slate of trustees and a mayoral candidate against the current mayor. On a one-thousand-dollar budget, against the mayor's ten-thousand-dollar budget, they narrowly lost.

Peterson half winked. "I think I made everyone nervous after all this." His main goal in running candidates was to bring about change, hopefully to replace the police chief, and to help wipe out corruption. "They watched me closely after this."

A defining characteristic of Peterson's personality certainly seems to be his willingness to fight back. In true American spirit, the harder things got, the tougher he became. He is falsely accused of corruption, and fights back, wins, and then runs candidates to sweep away the corruption of others. He loses all his money in the process, his house, his marriage, but through it all he keeps his bar business, opened with Victoria shortly after they married. Even after they're divorced, she remains his business partner.

They stayed partners and friends for a long while, although in the end Peterson bought out Victoria for $100,000 and ran the business as a sole proprietorship after that. Again, with true entrepreneurial spirit, he drove the bar on to resounding success. Full-time cop, full-time bar owner, now single again, and playing the field. Peterson continued as her friend for a while, even co-signed on her house, but eventually they drifted apart, became strangers again. Marriage number two became a distant memory.

"I have fun with everything, so I'm up for anything"

Peterson's very unique sense of humor—not so much abrasive as I-don't-care-what-anyone-thinks—remained a defining characteristic of his fascinating and tumultuous life. Never one to dwell on the past, he put up his humor like a shield, never allowing anything to get him down for longer than a day or two. "I'm not wired like other people that way," Peterson said, in our third straight day of interviews. "Why dwell on the bad things? I have fun with everything, so I'm up for anything."

"It gets you in trouble with the media, though," I commented.

"Yeah. But really just the media. And I don't care." He laughs, as always. "People can say whatever they want. I only get mad when they bring my children into it. The media really are persecuting my children."

"So you're a decent upstanding guy?" I try not to sound sarcastic.

"I like the girls. I like my beer. I like to party. I like to be the clown. But I never got into illegal stuff, drugs, any of that. It doesn't even interest me. I get high on practical jokes."

The practical jokes thrived at Peterson's bar, keeping it popular with the locals. The pub was in a blue-collar neighborhood, and the crowd were pretty much hard-working people who liked a good laugh. Arm wrestling was the big sport in Peterson's bar, a nightly contest. Everyone was fair game in the arm wrestling, and everyone wanted a turn at Peterson. All the patrons knew he was a martial arts–trained, black belt, cop-trained, tough guy, but this crowd took that as a challenge. Every night he'd be challenged. Peterson figured out a way to stop the challenges once and for all.

One of the bar's regular patrons, a giant construction worker with biceps the size of watermelons, was the undefeated champion of the arm wrestling bouts. Peterson had made him his bouncer and later his friend. One night, Peterson revealed his plan. He took his friend into the office and said, "Here's what we're going to do. We're going to arm wrestle. We're going to bet a hundred bucks." He gave his friend a hundred bucks. The plan? His friend would throw the arm wrestling to Peterson, who knew that, martial arts notwithstanding, he could never beat this guy. The plan worked perfectly. The giant bouncer threw the contest, barely, tossed Peterson a hundred bucks, feigning anger, and from that night on, Peterson was able to deflect all challengers by pointing at his giant friend and saying, "You beat him, you can have a turn at me." His friend made a bundle every week as challenger after challenger came forward, hoping to beat the bouncer to have their turn at Peterson.

After hours, the bar became famous for its "green felt club," a quasi after-hours consensual sex club, where after the bar closed, daring couples would have sex on the pool tables.

Kathleen Savio on her wedding day.

"Kathy was a blind date"

"The village of Montgomery was constantly up my butt for stupid things," according to Drew—not the after-hours sex club, but little things like parking and liquor licenses. The chief of police in Montgomery was a friend of the Bolingbrook police chief, who hated Peterson.

Peterson had by now bought out Victoria's share of the bar, and their divorce was almost final. His friends fixed him up. "Kathy was a blind date," Peterson said, smiling.

Kathy is better known as the famous Kathleen Savio, wife number three in Peterson's world, found dead in a bathtub in her home in 2004.

Kathy, as Peterson called her, was beyond simply glamorous and gorgeous. "I had the hots for Kathy from the beginning," he said in an interview, holding a picture of her to show me. "Very voluptuous, very beautiful." Of course she knew she was beautiful. Vivacious and fun, Kathy laughed at Peterson's jokes, enjoyed many of the same things he did—their first date was a comedy club and dinner—and she was tough as nails. "No one, myself included, could stand up against Kathleen," Peterson said, smiling. "When her temper got up, you stayed clear. When she swung, you ducked. She did things no one else dared to do, so life was an adventure in the beginning. We did things I never did with Victoria. She was a lot of fun. And she was gorgeous."

Every week they went to a new stage play or club, ate dinner out any chance they could, and their relationship was "very romantic." Kathleen, like Peterson, enjoyed meeting new people, parties, telling jokes, the crazier the better. She was almost a personality twin for Drew Peterson in most ways except one. "She had this temper. And she liked to be the boss. But mostly we had a lotta laughs. She was a good time."

Drew's pre-teen kids, Steven and Eric, children by Carol, liked Kathy a lot, in ways they never really grew close to Victoria. And Kathleen took charge, quickly becoming the boss of the family unit, in charge of everything.

The defining characteristic of the relationship was "fun." Everything they did had the simple objectives of amusing, entertaining and "trying new things."

"They were an odd group."

Perhaps atypically for Drew Peterson, Kathleen was only ten years younger. More typically, their engagement was quick and they married six months after their first comedy-club date. He was mid-thirties, she was mid-twenties, and she drove the relationship. The one roadblock to happiness on their detour through marriage was the inlaws.

"They were kinda an odd group," Peterson said, squinting as if concentrating on the memories. By this time in the interviews, hundreds of hours in, I've learned that he has a perfect mind for details, able to recall names from thirty-five years ago without prompting, even knowing how to spell their names, the names of their children, what they did, where they lived, their address. He has the mind of a sharp cop, in other words. When he analyzes Kathy's family, he does it quite coolly, as if able to detach himself from the idea that he was a person involved in their life, and presenting them almost as a third-party witness might.

"They didn't like me much, either," Peterson said, sounding regretful. "They were instantly against the idea of their daughter dating a policeman."

Peterson tried to be sociable and used his humor to try to disarm them, to draw them closer, but they never got past the idea that he was a cop. "They seemed to think all cops are cheaters. Policemen are dishonest. They were always looking at me out of the corner of their eye. In ten years of marriage, then never warmed up to me."

The wedding was a "nice-sized" affair with close to three hundred attending in spite of family disapproval of policeman Drew Peterson. Kathy's father planned on giving her away to Drew at the ceremony, but unfortunately, two weeks before the marriage, Kathy's mother passed away. "She was close to her mom," Peterson said. Kathy's father and mother were divorced, but her father used the mother's passing as a reason to not give her away at the wedding.

The wedding was marred, slightly, by tearful moments as both Kathy and Drew Peterson reminisced on their recently passed-

Elaborate wedding cake at Drew and Kathy Peterson's wedding (Kathy, also known as Kathleen Savio).

away parents. Peterson was close to his father, who had just passed away, and Kathy was very close to her mother. But differences and memories were put aside and the event itself was mostly social and enjoyable, and both Kathy and Drew were ecstatic to learn they were pregnant with future music star Tommy.

Tommy's birth would change everything.

"She was suddenly the boss."

Peterson first noticed Kathy's bossiness shortly after Tommy was born. Tommy was a delight to both of them, but after his birth Kathy wanted to be active and professional. Peterson had just bought out the bar from Victoria, and Kathy asked to manage it. Peterson, a full-time cop, part-time wedding photographer and sometime chimneysweep, agreed, with a few reservations.

"You have to understand," he explained, still staring at the wedding pictures of Kathy and family, "we were a close-knit family,

Main: Kathy Peterson (Kathleen Savio) as a bride on her wedding day.

Inset: A goofy Drew Peterson, happy husband of Kathy, being slung around by best friend/best man at the wedding.

my crew at the bar. I could leave them to do their own thing and trust them to do it. It was a fun place. Kathleen—Kathy—wanted to change all that. To make it a real business. Maybe it was having another child in the house, the financial obligations, but whatever it was, she was suddenly the boss."

The aggressive persona, the dominant personality, originally surfaced only at the bar, where she became somewhat unpopular with the easygoing crew. Employees began to complain. Later, she'd import the bossiness to their home.

"She was all about the bottom line," Peterson said. "That's a good thing in a business, as long as you don't lose your employees. It's a service business."

At first Kathy was very good for the business. "She was very, very organized. And she could spend her entire day at the bar." He sighed. "She was very good with figures and dollars and numbers, but she wasn't a people person."

Tommy's birth marked the change in her personality. He was not the cause, but it was the birth that seemed to trigger her dominance. Everything had to be handled a certain way. Employees who argued were threatened with termination, unless Peterson intervened. He often did speak on behalf of employees, but this only created a new distance between him and his new wife.

The anger wasn't entirely natural, though. She would get angry quickly, but it would last for days, and she'd yell at employees, slam doors, threaten more firings. A thinner shadow of this temper monster materialized in the Peterson household as well. So much so, they actually consulted six different councilors over time: a psychiatrist, psychologists and family councilors. Kathleen would always terminate the sessions if they probed too deeply into her family's abusive past. In the end a psychiatrist prescribed Zoloft, an anti-depressant often given to people with clinical depression, Asperger's Syndrome or bi-polar disorders. This helped clear moodiness after the anger, but not the anger itself. By this time employees were jumpy, trying to stay clear of the boss.

Peterson was always a good listener, and coped well with anger. Over time, at counseling sessions, and in their own talks, he discovered what Kathy believed her issues were. She said, "My stepparents were very violent." According to Kathy, her stepmother was somewhat physically abusive with her. She tried to live with her father and stepmother for some time, later with her mother and stepfather. The stepfather, according to Peterson, sexually abused Kathy and two of her sisters. At the age of sixteen, she was on her own, unable to live in either home.

Their marriage would last ten years, a garden with more rocks and thorns than flowers, rewarding and wonderful and beautiful, yet very prickly. Their children were the cement that bonded them together for ten years, through the lows of depression and the growl of anger. Peterson desperately wanted to avoid another divorce—"it's a terrible thing, to be divorced"—and Kathy didn't want to be divorced, period. "We did what we could." Peterson had grown up believing that "you don't get rid of somebody if they're sick" and to him, both Kathy and their marriage needed loving care. To him, Kathy needed love and nurturing, not the stress of a divorce and more anger. "I did love her very much, and she wasn't like this all the time, so I wanted to be there for her."

Still, the fights became shorter but more frequent. The bar employees lived in terror. And Peterson, while not terrified, realized that they could not stay together. On rare occasions, Kathy would even become violent, striking out either vocally or physically at anyone within reach. Eventually, for the good of the kids, they would have to divorce.

"We always fought about money."

Eventually, the excitement of owning a bar lost its allure for Peterson. Always the entrepreneur, he got into the printing business, mostly because of his brother.

"On my father's deathbed—this was actually before I married Kathy—my father looked at me and said, 'you take care of him,' meaning my little brother," Peterson told me when I asked what happened to the bar. "Together, we put together this printing and prepress business."

Again, though, Kathleen kept control by force of her dominant personality. Peterson was so-called president, Kathy was the director of finance, brother Paul did production, and they had one more person for sales. It was a successful business, but the reality was that Kathy, Paul, and the sales director came to "hate each other." Peterson became the referee in a war between his brother, his wife and the sales director. "It was awful."

History seemed to repeat itself as Kathy's curt management style and anger issues alienated all the employees, not just brother Paul. "It's no exaggeration to say that all the employees hated my wife."

"I remember one time these three sales guys came in to hard sell us," Peterson laughs. "They were big tough guys. I pointed to Kathy's office and said, 'Sell it to her—if you can.' He laughed, watching from outside the office as Kathy tore them to shreds. They left the building in a visible sweat, looking pale, with Peterson laughing on the floor. It was in moments like this he felt a fierce pride. She was a toughie, no doubt about it. No one went up against Kathy—especially on issues of money—and won.

"Kathy and I were always fighting about money," Peterson said, "so it was nice to see other people lose these fights too. I don't know why we fought about money. We had money, our businesses did well, but we always fought about money."

"Old Golden Tongue"

Peterson kept his two lives separate—entrepreneur and cop. It wasn't possible to separate family life and business, because his wife was his active director-partner, but as a cop, his only run-ins were with dangerous perps.

As an entrepreneur he was successful, albeit always in a referee position, mediating between Kathy and employees, Paul and Kathy, the suppliers and Kathy. As a cop he was also the big referee, but here he took great personal satisfaction from his ability to put people at ease.

"For years after I'd arrested people, they'd come up to me and compliment me on how I put them at ease when I arrested them." A low rumble of laughter. "I always joked around, even with perps. Reason being, I didn't see any reason to create hardship or make things harder than they needed to be. So I never had any problem with people on arrests." Peterson was in demand as "old golden tongue" for his ability to defuse difficult situations. He could resolve hostile domestic disputes. He could talk almost anyone into surrendering.

Memorable and perhaps telling of his personality and

relationships, one night his team responded to a violent domestic dispute involving a gun in Bolingbrook. The police converged on the house and found the husband in the family room, sitting at a chair, with a gun in his hand. The depressed man had decided he was going to go out fighting. The team took cover behind walls and doors, guns drawn, but it was left to "golden tongue" to talk the guy down. Outside, they had a sharpshooter, focused on him through the window. The easy solution: they could kill the distraught husband.

This came down to life or death. In this situation, no one is going to risk their life to save a guy with a gun.

Peterson called out, from behind the door, "Hey, why you wanna hurt us?" The guy didn't look up. "You having trouble with your wife? Everybody here has trouble with their wives. Jim[86] over here, his wife won't let him see the kids. Bill, his wife took him for everything he had. My last wife just divorced me." He went on, listing off all the problems he knew his fellow officers were having, common knowledge from drinks-after-work talk. First one of the cops laughed out loud. Then the husband with the gun smiled. His lip trembled a little bit. Peterson went on rhyming off the long list of problems they each had with their wives. Now the husband laughed for real, and so did all the cops. An hour later, the guy gave up, surrendering to the "class clown," Drew Peterson.

"Kathy, the husband beater"

The main flashpoint for marital discord became the multi-generational family. Steve and Eric were fast approaching college age. "If I'd put aside money for their college education, Kathy'd take it as I'm taking food out of the mouths of our younger kids." He shakes his head. "We had money, we were successful, but I had to argue for every penny for Steve or Eric."

Kathy was the consummate money person, a financial whiz, and very quick to find a dollar missing in the ledger. Peterson would sneak Steve and Eric money on the side, when Kathy wasn't around. It became more difficult as they got to college age and the money needs increased. "I had to sneak them money, otherwise there'd be a big battle about it."

When they sold the prepress business, Kathy insisted on splitting the money into two TD Waterhouse accounts, one as "Drew

Peterson in joint tenancy with Kathleen" and the other "Kathleen in joint tenancy with Drew Peterson."

A peculiarity of their marriage, which became evident in the later divorce and the various calls to law enforcement over domestic disputes, was Kathy's violence, particularly after Peterson met seventeen-year-old Stacy Cales. In a complete turnaround from average marital situations, Kathy became known as a "husband beater." Her temper, when let loose, knew no bounds. People ran for cover. Only Peterson had nowhere to run.

Before Kathy and Drew's divorce was finalized, Drew began dating young Stacy. Kathy and Drew continued to fight after their separation, and Stacy became the gasoline on the Drew-Kathy fire. At one point their relationship became so volatile that Kathy physically assaulted Stacy.

Oddly, an audit of the much publicized eighteen domestic dispute complaints at 392 Pheasant Chase Court—often mentioned in media reports to demonstrate Peterson's "dangerous" personality—reveals that almost half of the calls were from Peterson with complaints about Kathy. All of these complaints were filed after their breakup, during their custody battle, but they do give credence to Peterson's claims:

- Of the nineteen calls after their separation, including one from Stacy and Drew's home, nine were from Drew, ten from Kathy
- Of the ten calls to police from Kathy, eight were for "being late returning the children" and one was for an alleged break-in (which was called in two weeks after the incident)
- Of the nine calls from Drew, three reported domestic battery by Kathy, perpetrated either on him or on Stacy Peterson.

"She was just a little bitty spitfire," Peterson said "I mean she could be vicious. But I wasn't threatened at all because of her size. But you always backed down from Kathy. What she didn't have in weight, she made up for in temperament. She'd physically swing at me, all the time." What didn't work in their fights, though, was Peterson's sarcasm. Kathy would be deadly serious, physically pounding on him, and he'd be either laughing at her or sarcastic, because he knew that hurt more than anything else he could do.

Domestic Trouble

According to Bolingbrook Police, "Domestic Trouble" calls were a regular occurrence at 392 Pheasant Chase Court (the residence of Kathleen Savio) and a one-time occurrence at 6 Pheasant Chase Court (the residence of the Peterson family). All calls seemed to relate to custody of the children and Kathleen Savio. Interestingly, all of the Domestic Battery Charges are from Drew Peterson, claiming he or Stacy were "battered" by Kathleen Savio,[87] while most of Kathleen's calls on Drew related to being late with the children visitations:

392 Pheasant Chase Court (the residence of Kathleen Savio)			
Bolingbrook Police Record 2002			
Date	**Complaint**	**By**	**Event**
02/2/2002	Domestic Trouble	Drew Peterson	An argument between Drew Peterson and Kathleen Savio
05/03/2002	Domestic Trouble	Kathleen Savio	Kathleen Savio reports Peterson took her car, although both are still registered owners and they are still married. Vehicle returned
05/03/2002	Domestic Battery, Disorderly Conduct	Drew Peterson	Peterson claims that Savio struck him, pushed him and spit on him. He does not press charges.
05/26/2002	Battery	Drew Peterson	Savio punches Stacy in the face when Peterson drops their children off. This time Savio is arrested and witnesses corroborate. Drew keeps custody of the children. Although Savio is charged, the record is later expunged by the court
05/26/2002	Domestic Trouble	Drew Peterson	Savio complains that she has sole custody of children. It is later determined there is no such court order. Again Peterson keeps children.
06/25/2002	Visitation Interference	Drew Peterson	Peterson claims Savio will not release children for visitation
06/05/2002	Criminal Trespass, Unlawful Restraint, Domestic Battery	Kathleen Savio	Two weeks after the claimed occurrence (allegedly 7/18/2002), Savio retroactively claims Peterson broke into the house, and even restrained her. Savio did not file a complaint but report was forwarded to state's attorney.
07/11/2002	Visitation Interference	Kathleen Savio	Savio claims Peterson violated a court order. Logged.
12/05/2002	Well Being Check, Visitation Interference	Kathleen Savio	Savio claims Peterson pounding on door and she refuses visitation because the children "are sick." Logged and referred to lawyers.
12/05/2002	Alleged Violation of Order of Protection, Visitation Interference	Drew Peterson	Savio again blocks Peterson from getting children even though no Order of Protection standing. Logged.
12/20/2002	Notification	Kathleen Savio	Savio notifies police she has advised Stacy by certified letter she will be arrested for trespassing for future violations. Logged.

392 Pheasant Chase Court (the residence of Kathleen Savio)			
Bolingbrook Police Record 2003			
Date	**Complaint**	**By**	**Event**
01/02/2003	Notification	Kathleen Savio	Savio calls again stating the kids have a late doctor's appointment and she will not drop off children. Logged.
02/18/2003	Citizen Assist	Drew Peterson	Savio again will not turn over children for visitation because they "are sick." Logged.
06/02/2003	Residential Burglary	Kathleen Savio	Savio claims someone enters the rear sliding glass door and takes diamond jewelry and a camera. Peterson denies involvement. No witnesses or evidence.
09/04/2003	Visitation Interference	Kathleen Savio	Savio claims Peterson does not drop the Children at appointed time. Logged.
09/09/2003	Visitation Interference	Kathleen Savio	Savio again upset that Peterson is 10 minutes late with children. Logged.
09/09/2003	Disorderly Conduct	Drew Peterson	Savio claims Stacy calls her insulting names when Peterson drops off children. Referred to the state's attorney's office.
11/11/2003	Visitation Interference	Kathleen Savio	Savio claims Peterson has children past appointed return time. Logged.

6 Pheasant Chase Court (residence of Drew and Stacy Peterson)			
Bolingbrook Police Record 2002			
Date	**Complaint**	**By**	**Event**
04/38/2002	Domestic Battery	Drew Peterson	Savio came to Peterson's residence and started removing items from Peterson's truck. When Peterson asked her to stop, Savio hit him in the back leading to Peterson filing a report. He never followed up with charges.

"She was an embarrassment"

Perhaps signaling the end of the marriage, Peterson started to notice they were less and less welcome at police or public social occasions due to Kathy's "hellcat" behavior when drinking. Shortly before they broke up for good, they attended a function with the mayor of Bolingbrook and other dignitaries—"these are all prominent people I work for"—and she became uncontrollably drunk.

At this memorable event, she climbed over the table and whispered in the mayor's ear. When one of the village managers tried to intercede, she spilled her drink on him. "She was an embarrassment when she'd be drinking," Drew said.

Drew insists she was not an alcoholic. "When she would drink, though, whatever mood she was in when she started became magnified a dozen times over. She could be a happy drunk, or a mean drunk." Social drinking became a crazy adventure.

"I was walking on eggs all the time, not to piss her off." He still didn't want a divorce. He still loved her. But more and more Kathy's antics ostracized them socially and even in their own businesses with their employees. Peterson realized the marriage was dysfunctional, and he accepted that it was every bit as much his fault as Kathy's. In the casebook of marriage counseling, "irreconcilable differences" could have been perfectly illustrated by their marriage. More and more his sarcasm and humor grated on Kathy's nerves. More and more often her temper drove him away. Even the kids felt it.

Towards the end of the marriage, on a typical night:

- Kathy would shout at him
- In defense, Drew would crack an insensitive joke—the same sort of humor that gets him in trouble with the media today
- Angered more by his flippant attitude, she would get physical, often hitting or striking, even biting.

Or the flipside:

- Drew would crack an insensitive joke
- She'd yell at him
- He'd crack another Drew-ism
- She'd hit him.

"She was a tiger. All of a sudden, all you see is teeth and hair coming at you."

The tub in which Kathy Savio was found drowned. She had a contusion on the back of her head and was found in a fetal position on her left side. She was found by neighbors who entered the house when Drew Peterson became concerned after she didn't answer the door or phone when he returned their children from visitation.

Guilty?

"Healthy adults don't drown in bathtubs accidentally."

This account of February 27, 2004, the night Kathleen Savio was found drowned, is dramatized from renewed speculation in national media after the 2008 findings of Doctor Michael Baden, forensic pathologist. Compare this to the "Innocent" account of Peterson and the original coroner's inquest. The main rationale for building this "guilty" scenario is the "intimates theory" and the financial gain motive. In my analysis, this is the only way it could have happened—if it did happen—simply because Kathy, in a homicide scenario, would have to have been "surprised." She was more than capable of defending herself, known for her temper and her strength.

Assets and liabilities. That's what life comes down to in the end: assets and liabilities. The things you do, or don't do, are risk factors. The goal is simply, in the balance sheet of life, to come out with more assets than liabilities.

As he picks the complex lock, focused on the task, he keeps his mind fixed on assets. Liabilities are to be eliminated. The kids, the houses, the businesses, his jobs—all assets.

Kathleen—she's been a liability for eight or more years. She embarrasses him in public. She beats his fiancée. She wants half his pension. She is a hellcat, hard to handle at the best of times, impossible when angry.

A liability, and an unpredictable one at that.

The lock is troublesome. He has no training in lock picking, and this is a major lock. The other troublesome factors: the snow, the neighbors, the streetlights, Kathleen's wariness—it is a long shot. How is he going to eliminate the evidence of his visit? He can see his footprints in the salted sidewalk. The only solution for that will be to create traffic on the sidewalk from neighbors, the police and others. This means he has to engineer the "discovery" of the accident. He also knows his lock picking will leave trace scratches, evidence of a break-in. Maybe it would be better just to break a window. Then the police will believe it was a burglary. In many ways, it is a better solution, since it will remove suspicion from him as an "intimate."

No, he's committed to the impossible task of making it look like an accident. It will be nearly impossible. She'll fight back. She'll scratch at him and leave marks on his face if he gives her a chance. He has to catch her unawares, because one slip and she'll have the better of him. The sirens will wail, the police will question, and she'll file charges.

Finally, the lock gives. He removes his shoes, so the salt from the walk won't mark the floor. If this is to be an accident, rather than a simple break-in homicide, he can leave no evidence. He has to use all his knowledge of police and forensic methods. Even so, the risks are gigantic. There'll be hair, salt traces, and even with his hat and gloves, a big chance of DNA evidence. One slip and he's done. He'll never see his kids again. He'll never work the watch.

No point in thinking about risks. No one ever beats him. He is far too smart for anyone else. It's like a game. No one ever wins against him in the game of life.

He forces all thoughts from his mind. He hears the television.

He hesitates, making sure no one has seen him. It's a busy neighborhood, with neighbors on both sides. It has taken him more than thirty minutes on the lock alone. He hasn't raised even a light bead of perspiration. Nothing ever frightens him. His heartbeat remains steady. This is easy for him. Even if they had questions afterward—they always suspect the intimates, he knows that—he feels sure he can handle it all, as long as he leaves no evidence. No one, and nothing, can stand against his perfect planning.

The television is loud enough to cover the sound of his approach, even with the creaking of the third step on the staircase.

He almost smiles. The risk is worth it. Like any business risk, you weigh the dangers against the net gain. Except this is almost more of a crapshoot than a business proposition. He knows that, as a law enforcement expert. He'll automatically be suspected not only as a past intimate, but as someone with an emotional and financial motive. One slip, just one, and it's game over.

Finally, he'll be rid of this liability.

Analysis: This is perhaps not a very convincing reconstruction. I have trouble with this myself. There are no signs of struggle in the house. To pull off a homicide this complex, without leaving forensic trace, would require something of a criminal genius. Even then, the risks and variables were overwhelming. The reason, I believe, the Illinois State Police and the forensic teams came to believe the theory of accident was simply that the obstacles to this "perfect crime" are very great. To accomplish a homicide like this would require:

- **A struggle confined to her tub, since there was no trace of blood elsewhere, or a total surprise and no struggle as I've theorized here.**
- **The murder committed elsewhere, and the body brought back to the house; this should have left trace as the body was carried.**
- **Picking the lock, a major obstacle as it would require expertise, a cool head, and escaping detection by neighbors, passersby and the "victim." Or a key. Only Kathy and her latest boyfriend had these keys. The lack of forced entry is therefore problematic.**

The scenario I've given is the only one that works, assuming the suspect is a criminal mastermind, a master lock picker, and very cool-headed. A degree of luck would also be required.

March 2, 1997 Last Will and Testament of
Kathleen Savio and Drew Peterson

This day March 2nd 1997 Drew Walter Peterson and Kathleen Savio Peterson, both being of sound body and mind, do hereby bequeath all of our worldly possessions to each other in the event of either of our individual deaths.

In the unlikely event we should die on or about the same time we do hereby bequeath all of our worldly possessions, to be divided equally among, our four surviving children, Eric Drew Peterson, Stephen Paul Peterson, Thomas Drew Peterson, Kristopher Donald Peterson. Property included but not limited to the following:

1) Golden Rule life insurance policy $100,000.00*
2) Monumental Life Insurance policy $125,000.00
3) Prudential Life Insurance policy $308,137.59
   Beneficiary Merchants Bank Oswego to pay off note for Suds Pub in Montgomery. Remaining funds to be divided.
4) Bolingbrook Police Pension fund in excess of $50,000.
5) Real Estate: 1040 Walden Ct in Bolingbrook, IL, including ALL Contents. 1993 Ford Van, 1992 Nissan Pathfinder.
6) Real Estate: 9 Clay Ct, in Montgomery, IL.
7) The Blue Lightning Corp. (Suds Pub in Montgomery 1250 S. Broadway in Montgomery) 100%
8) Da Page Corp. (Fast 'N' Accurate Graphics - 87 Eisenhower South, Lombard) 100%
9) CMYK Corp. Lombard-Naperville (Printing) 25%

We Drew Walter Peterson and Kathleen Savio Peterson do also name James B. Carrol to be executor of this will and to have full control to handle all of our financial affairs in the event of our deaths.

It is also the desire of Drew Walter Peterson to have his remains cremated and buried with the remains of his wife, Kathleen Savio Peterson.

We Drew Walter Peterson and Kathleen Savio Peterson do hereby make this our last will and testament.

Drew Walter Peterson | Kathleen Savio Peterson

Witnesses
Alex J. Morelli 03/02/97 | Gary L. Marcolina 3/2/97

---

* These were the only spousal policies. Kathleen also took out a million-dollar policy on her two children, payable in trust.

Timeline for the Peterson Family from Various Media Sources

Note: For a detailed timeline of Stacy's disappearance, see page 47.

2001
• *Chicago Tribune*—"Stacy Cales graduated High School"[88]

Note: A key factor in assuming Peterson's guilt in Savio's death derives from his moral character, illustrated in sensational headlines and stories regarding Stacy Cales' age and the thirty-year difference in their ages.

2001
• "When my brother left for the military, she (Stacy) started dating Drew and we haven't seen her since because he cut off all ties with us," he (Scott Rossetto) said."[89]

Note: Relevant to the timeline since Peterson claims Rossetto is one of Stacy's infidelities, contributing to Stacy and Drew's marital woes.

2001
• "The couple (Drew Peterson and Stacy Cales) met six years ago (2001) he said. She was 17. He was 47. At the time, she was working at a SpringHill Suites hotel in Bolingbrook … A friend of Stacy's, Jen Kaye, said she and others were surprised by the relationship. Because Stacy Peterson was not close to either of her parents, 'we chalked it up to Stacy looking for a father figure to fill a void that she had in her own life,' Kaye said."[90]

Note: Relevant to show Stacy was not close to her parents as indicated in various accounts.

Various 2002-2003
• *On the Record with Greta Van Susteren*, FOX News: Bolingbrook Police Chief Raymond McGury:

> There was a series of complaints. And as I was speaking with your producer, I noted eighteen different reports that were placed on file beginning, I believe, somewhere in February of 2002. And the last one was somewhere like November, I believe, of 2003… And so that's why we have eighteen separate

reports. And of those eighteen*—I spent my weekend going through all of these meticulously—nine of those are visitation issues. You didn't drop the kids off on time. Call the police, document it, so I can use it in court. You didn't drop the kids off, or you're not giving me the kids. So 50 percent of those had to do with that type of thing.

Note: Supports my analysis that most calls related to the visitation rights. Of the remaining calls, three involved domestic battery but were filed against Kathy by Drew and one was filed by Kathy but later dropped.[91]

11-2002

• *Chicago Tribune*—"And in a November 2002 letter to a Will County assistant state's attorney, Savio mentioned Peterson's relationship with his current wife ... There have been several times throughout my marriage with this man where I ended up at the emergency room in Bolingbrook for injuries, and I have reported this only to have police leave my home without filing any reports."[92]

Note: Media have freely used this filing and a dismissed order of protection to allege a pattern of abuse. However, out of nineteen total domestic calls from both addresses, no alleged abuse calls from Kathy were ever pursued, while Peterson filed three abuse calls against Kathy (normally involving battery of Stacy), per this report:

• "Sources tell CBS 2, Bolingbrook police were called to the home nearly twenty times for domestic disputes during that marriage." [93]

10-18-2003

• *Suburban Chicago News*—"Peterson married Stacy Peterson eight days later (eight days after divorce from Kathy finalized[94]). At the time of their marriage the couple had an infant son."

Note: This sensationalizing doesn't take into account the two years of failing marriage leading up to the divorce, fairly average and typical in America.

03-01-2004

• *NBC5*—Steve Carcerano, who was Peterson's neighbor when

---

* Complaints at 392 Pheasant Chase Court (the residence of Kathleen Savio).

he was married to Savio, said finding the body would be forever fused into his memory. "It's something you'd see in a movie; it was something I'll never forget," he said. Peterson had summoned his neighbor to the house because Peterson said he hadn't heard from his estranged wife in nearly two days, Davlantes reported. Peterson told Carcerano to open up the house and see what was going on. "I went from the closet to the bathroom," Carcerano said. "It looked like there was a rubber exercise ball or something in the whirlpool. When I looked down, it was Kathy. She was naked—she was dead— hair over her face." Carcerano, who said Peterson was steps behind him when the body was discovered in the home that Savio and Peterson owned, described Peterson's reaction when he saw Savio's body. "He ran upstairs and upon seeing her, he just broke down and started screaming, 'Oh my God, oh my God! What am I gonna tell my kids?'" Carcerano said."[95]

Note: This is more or less in line with the Coroner's Inquest and official reports. Not mentioned is the locksmith, although this is possibly a reporting oversight.

• *Today*—Transcript[96] (Matt Lauer host):

Lauer: Why didn't you go in the house?
Peterson: Kathy was always accusing me of things like she didn't want me in the house ever because she was afraid I was going to steal something.
Lauer: But you're the police officer.
Peterson: Right.
Lauer: The watch commander.
Peterson: Right, exactly.
Lauer: And it's your job to investigate crimes if they've been committed.
Peterson: So when I heard screaming, I went inside and there she was in the bathtub.
Lauer: What did you see? And did it look like an accidental drowning to you at that time?
Peterson: I felt the p– I didn't know if she was dead or alive, so I felt her pulse and, you know, being a policeman, I basically didn't want to touch anything or disturb anything.
Lauer: True or false: you ended up with a million* payout life insurance policy you had on her?

---

* Kathleen took out this million-dollar policy on her two children, payable in trust.

Peterson: My children did, and the money is in a protected account for them when they're older.

Lauer: Can you look me straight in the eye and tell me that you had nothing to do with the death of your third wife Kathy or the disappearance of your fourth wife Stacy?

Peterson: I can look right in your eye and say I had nothing to do with either of those incidences.

3-24-2004

- *Chicago Tribune* Obituary—"Kathleen Savio, age 40, suddenly March 1, 2004, at her residence in Bolingbrook, formerly of Glendale Heights. Survived by her loving children Thomas and Kristopher Peterson; devoted daughter of Henry (Marcia) Savio; sister of Anna Marie Savio-Doman, Susan M. Savio, Henry M. (Mary) Savio and Nicholas Savio; aunt of Charles H. Doman, Melissa (Tom) Moore, Michael E. Lisak, Angela M. Lisak, Elizabeth Savio, Robert Savio and Noelle Savio; niece of Mike Szpak; dear friend of Steve Maniaci; preceded in death by her Mother, Mary Savio. Visitation Friday 3 to 9 p.m. at the Anderson Memorial Chapel, 606 Townhall Dr., Romeoville. Funeral Saturday, March 6, 2003, 9:30 a.m. from the funeral home chapel to St. Andrew Catholic Church for a 10 a.m. Mass. Interment Queen of Heaven Catholic Cemetery in Hillside."

Note: Worth noting, even back in 2004, the family excluded Peterson from the obituary. He did attend services and paid for the funeral.

3-2004

- A coroner's jury ruled the death accidental. The state police investigation yielded no criminal charges. "Nobody looked at my sister's case close enough," Doman[97] said. "I never got a call back. It was like they couldn't be bothered."[98]

Note: The Will County Coroner Patrick K. O'Neil ruled the death accidental based on evidence of drowning. Water was demonstrated to have drained from the tub over time. It is extremely doubtful the police "couldn't be bothered." If anything, with a case involving a police officer, the police tend to be more diligent. The ruling came from the Coroner and not from the police.

• *Larry King Live*, interviewing Sue Doman, sister of Kathy—"I had gotten a call at 1:30 in the morning from my sister. And she had said to me that my sister was dead. And the first thing I said to her, did he kill her? ... Larry, I don't know why this was not investigated. It was ruled an accidental drowning. The next day, everyone was in the house. Drew was in the house. We were in the house. I don't understand accidental drowning. How could you go in a house and look at someone and say—that's in a dry bathtub and say, oh, it's an accidental drowning?"[99]

Note: As an impartial analyst, this seems clearly to be "evolved recall" or the phenomenon of "convincing oneself" of past events based on prevailing current opinion, similar to the issues faced in finding impartial juries in jurisdictions with aggressive media coverage. I make this analysis based on past media reports from 2004, comparing them to this 2007 interview, and also because it doesn't ring true that they'd be talking about "accidental drowning" the day after Kathy died. That call wasn't made until the coroner's jury ruled, much later.

5-2004

• *Bolingbrook Sun*—"The testimony from Special Agent Herbert Hardy at the May 2004 coroner's inquest of Kathleen Savio's death painted the 40-year-old's demise as anything but fishy ... And our investigation shows that basically, after the coroner's report and toxicology, that she died from drowning ... We believe that the laceration from her—that she sustained to the back of her head was caused by a fall in the tub ... There was nothing to lead us to believe that anything else occurred." [100]

Note: A volunteer medical examiner of some repute, Dr. Michael Baden, re-evaluated the findings and an exhumation was performed in 2007 at the request of the family and based on suspicions created by the media coverage of Stacy's disappearance. Baden indicated that his finding was "consistent with a homicide." Typically, "consistent with" language is used in reports as a non-conclusive statement.

• *On the Record with Greta Van Susteren,* FOX News—"At the time, a Coroner's jury declared it an accident, but now there's a new prosecutor, James Glasgow, and he's investigating whether her death was really a homicide." (Images of the exhumation tent, as Kathleen Savio's body is exhumed.) "What will we learn about Kathleen Savio and when? Dr. Baden is going to tell us."

Baden: "Well, I think what's happening is that a mistake may have been made back in 2004. The family members, Anne and others, are questioning how much to believe about what authorities tell her this time … Having a second set of eyes on the autopsy will reassure them they're getting as independent an opinion as possible."

Greta mentions the leak in the casket and water damage and deterioration. "The soft tissues are going to be important, because there's an issue of whether or not she was beaten up before the drowning."

Note: Baden stipulates there was a drowning, contrary to the notion in various media reports that it was silly that someone could drown in an empty tub.

• FOX News, "Dr. Baden responds to charge his autopsy findings were self-fulfilling prophecy"—Excerpt from *Today* interview:

Brodsky: Dr. Baden, with all due respect, he's a renowned pathologist, but he had a pre-existing opinion before he did the autopsy.

Matt Lauer: Mr. Peterson, are you upset to learn that she may have been murdered?

Peterson: Yes, I'm upset to hear something like that. Very much so.

Brodsky: We do disagree with his findings. The first autopsy … was very thorough. They concluded it was an accident. Dr. Baden is a paid commentator for FOX Entertainment Group.

(Cuts back live to Dr. Baden)

Baden: It's up to Coroner O'Neil who will eventually issue the determination … Here was a woman who had been beaten up before she drowned. Adults don't drown in bathtubs if they're healthy and don't have drugs on board. She had all kinds of bruises, and a bleeding laceration of the head … It should have been called a homicide …

Note: Baden went on to indicate that the findings of the original autopsy were not incorrect, the cause of death was drowning. He disputes the determination that this was an accident versus "consistent with a homicide made to look like an accident." In other words, he gives his expert opinion. All experts, Dr. Baden included, tend to find in favor of the team who engages them—the same pathologist often interprets differently as an expert for the prosecution than for the defense, for example.

"Of sound body and mind"

"We were well prepared. We've always thought of the kids, no matter how bad things were." Peterson is driving us to pick up his son Tommy at Bolingbrook High school as I cling to the safety belt of the tall Yukon. I guess that he's not too intimidated by local police, since he's driving faster than I would in my wildest mood.

"It's all about the kids," Peterson said. I believe him, not because I believe he's innocent in the matters of his wives—I'm undecided there—but because I've spent time with him and his kids. They can't get enough of him. Lacy clings to his thigh like a third leg and says nonstop, "I love you, Daddy" and he replies instantly, "I love you, Princess." She's his princess. He always has time for his sons. These are not things you can hide from someone who spends a lot of time in the house, as I did. Artificial emotion doesn't play. He never raises his voice to them, except the occasional "Knock it off!" They come to him for help. They talk to him. He talks to them. His life is, clearly, his kids.

In blogs, I've seen the comments "Oh, he leaves those kids on their own" or "He's gone off to Florida without the kids." They're never alone. During my long interviews, rather than give them the run of the house, adult son Steve, the police officer, comes over to babysit. Sometimes it's Uncle Paul. These are kids who want for nothing.

Love or hate Drew Peterson, he's at least a very good father, probably better than most. He's both dad and mom, now.

The children are well taken care of. The life insurance policy paid out on the death of Kathleen Savio went straight into an untouchable trust fund for the kids. "They'll be well taken care of if something happens to me."

"Something" of course means—and he isn't coy about the possibility—"if I'm arrested." He's given Steve a line of credit on his house and cash. There's the trust fund for the kids, now containing most of the family assets built up over thirty years.

"The only thing my kids need is a mom," Drew says sadly.

"Was there ever a time you were physically abused?"

A common accusation against him, since Peterson became

national news, is "child abuse." No one seems capable of believing that his is a normal single-parent household, and the more cynical put in anonymous calls to the Illinois Department of Children and Family Services. Peterson believes it's most likely Sharon Bychowski, or one of the other "well-meaning neighbors" as they're called in blogs—"the old biddies" as Peterson more colorfully calls them.

One such call came in late December 2007. The Illinois Department of Children and Family Services called Peterson first, around one PM and told him, "by law we are required to come to your house and investigate and interview the children." They were already on their way.

Peterson had been accused of everything and anything since October 2007, from being a monster preying on the neighborhood, to being a wife-killer, but he drew the line at child abuse. His life is his children. He was not surprised by the call. He phoned Reem Odeh of Brodsky & Odeh immediately. "The old biddies have called child services," he fumed.

Reem knew the children well. She had handled DCFS complaints for other clients, never for Peterson, but she was one of the Peterson team. In her visits to the house to interview Peterson, she had become close to the kids, and even visited them socially since she lived ten minutes away. Like everyone, she adored them.

Reem is herself a single mom with three kids, including a six-year-old son and ten-year-old daughter. She knew that a visit from DCFS would be more traumatic for the children, especially after all the media interest in the case. They'd been through enough at the hands of well-meaning neighbors, including an incident when Bychowski, a neighbor, cornered the kids and wouldn't let them go home as she probed them about their home life. Peterson had complained to police over that incident.

Reem is one of those people you instantly trust. She has the looks of a cover-girl model, with long legs and impeccable taste in fashion. She is breathtakingly beautiful, and the last thing you might expect her to be—at least in a television-educated society—is a lawyer. Her life has been a stunning triumph. Brought up in an "old world" family, she was betrothed at thirteen years of age to a Palestinian man. By the age of fifteen, she was married and a year later was with child. Her husband was abusive and both an alcoholic and a gambler. By seventeen, she managed to get herself out of the abusive relationship. Her second marriage was nearly as bad. They moved from America to Amman, where her husband took away her passport and she was cruelly abused. She sought refuge at the US embassy, obtained a new passport, and fled back to the United States. If anyone knew abuse, it was Reem Odeh.

Now, years later, an esteemed lawyer, she raced out to the Peterson house to handle the DCFS for Peterson, a forty-five-minute drive from Brodsky & Odeh's office. Brodsky called the case-workers and informed them Reem was on the way and not to commence without her there. Among other concerns—because it had happened before—the case-workers could be undercover police seeking to interview the children without a lawyer present.

Reem greeted the case-worker, a tall fiftyish white male named Charles. He was not a typical case-worker, and in fact did very much resemble a police officer. Reem accompanied him on a walk through to make sure the house was a good and safe environment for the children. He argued with Reem over interviewing the children. "I must interview them alone," he insisted. Reem merely denied his request, over and over, until he finally understood he would not be allowed to interview them without her present. Finally, he agreed. He had no choice, since the law sided with the Peterson family on this issue.

Charles interviewed Tommy and Kris, in that order. He probed them over and over about physical abuse, then mental abuse. Tommy and Kris pretty much laughed at him. "Uh-uh. No way," Tommy said. When Charles asked if they felt safe, Kris said, "Sure, why wouldn't I be safe?" When Charles asked directly if they wanted to go somewhere else, to be safer, they both very maturely and firmly said, "No way!" Tommy seemed amused by the whole thing. Kris seemed to not like Charles.

The younger children are always more emotional. It's harder for them to understand, and they're extremely close to their father. So Charles used more age-appropriate language. "Did any one ever hit you? Did Daddy every hit you? Did Daddy ever yell at you? Did Daddy ever touch you?"

The kids thought the man was a kook. They said "no" to each question, and they couldn't wait for the man to leave.

A reassuring presence through all this was Reem. They loved Reem and it helped the younger ones especially to have her there.

DCFS

Illinois Department of Children & Family Services

INVESTIGATION OF SUSPECTED CHILD ABUSE OR NEGLECT--UNFOUNDED

FEBRUARY 04, 2008

Drew Peterson
6 Pheasant Chase Ct
Bolingbrook, IL 60490-4513

Dear Mr. Peterson,

RE: SCR# - 1785451-A
Name - Peterson, Drew

You were previously notified that this Department was investigating a report of suspected child abuse or neglect in fulfillment of its responsibilities under law.

After a thorough evaluation, we have determined the report to be "unfounded." This means that credible evidence of child abuse or neglect has not been found.

The Abused and Neglected Child Reporting Act permits you to request that a report that was falsely filed be retained by the Department. If you believe that the report was falsely filed, you must within ten (10) days request in writing that the report be retained.

The request must be submitted to the State Central Register, 406 East Monroe Street, Springfield, Illinois 62701, postmarked within ten (10) days of the date of this letter. If such written request is not received in accordance with the prescribed procedures, the information identifying you and all other persons named in the report will be removed from the State Central Register and destroyed.

Thank you for your cooperation in this investigation. If you have any questions, please write me at the address below.

Sincerely,

Linda Everette-Williams

Linda Everette-Williams, Administrator
State Central Register

Photo of the DCFS letter indicating that the investigation of Peterson's home, managed and attended by lawyer Reem Odeh (inset) concluded "child abuse or neglect has not been found." The investigator apologized. A common theme in blogs is that he "must be a child abuser." In author visits, the children clearly adored their father. Photo of Reem Odeh (inset) courtesy Brodsky & Odeh.

Stacy took this photo of Drew holding two-year-old Lacy and three-year-old Anthony, standing with son Kris, during their trip to Disney World.

When Charles couldn't elicit the responses he wanted, he proposed a follow-up session. Reem firmly denied his request. "These children go through enough from the media. There's no need to put them through this." She convinced him that the complaints were either a concerned person who assumed the worst, or a purposely misleading complaint—but in either case a complaint without any knowledge of the family. The DCFS case-worker accepted her comment, and in the following eight months there has been no further investigation.

Charles actually apologized to Peterson and told him he was doing a fantastic job with the kids. "They are obviously good kids who are happy and well cared for." A letter came a week later indicating all complaints of abuse were unfounded.

Case closed.

Drew and Kathleen Peterson at their wedding banquet.

Innocent?

"Did you see your ex-wife Kathy alive?"

This account of March 1, 2004, the night Kathleen Savio was found drowned, is dramatized from interviews with Drew Peterson recorded in July, 2008, supported by the testimony of Steve Carcerano and the formal Coroner's Inquest. We'll call this the "Innocent" of our "Guilty & Innocent" presentation. Peterson took two polygraphs to help us establish the truth or falsehood of his claims. Refer to the chapter "Did you have any involvement in the death of your ex-wife Kathy in 2004?"

Weekends are special. He has Tommy and Kris, and they do all the things they enjoy as a family. The time together is always too short, but they are happy times, filled with hours of play, Ping-Pong, TV, video games, the regular weekend movie at the theater, spoiling them with fast food and popcorn, and father-son moments. When they are together, it feels like they are always together. They each have their own rooms in the house, and both Tommy and Kris love Stacy and their half-brother Steve. Even though Kathy hates Stacy, the kids have bonded with Stacy. She takes Tommy and Kris places. On weekends, they feel like a regular family unit.

He always dreads the Sunday nights, though, because for the rest of the week their big house feels empty. On return times, there are often shouting matches, sometimes with the police called, because Kathy is documenting the return times for a future review of custody, and she calls in reports even when Peterson is just ten minutes late.

Last Friday night had been fairly painless as post-separation Kathy events went. He went up to her door, wondering how it would go. He noticed a dead crow on the porch, which, if he had been superstitious, he'd probably have considered not a very good omen, but it became just another Drew-joke opportunity. He complimented Kathy on how good she looked—she looked like she was going out for the Friday night.

"You've got a dead bird on your porch," he said.

She stole his joke, a bit of the old feisty Kathy showing through. "Probably dead 'cause you're here."

They laughed together. The kids were happy as always to see him, and they'd have a great time.

She smiled. "I'll see you when the weekend's over."

"Have a good one."

"I will. You too." It was all so very cordial and unusual. He guessed she had exciting plans, because she was looking hot, as only Kathy could look, and she was smiling.

It's a full house on the weekend, with Stacy and the baby, Steve and his girlfriend Jennifer Shone, Tommy and Kris and Peterson. They watch a movie Saturday night, play Ping-Pong, eat out, and everyone has a great time, even adult son Steve and his live-in girlfriend. The next day is a highlight of their weekend with a visit to Shedd Aquarium in Chicago on Sunday. Tommy loves the dolphins in the Oceanarium and Kris likes the Green Sea Turtles and Hammerhead sharks in the Caribbean Reef. They eat junk food, and then the race is on to get back to Kathleen's because she isn't patient with tardiness.

He leaves the car running in the driveway, with the heater on for the kids, and runs up to the porch. Oddly, the light is off. He knocks on the door, then he knocks again. And again. It's unusual. Kathy is stern about visitation times. He tries phoning a few times.

Home is nearby, so he drives the kids home and tries her by phone again, both cell phone and land line. He even leaves "bitchy" messages for her: "Hey, Kathy, the kids are worried. Where are you?" He's a little worried, only because she really hates when he's late, but he remembers she was dressed "to the nines" on Friday. Maybe it's a big weekend for her. He doesn't have to work until five o'clock on Monday night, the night shift as usual, so he shrugs it off. At least he gets more time with his kids.

The next day is an impromptu good time with Tommy and Kris, more Ping-Pong, more video games, lots of TV. He tries Kathy all day, but no answer. Now it really is worrying him. This is just not like her at all.

He has to go to work at five in the afternoon, but Stacy offers to look after everyone. He goes on patrol as usual, but he can't get Kathy out of his mind. Even if she had planned a big weekend and forgot to tell him, she'd have called by now.

At seven o'clock he swings around Kathy's neighbor's house, Mary Ponterelli. "Have you seen Kathy?" Mary hasn't, and now Peterson can't get past the worry. "Do you think you can call her boyfriend Steve? He'll know where's she's at." Steve doesn't like getting calls from Peterson.

Ponterelli tries Kathy's phone herself a few times. She agrees it's really odd. "Do you have a key for Kathy's house?" Peterson asks her. She doesn't. Peterson drops by neighbor and old friend Steve Carcerano. While there, Ponterelli calls him back and says, "I want to go in to Kathy's house now."

"This ain't like her at all," Peterson agrees. "She's normally screamin' at me if I'm late."

Everyone agrees they should enter the house. Peterson says, "We can get a locksmith. No way I'm breaking down Kathy's door."

"You're the police," Ponterelli says.

"I can't enter the house," Peterson says. "She'd have a fit." Peterson calls for a locksmith. Carcerano, Ponterelli, and her son meet Peterson and the locksmith at the house. Even though Peterson's on duty, it isn't a probable cause entry, just concerned neighbors. He knows Kathy. If he's in the house, she'll have him charged with break and enter.

Carcerano goes first, followed closely by Ponterelli and her son. Peterson hangs back. He knows Kathy will freak out if she discovers him in the house.

A woman's scream, sharp and piercing, has Peterson running through the door and up the stairs. They're in the bathroom, looking down into the tub. Kathy's there, naked, on her left side, in a fetal position, hair over her face.

"Oh my God," Peterson says. Instinctively he checks her vitals, but she's cold to the touch. Clammy. She's dead.

He hears himself yelling, "Oh my God, oh my God! What am I gonna tell my kids?" The rest is a blur. He calls the department, and within minutes Officer Sudd shows up to secure the scene, then Sergeant Ken Teppell, then the Bolingbrook brass, detectives, the chief. Within an hour, the entire department seems to be there.

The numbness sets in. All the officers and detectives nod at him one by one and he can see they're as shocked as he is. He doesn't know what to say for the first time in his life.

Peterson moves outside, to give them all room. He's just a witness ex-husband here, not a cop. He sits on the hood of his car, watching as the coroner drives up, then more police, then Kathy's boyfriend Steve Maniaci. It is all a numbing blur.

Steve, Kathy's boyfriend, approaches Peterson. They look at each other. Peterson nods. "What's going on?" Steve says, oddly calm. "What's going on?"

Peterson shakes his head. "I don't know. I really don't. I was hoping you'd know. Weren't you with Kathy this weekend?"

"We were fighting," Steve says. "We broke it off." He isn't crying, but he does seem upset. Steve hangs around a while longer, looking bewildered. He talks with the police for a while, and emerges later with Kathy's cat.

Official Timeline
from Drew Peterson for the night Kathy Savio died

Friday Afternoon 2-27-04
- Pick up Tom and Kris for visitation.
- Friday night: Home with Kids and Stacy.

Saturday 2-28-04
- Home all day and night with Stacy and kids.
- Stephen his adult son living in basement of house with his girlfriend, and the two younger sons have bedrooms upstairs next to Drew and Stacy. There is a house full of people.

Sunday 2-29-04 (leap year)
- Drew took Stacy, Tom and Kris to the Shedd Aquarium in downtown Chicago and then home.
- Tried to return kids from after visitation at 8:00 pm.
- No answer at door, no answer on phone. Very unusual.

Monday 3-1-04
- Called and left several messages throughout day for Kathleen. No response.
- 5:00 pm—Went to work at Bolingbrook PD
- About 7:00 pm—Went to Kathleen's neighbor's home, Mary Ponterelli, and asked about Kathleen.
- Between 8:00 and 9:00 pm—Went to Kathy's house with Mary Ponterelli, Steve Carcerano, and Nick Ponterelli (Mary's teen son), and a locksmith. Mary, Steve and Nick enter the home and find Kathy's body in bathtub. Drew hears scream, enters house, checks Kathy for vital signs and finds none, then Drew calls Bolingbrook PD dispatch to report situation.

"The subject is unclothed."

An important element of the "Kathy Savio" story comes down to a battle of experts. Dr. Bryan R. Mitchell and Coroner O'Neil, with an empanelled Coroner's Jury originally made a determination of accident. Dr. Blum, brought in by Coroner O'Neil for Kathy's controversial exhumation, will not disclose his findings except to the police. Dr. Baden conducted his own expert review.

While Doctor Mitchell and Coroner O'Neil made official calls, and eventually so will Dr. Blum, at least as a state's expert, Dr. Baden's opinion is limited to the context of an expert on behalf of the family, who have already announced a lawsuit against Drew Peterson on behalf of Kathleen Savio.

For this reason, it is important to review the actual autopsy performed by Dr. Mitchell. No one, including Dr. Baden, disputes his findings. In fact Baden goes out of his way to state "the findings of the original autopsy were not incorrect."

"Dueling pathologists"

"I, Bryan R. Mitchell MD, have made a necropsy on the body identified to me by the coroner of this county as being:

Kathleen S. Savio Date of Death: 3-1-04
Place of death: Bolingbrook, IL.
Place of examination: Crest Hill, IL.
In my opinion, the cause of death was as follows:
Immediate cause: Drowning."

None of the experts dispute the finding of "drowning" in spite of playful jousts from Geraldo and Mark Fuhrman on television spots about "drowning in a dry tub." The tub was tested, and drains in a few hours.

Dueling pathologists became headline news as forensic pathologist Doctor Michael Baden, famous for his handling of the O.J. Simpson case, urged a new ruling of homicide while state's expert Dr. Blum remained quiet on his findings. It is now accepted that the state has suggested homicide.

The contradictory rulings led to a flurry of forensic bickering, set against the current climate of US Senate Hearings on Crime Lab Funding, that revealed on January 18 of 2008: "The Inspector General of the US Department of Justice issued a report showing that the federal government is failing to provide critical forensic science oversight ... The federal programs at issue provide funds to assist federal and state authorities to realize the full potential of DNA to solve crimes and protect the innocent."[101]

"We know that Dr. Michael Baden was paid $100,000..."

Recently, FOX News (division of FOX Entertainment) engaged Doctor Michael Baden to conduct a review, followed by the sensational exhumation and announcements of new findings. Doctor Baden is often engaged by victims' families, and is "a highly skilled forensic pathologist" according to Mark Fuhrman in his book *Murder in Brentwood*. He went on to write:[102] "I once worked on a case where he was brought in by the victim's family to give a second opinion. At first the case was deemed an accidental death, but Baden's review of the autopsy allowed police to reclassify it as a homicide." This was prior to the O.J. Simpson case in 1994, so clearly Baden has a track record of helping victims reclassify rulings as homicides. Of course in the O.J. case Baden was retained by the defense team, according to Fuhrman: "We know that Dr. Michael Baden was paid $100,000 for his services ..."

In an interview with Van Susteren on *On the Record with Greta Van Susteren* in November, 2007,[103] Baden said: "It is not an accident. The hair, her head hair, was soaked in blood, as the medical examiner says, and she had a laceration, a blunt force laceration on the top of her head. She had a dozen other black-and-blue bruises and scraping abrasions of the extremities and of the abdomen. It looks as if she—from the description that she was beaten up, apart from drowning. Her heart was good. Her brain was good. There were no drugs in her body on toxicology. There's no reason for her to have drowned. Adults don't drown if they're in good health."

Type of Accident or Manner of Injury	Total Deaths in 2000	One Year Odds [1 in #]	Lifetime Odds [1 in #]
Struck by or against another person	61	4,513,213	58,689
Bitten or struck by dog	26	10,588,692	137,694
Bitten or struck by other mammals	65	4,235,477	55,078
Bitten or stung by nonvenomous insect and other arthropods	9	30,589,556	397,784
Bitten or crushed by other reptiles	31	8,880,839	115,486
Other and unspecified animate mechanical forces	12	22,942,167	298,338
Accidental drowning and submersion	3,482	79,065	1,028
Drowning and submersion while in or falling into bath-tub	341	807,349	10,499
Drowning and submersion while in or falling into swimming-pool	567	485,549	6,314
Drowning and submersion while in or falling into natural water	1,135	242,560	3,154

http://danger.mongabay.com/injury_death.htm

Excerpt data National Safety Council 2000, "Most Common Causes of Death Due to Injury in the United States"

Statistics (highlighted) of drownings in bathtubs contradict the subsequent expert opinion of pathologist Doctor Baden that "healthy adults don't drown in bathtubs" here showing 341 bathtub drownings in 2000.

"Do adults drown in bathtubs?"

Joel Brodsky, attorney for Drew Peterson is quick to point out that "adults do drown in bathtubs."

The US Consumer Product Safety Commission reported 341 bathtub deaths in 2000, many featuring lacerations, contusions and abrasions. This is consistent with the original autopsy report and seems to contradict Dr. Baden's assertion that "adults don't drown if they're in good health."

Many of these were people in good health between the ages of twenty-one and sixty-five. The same commission extrapolated 126,563 overall bathtub injuries (not deaths) based on 341 reported incidents, on the assumption that many incidents are unreported. On this scale, if it is statistically sound, the actual number of bathtub deaths of healthy people could be substantially higher than the

```
 1              MR. O'NEIL:  Ladies and gentlemen, this is an
 2    inquest into the manner of death of the late
 3    Kathleen Savio, a 40-year-old female, who, on
 4    Monday, March 1st, 2004, was found to be deceased.
 5                      This is neither a civil nor a
 6    criminal hearing, but merely an inquest to determine
 7    the manner of death of the late Kathleen Savio.
 8                      We have available Susan Savio.
 9    Susan, can you step forward, please?
10                      (Witness sworn.)
11                      SUSAN SAVIO,
12    having been first duly sworn, was examined and
13    testified as follows:
14                      DIRECT EXAMINATION
15    BY MR. O'NEIL:
16         Q.   Please state your full name and spell
17    your last name for the record.
18         A.   Susan Savio, S-A-V-I-O.
19         Q.   Your current address, ma'am?
20         A.   485 Thornhill Drive, Carol Stream.
21         Q.   What is your relationship to the late
22    Kathleen Savio?
23         A.   Sister.
24         Q.   We have your sister's age listed as 40,
```

                                                          1

George B. Rydman & Assoc., Joliet, IL (815) 727-4363

> Witness's sworn testimony at the
> inquest into the death of the late
> Kathleen Savio, March 1, 2004.

number of reported bathtub deaths.[104]

So, O'Neil's original ruling, and Dr. Mitchell's autopsy may not be so easily rejected as incorrect by a review several years later.

"The subject is received in a body bag"

The full autopsy report is included here in picture form for those interested in the details. *Warning: Do not read if you are sensitive.* The overall finding is "drowning" and the determination is "accident."

Here is my own analysis as a layman (I am not a pathologist) who has studied autopsies as a crime writer:

The abrasions and contusions listed seem relatively minor and consistent with a fall in a tub, not necessarily the result of a "beating" as indicated by the family's pathologist, Dr. Baden. I tend to believe the less sensational finding of Dr. Mitchell and O'Neil's Coroner's Jury, since there is very little overt evidence of physical abuse. Drowning is definitely the cause of death. However, there are the issues of the missing water (the tub was later shown to drain away) and the contusion on the back of the head when she is on her side in the tub. Dr. Mitchell, however, states "the laceration to posterior scalp may have been related to a fall in which she struck her head." In my own amateur re-constructions in a similar sized bathtub, it does seem possible to fall backwards, hitting your head, then roll over on to one's side, assuming there is water in the tub. Without compelling evidence of a struggle (skin under Kathy's nails from an assailant, some evidence she fought back—she was a "fighter" according to all witnesses) the only way this can be a homicide is if she was instantly incapacitated. The minor bruising on her abdomen and thigh would not be consistent with a struggle, but could be consistent with a fall in the tub.

To allow others to make their own evaluations of Kathleen Savio's autopsy, the entire original report is reproduced below.

AUTOPSY REPORT

COUNTY: WILL	AUTHORITY: PATRICK O'NEIL CORONER

NAME: **KATHLEEN S. SAVIO**   CASE#: **W 04-0057**

SEX: FEMALE	RACE: WHITE	AGE: 40 YEARS

PLACE OF DEATH: BOLINGBROOK, IL

EXAMINED BY: BRYAN MITCHELL, M.D.	WITNESSES: KEVIN STEVENSON, DEPUTY CORONER; BOB DIEHL, ISP; & BILL BELCHER, JR.
DATE OF DEATH: MARCH 1, 2004	TIME OF DEATH: 11:17 P.M.
DATE OF AUTOPSY: MARCH 1, 2004	TIME OF AUTOPSY: 2:20 P.M.

EXTERNAL EXAMINATION:

The subject is received in a body bag with appropriate identification. The subject is unclothed. The hands are bagged. About the neck, there is a yellow-metal necklace.

The decedent appears to be of normal development, an adequately nourished and hydrated, adult, and white female weighing 154 pounds and measuring 65 in. in length.

The body is cold to touch. Rigor mortis is absent. Postmortem lividity is purple and fixed over the anterior surfaces of the body. There is fingerprint blanching noted over the right medial breast and blanching over the areola and central portion of the left breast, the left thigh, and calf.

The hair is long, brown, and straight. The hair is soaked with blood. The eyes are closed. The irides are brown. The corneae are cloudy. The sclerae are white. The nasal skeleton is intact. There is a foam cone emanating from the nostrils. The lips and frenulum are intact. The lips are purple. The teeth are natural. Dentition is in good repair. The tongue is partially clenched between the teeth. Each ear lobe is pierced once.

The chest is symmetrical. The breasts are of normal development. No palpable masses or nipple discharge is noted. The abdomen is soft and mildly protuberant.

The upper extremities are symmetrical. The fingernails are short and clean. There is wrinkling of the fingers and palmar surface of the left hand.

1

The external genitalia are that of a normal, adult female. No trauma is noted.

The lower extremities are symmetrical. The toenails are short and clean.

The back and buttocks are symmetrical and free of significant injury.

EXTERNAL EVIDENCE OF INJURY:

1. On the left parieto-occipital scalp, there is a 1-in., blunt laceration.

2. On the left buttocks, there is an irregularly shaped, red abrasion measuring 3 in. x 1 in. in greatest dimension.

3. On the left lower quadrant of the abdomen, their are 3, oval-shaped, purple contusions ranging from 1 in. to 2 in. in greatest dimension.

4. On the left anterior thigh, there is a faint, 1 in. x ¾ in., purple contusion.

5. On the mid shins, there is a 3/8-in., circular-shaped, purple contusion on each.

6. On the right outer wrist, there are ½ in. and ¾ in., linear, red abrasions.

7. On the dorsum of the right 1st finger, there is a circular-shaped, 1/8-in. abrasion.

8. On the left elbow, there is a circular-shaped, 3/8-in., red abrasion.

EVIDENCE OF MEDICAL TREATMENT:

1. On the left upper back, right upper back, and left lateral back, there is an electrocardiogram lead.

INTERNAL EXAMINATION:

Body Cavities: The body is entered through a Y-shaped incision. The internal organs are in their normal anatomic positions and normal anatomic relationships. No excess in fluid is seen in the pericardial sac, pleural spaces, or peritoneal cavity. The pannicular fat measures 5.1 cm.

Neck Organs: The tongue is pink-tan and soft. The hyoid bone, thyroid, and epiglottic cartilages are intact. The larynx and its lumen are patent. The vocal cords are intact. The strap muscles are free of hemorrhage.

Cardiovascular System: The heart weighs 260 g. There is a mild amount of epicardial fat. The myocardium is red-tan and homogeneous. The left ventricle measures 1.0 cm. The right ventricle measures 0.3 cm. The valves and chordae tendinae are thin and delicate, except for mild thickening

2

of the leaflets of the mitral valve. The chambers are of normal size. The septa are intact. The coronary ostia are patent. The coronary arteries pursue their normal anatomic course. No atheromatous plaques or thrombi are seen. The great vessels are patent and pursue their normal anatomic course. The intima of the aorta is red-tan and smooth with hemolysis.

Respiratory System: The trachea and bronchi are patent. The mucosa is tan and smooth. The lungs combined weigh 900 g. The pleural surface is smooth and gray. The parenchyma is red-purple and soft with mild congestion and moderate edema. No areas of consolidation, tumor, infarct, or fibrosis are noted. The pulmonary arteries and veins are patent and unremarkable. No thromboemboli are seen.

Hepatobiliary System: The liver weighs 1,530 g. The capsule is smooth and glistening. The parenchyma is red-brown, soft, and congested. No tumor or fibrosis is noted. The gallbladder and biliary tree are patent. No stones are identified.

Gastrointestinal System: The esophagus is without special note. The mucosa is gray-white. The stomach contains approximately 2 cc of tannish-colored fluid. The rugal folds are gray-tan and partially flattened. The duodenum, small and large intestines contain their normal contents. The serosal surface is smooth and glistening. The mesenteric fat is yellow-tan and unremarkable. The appendix is present and unremarkable.

Endocrine System: The pituitary is of normal size. The thyroid is red-tan and soft. The pancreas is tan and lobulated. The pancreatic duct is patent. The adrenal glands have a yellow cortex and brown medulla.

Musculoskeletal System: The muscles are red-tan and soft. The bones are white-tan and hard. No fractures of the spine or pelvis are noted.

Genitourinary System: The kidneys combined weigh 270 g. The capsules strip with ease. The cortex is red-brown, smooth, and congested. The corticomedullary junction is sharp. The pelves, ureters, and urinary bladder are patent.

Hematolymphoid System: The spleen weighs 140 g. The capsule is smooth and gray. The parenchyma is red-purple, soft, and congested. No tumor or fibrosis is noted. No significant lymphadenopathy is seen. The bone marrow is red-brown and unremarkable.

Reproductive System: The uterus, ovaries, and fallopian tubes weigh 130 g. No pathologic abnormalities are noted. No intrauterine pregnancy is noted.

Central Nervous System: No other lacerations are seen on the scalp. The skull is intact. No subdural or epidural hemorrhage is seen. The leptomeninges are clear. The subarachnoid space is unremarkable. The brain weighs 1,160 g. There is flattening of the gyri with notching of the cerebellar tonsils. Serial coronal sections of the brain reveal no other pathologic abnormalities. The ventricles are of normal size. The cerebrospinal fluid is clear. The cerebellum is of normal development. The arteries at the base of the brain are patent.

3

NAME: KATHLEEN S. SAVIO   CASE #: W 04-0057

Samples of fluids and tissue are submitted for toxicologic analysis. A DNA card is submitted for storage. A stock of tissue is submitted for storage.

DIAGNOSES:

1. Cerebral edema with cerebellar tonsillar notching.

2. Moderate pulmonary edema.

3. Water in the ethmoid sinuses.

4. Hepatic, renal, and splenic congestion.

5. Laceration of the posterior scalp.

6. Mild mitral valve thickening.

7. No tumor, significant trauma, infection, or congenital anomalies.

8. Toxicology is negative.

OPINION:

In consideration of the circumstances surrounding her death, the available medical history, and autopsy findings, the death of this 40-year-old, white female, **Kathleen Savio, is** ascribed to **Drowning.**

Comment: The laceration to posterior scalp may have been related to a fall in which she struck her head.

Brvneiuul mb   3/20/04

Bryan Mitchell, M.D.   Date Signed
Forensic Pathologist
IL #036-089797

4

St. Louis University Toxicology Laboratory Report
6039 Helen Ave, Berkeley, Missouri 63134

Name: SAVIO, KATHLEEN
Age: 40 years   Race: White

Tox # 2004-1074
Sex: Female

Requesting Agency: WILL COUNTY CORONER
===
Vitreous:

    Alcohol: Negative
        Ethanol: _____ Negative
        Acetone: _____ Negative
        Isopropanol: _____ Negative
        Methanol: _____

    Liver:

    Drug Screen: Negative
        Amphetamines: _____ Negative
        Antidepressants: _____ Negative
        Barbiturates: _____ Negative
        Benzodiazepines: _____ Negative
        Cannabinoids (THC): _____ Negative
        Cocaine/Metabolites: _____ Negative
        Lidocaine: _____ Negative
        Non-Opiate Narcotic Analgesics: _____ Negative
        Opiates: _____ Negative
        Phencyclidine (PCP): _____ Negative
        Phenothiazines: _____ Negative
        Methadone: _____ Negative
        Propoxyphene: _____ Negative
        Acetaminophen: _____ Negative
        Salicylates: _____ Negative

    Individual Drug Quants: Negative
        Codeine: _____ Negative
        Morphine: _____ Negative
        Hydrocodone: _____ Negative
        Hydromorphone: _____ Negative
        Dihydrocodeine (Hydrocodol): _____ Negative
        6-Monoacetylmorphine: _____ Negative
        Oxycodone: _____ Negative
        Oxymorphone: _____ Negative

===

Requested by: : WILL COUNTY CORONER   Date/Time: 03/02/2004//02:40 PM

Received in Lab by: Judy L Barr   Date/Time: 03/04/2004//08:45 AM

Report by: DR. CHRISTOPHER LONG   Date/Time: 03/16/2004//02:44 PM

MAR 2 5 2004

NEC 1
(Rev. 3/69)

Department of Public Health
State File No.

Report of the Coroner's Physician to the
Coroner of Will County, Illinois

I, Bryan R. Mitchell MD, have made a necropsy on the body identified to me by the coroner of this county as being: **Kathleen S. Savio** **Date of Death:** 3-1-04

Place of death: Bolingbrook, IL.

Place of examination: Crest Hill, IL.

In my opinion, the cause of death was as follows:

Immediate cause
(a) Drowning

due to, or as a consequence of
(b)

due to, or as a consequence of
(c)

Other significant conditions contributing to death but not related to the terminal conditions

My conclusions are based on the following observations and findings,

1. Autopsy findings.
2. Coroner' reports.
3. Toxicology

Date: 3-20-04   Signed Bryan Mitchell MD

Coroner's Physician

Polygraph

Regarding the Death of Peterson's Third Wife Kathleen

Polygraph Subject: Drew Peterson
Session: Kathleen Savio
Polygraph Examiner: Lee McCord, over thirty years' experience
Conditions in the Examiner's words: "We were in a large conference room, sitting at a conference table, facing Millennium park. During the session, we closed the Venetian blinds. There was some daylight, and the only other light were the ceiling lights. As a typical polygraph room would be, it was not dark, but certainly closed off from outside view. This was a Sunday, so there was no traffic in the office. The park was full of people. As I looked out the windows, the park was full of people and it was a very bright sunny day, and a good warm day for Chicago. The room was warm. The air conditioning seemed to be off in the building on Sundays. It wasn't uncomfortable. The conditions wouldn't have made any difference to a polygraph. We both had water and were comfortable."
Result: Conclusive Results.

Drew Peterson is at his least jovial. He's not cracking jokes. He's subdued. He's about to take a polygraph—against the advice of his lawyer Joel Brodsky.

Everyone in the nation is hounding him to take one, from guests on *Larry King Live* to police to bloggers. "If you're innocent, take a polygraph," is the most commonly repeated phrase.

He's here to prove them wrong. Here, in the boardroom of Brodsky & Odeh. Everyone is breathless to see the results, although it will be a lengthy ordeal. Several hours of questions precede the real test, questions designed to test responses.

Peterson is scruffy but relaxed, wearing a white Polo shirt and jeans. He waits patiently in Brodsky's office, staring down at the lakefront view. In the other room is Lee McCord, a thirty-year veteran and one of the best polygraphers in Illinois. He sets up his equipment methodically, calmly, without emotion. He's gentle and soft-spoken and polite, very un-intimidating. He draws all the blinds in the boardroom, black blinds designed to completely filter out daylight. The room transforms from a cheerful boardroom overlooking the Magnificent Mile, to a bare room, made austere by venetian blinds.

Finally, he is ready. He politely addresses Peterson as Mister Peterson, and carefully rigs him in the elaborate measuring tools. The chest sensors and cuffs will measure four separate physiological responses to question inputs.

Lee McCord's silver and black pen hovers over the chart, ready to mark questions on the output, and his analysis. There's no guesswork here. The responses are the responses. One polygrapher can take the chart to another polygrapher and the results read the same way.

"Are you ready, Mr. Peterson?"

"Yes, sir." Peterson sounds subdued and respectful. He nods at Mr. McCord, then swivels in his chair to face the wall.

Two hours later, McCord is satisfied, and the real questions begin. He has not allowed Brodsky to write the questions. "I won't work that way," he told Brodsky. They've told him what they want to discover, and he will ask in his own words.

Firmly, he says, "Did you see your ex-wife Kathy alive anytime after you picked the kids up from her house on Friday, February 27, 2004?"

Without hesitation, Peterson says, "No."

McCord is establishing that Peterson didn't see Kathy alive after the kids were picked up. This would, in theory, establish innocence. If the answer was not deceptive.

"Did you have any type of contact with your ex-wife Kathy after you picked up the kids from her on Friday, February 27, 2008?"

"No."

Fine. He's establishing now whether Peterson called her or in any other way contacted her. Good.

"Did you have any involvement in the death of your ex-wife Kathy in 2004?"

"No."

Fantastic. A direct. Considering the 80-98 percent reliability of the polygraph test, this answer would be the most important of all. A non- deceptive "no" would mean he is innocent. A deceptive answer would mean he was guilty. Everyone is anxious for the answer.

"Were you present at the time of your ex-wife Kathy's death?"

"No."

Beautiful. No worming out on a technicality.

"That's it, then."

Peterson nods. "Thank you."

McCord walks around the table, and gently pries off the Velcro clasps, pulling off the cuffs and then the chest chords. McCord calls Joel Brodsky back into the room.

He returns to his seat, picks up his pen, and says, "Do you want to know the results now?"

As calm as can be, Peterson nods. "Sure. Why not?"

"To the question, 'Did you see your ex-wife Kathy alive anytime after you picked up the kids from her house on Friday 27, 2004?' you answered no. There is no deception."

"Meaning I told the truth."

"You're being truthful, Mr. Peterson, yes." The pen taps the paper. "To the question, 'Did you have any type of contact with your ex-wife Kathy after you picked up the kids from her on Friday, February 27, 2008?' you answered no. There is no deception."

Peterson nods. He was truthful. He's been saying this to everyone and anyone since this whole ordeal began.

"To the question, 'Did you have any involvement in the death of your ex-wife Kathy in 2004?' you answered no. There is no deception."

Peterson smiles.

"To the question, 'Were you present at the time of your ex-wife Kathy's death?' you answered no. There is no deception."

No deception. Assuming one accepts a polygraph as reliable, as indicated in various research studies, Peterson had nothing to do with the death of his ex-wife. Homicide or not, accident or not, he was not involved.

He should be a happy man. But he just looks tired. He knows that even the polygraph will not convince the real skeptics. But most will believe. And that's good enough for him.

McCord and Associates

SUMMARY OF EXAMINATION

RESULTS AND OPINIONS

On May 25, 2008, Drew Peterson voluntarily submitted to a polygraph examination at the request of his Attorney Joel Brodsky of Brodsky and Odeh. The examination was administrated by McCord and Associates regarding the death of his third wife Kathleen S. Savio

Prior to the examination the subject signed a form releasing Brodsky & Odeh of any liability which may results from the polygraph examination. The polygraph release form signed by the subject is on file in our office.

During the polygraph examination the subject was asked the following relevant questions:

1. Did you see your ex-wife Kathy alive anytime after you picked the kids up from her house on Friday, February 27, 2004?

> ANSWER - NO
> RESULTS - NO DECEPTION

2. Did you have any type contact with your ex-wife Kathy after you picked up the kids from her on Friday, February 27, 2008?

> ANSWER - NO
> RESULTS - NO DECEPTION

3. Did you have any involvement in the death of your ex-wife Kathy in 2004?

> ANSWER - NO
> RESULTS - NO DECEPTION

4. Were you present at the time of your ex-wife Kathy's death?

> ANSWER - NO
> RESULTS - NO DECEPTION

Lee McCord

Lee McCord
Polygraph Examiner

The second polygraph session, on May 25, 2008, with Lee McCord, expert polygrapher, this time probing the Kathleen Savio case. The test was conclusive and non-deceptive.

"Is there any way to beat a polygraph?"

There were two separate sessions with Drew Peterson, each lasting just over two hours on consecutive Sundays. Each time control questions were asked, followed by the "relevant questions." One session focused on Kathleen Savio and one session focused on Stacy Peterson.

I spent several hours interviewing expert polygrapher Lee McCord, a veteran of thirty-four years as an examiner. His answers are most enlightening, well thought out and easy for a layperson to follow. In particular, his answers on reliability and his opinion of Peterson's results are quite enlightening. Lee McCord speaks thoughtfully, with a gentle, persuasive, intelligent tone, and I believe his answers are balanced and credible.

Lee McCord doesn't want to be promoted in any way, shape of form in the book, due to the stringent regulations of his professional association. However, he understands the necessity of answering some key questions for people who may not have expertise in polygraphs, just as he could be called to testify as an expert. He also allowed me to reproduce his resume here, on the condition we indicate this is strictly for the credibility of the results, not to promote his name or company. I asked Lee McCord many questions relating to his background, but any personal questions I removed from the final interview reproduced here to satisfy the requirements of not "promoting" his name. This is about Drew Peterson, not Lee McCord:

Armstrong: *As an expert in polygraphs, Mr. McCord, how do you summarize their reliability in general?*
McCord: Certainly it seems to depend on the side you're standing on. I firmly believe in the reliability of the polygraph. There are studies that show the reliability is 95 percent. And, of course people question that reliability. We're all licensed in the state of Illinois. Polygraph is here to stay. Contrary to personal beliefs, the polygraph will always be a very useful investigative tool. Many people rely on it. Then again, it's certainly not the tell-all. I like to consider it, Mr. Armstrong, more an aid to assisting with investigations. It's never used as the final determiner of anything. It's definitely a good investigative tool and we never claim it to be 100 percent, but we

certainly know we're right far more often than we're wrong. It's totally credible.

Armstrong: *95 percent is virtually 100 percent.*

McCord: We can never claim 100 percent. We take it very seriously and if we write an opinion, we stand behind what we say. No matter what you say, people will question your conclusions, but if we state a person is right or wrong, we firmly believe that.

Armstrong: *How about as a straightforward determination of truthfulness?*

McCord: It's solely based on the polygraph chart. Now, personal opinions, or summations, or other persons' opinions matter not. We're not tainted by personal biases at all. We are guided by the graphs that come off the polygraph. Nothing more. So, regardless of what you think of that person, the only thing we can draw a conclusion on is the graph that comes off the polygraph. Any opinion given has to be based on something. And that's why we can tell you consistently that we believe "A" or "B." This is why we state in the report this is the opinion of the examiner based on the subject's polygraph—the person did tell the truth or didn't tell the truth—it's based on that graph and nothing else.

Armstrong: *And if you can't make a determination?*

McCord: We'd call it inconclusive—which you do not see in Mr. Peterson's test. Now, first of all, just so we're clear, no one ever passes or fails a polygraph test. The purpose of a polygraph is simply to verify a person's statement. We can conclude if that person is telling the truth or not telling the truth. Technically, we're verifying something that someone said. So when Mr. Peterson says that he had no involvement in his wife's death, I can verify that as being truthful based on what he said. Now, did he tell the truth factually? We're not concerned with that. We are concerned with what he believes to be true.

Armstrong: *In other words he believes it?*

McCord: Absolutely. Based on our experience we have to conclude that they're telling the truth. We can't determine factual truth, only their belief in whether it's true or not.

Armstrong: *Right. That they believe they're telling the truth.*

McCord: Absolutely.

Armstrong: *And, if two experienced examiners looked at the same chart they would come to the same conclusion?*

McCord: Absolutely.

Armstrong: Even if they weren't at that session?

McCord: Absolutely.

Armstrong: So, its reliability as an investigative tool is sound?

McCord: Yes, we believe it to be very sound.

Armstrong: How would you evaluate your session with Mr. Peterson?

McCord: He was very cooperative. There are some people who make a good polygraph subject and some who don't make very good polygraph subjects, meaning, they're difficult to interview, or just don't cooperate. He was very easy to interview and he was very cooperative. Then again, he was a thirty-year investigator, so I would expect him to be cooperative. Every question I put to him—he never made any attempt to avoid questions. I thought the interviews went very well.

Armstrong: Is there a way to deceive an experienced polygraph examiner?

McCord: To beat the test? No sir. As a polygraph examiner I think not. I don't recall anyone ever telling me anyone can beat a polygraph. We're trained to look for certain things, such as if their breathing is too controlled or if they're evasive in their answers. Can you beat a polygraph test? If you believe what you're saying to be true, of course. But if you can't do that, you can't beat a polygraph.

Armstrong: Any other ways to beat a polygraph? Training? Drugs?

McCord: No. There's a perception that there are ways, such as putting pennies under your tongue, or tacks in your shoe. It'd certainly be inconvenient, but no I'm not aware of any. It'd give you a false reading, perhaps, in that if you stuck a thumbtack in your toe, that would be uncomfortable, but that would show up as a negative on a polygraph test, not favorable, so no, that wouldn't work. The only thing that can throw a polygraph is an examiner who is not being professional or reporting correctly. It's bad, for example, to come to like the person you're giving a polygraph to, because you can be lax.

Armstrong: Would that have happened at all with Drew Peterson?

McCord: Absolutely not. This is too big of an integrity issue. If anything I scrutinized him more than I would have any other subject. I made sure I crossed every t and dotted every i. My most important goal here was to ensure the test was administered properly.

Armstrong: How long was each session with Drew?

McCord: About two hours.

Armstrong: Aside from the main questions you asked, what else did you ask?

McCord: There are control questions, relevant questions and the irrelevant questions. The irrelevant questions would be questions like his name, do you live in Chicago, things like that. The relevant questions are the ones you have. And the control questions are specifically for comparison purposes.

Armstrong: Can you give me a few examples of the control questions?

McCord: One was "lying to authorities." "As a child, did you ever lie to authorities?" "As a teenager do you remember lying to your parents?"

Armstrong: Do you keep a record of the control questions?

McCord: By law we keep the whole test for five years.

Armstrong: How did Mr. Peterson appear to you?

McCord: He looked a little scruffy. Very casually dressed. Very pleasant and low-key. He wore jeans and a sports shirt to both sessions.

Armstrong: Was he smiling a lot?

McCord: No, not at all. He was kind of somber. He greeted me. Joel led me to the conference room. He and Joel were working on the computer. Joel introduced him as Mr. Peterson and we shook hands, and then he and Joel went away and I set up my instruments. And when they came back, we three sat at the table and Joel, in front of Drew, explained the purpose of the test, exactly what the issues were. I wanted some detail. Everything I asked them for, they were very forthright in giving to me. And Joel and Drew left. I took a couple minutes to write things out. After I said I'm ready, Drew came in and we sat down, connected him, and started the test. It lasted about two hours. Drew never asked his results.

Armstrong: You can determine results immediately?

McCord: Yes. He didn't ask. He waited until I stopped and I finished and I called him and Joel back. Afterwards he just said, "Thank you." But he never asked. Often times, at the conclusion of a test, people

Lee McCord

Employment

Polygraph Examiner/Owner
McCord and Assoc.

January 1990 - Present
Chicago, IL

Administer structured pre-employment and specific Polygraph examinations for
private industry and law enforcement agencies including sex offender testing.
Administers psychological testing for pre-employment placement and conducts
security interviews.

Polygraph Examiner/Manager
London House

June 1985 - Jan. 1989
Park Ridge, IL

Manager, Polygraph and Interviewing services. Implemented Structured
Interview and Psychological Testing program; Conducted training sessions on
Structured Interviewing Techniques; Administered pre-employment and specific
polygraph examinations for law enforcement agencies and private industry.
Supervised fellow polygraph examiner including giving final review on all
polygraph testing. Responsible for daily operation of polygraph department.

Polygraph Examiner/V.P.
Lincoln Zonn, Inc.

June 1979 - June 1985
Chicago, IL

V.P., Mid-west region. Supervised five fellow polygraph examiners who traveled
throughout the mid-west conducting polygraph examinations and security
interviews. Responsible for daily operations of mid-west office, staffing and
supervision of office staff. Conducted polygraph examinations and security
interviews.

Polygraph Examiner/Manger
Wells Fargo, Inc.

Oct. 1974 - June 1979
Chicago, IL

Manager, Polygraph Department. Supervised two fellow polygraph examiners
and office staff. Responsible for daily office operations and conducted pre-
employment, routine and specific polygraph examinations.

Education

Bachelor of Science
Savannah State University

1970 - 1974
Savannah, GA

Polygraph training included an internship at Well Fargo, Inc. and study courses at John Reid and Associates.

Skills/Professional Associations

Licensed to conduct polygraph examinations in Illinois (1974) and Indiana (1984).

Member of the Illinois Polygraph Society since 1974. Past Chairman of the Grievance Committee.

Military Experience

United States Air Force 1966 - 1970. Held the rank of Sergeant and served in Viet Nam from 1968 to 1969.

Reference

Available upon request.

will ask. He never asked.

Armstrong: *His attitude during the session?*

McCord: I got the impression that he wasn't happy. Now, I don't know Drew. I met him for the first time in session. There were times he'd say something that made you smile, but overall he seemed kind of somber. I remember him standing by the window, looking out at Millennium park with his hands in his pockets when I was setting up, just standing there staring out the window looking thoughtful, and then he'd walk around, moving slowly, so there was nothing that made me think he was happy to be there, I didn't get that impression. He looked a little fatigued.

Armstrong: *Did he joke with you? Socialize with you after?*

McCord: No, no. There was very little conversation at all beyond our session.

Armstrong: *What does the polygraph measure?*

McCord: Breathing patterns. There are two tubes. Pneumatic tubes. One goes across your chest, one goes around your stomach area. And we simply record your breathing patterns. The tubes actually measure the expansion and contraction. We establish a breathing pattern. The average person, typically, will breath eight to ten times per minute at most. And then we attach leads to your fingers that measure galvonic skin response, typically on the index and ring finger of the person's hand. We record electrical impulses of the body. And we use a blood pressure cuff, the same cuff a doctor uses to take your blood pressure, except we use it to measure blood volume. We watch how fast your heart beats. We look for increases and decreases in a person's blood volume. It has nothing to do with blood pressure. Just blood volume. It's similar to watching an EKG in a hospital. You can see a person's heart beating on a monitor. We can see that. But we can also see breathing patterns, a person's chest expanding and collapsing, and there's a pattern to it. If a person is being less than honest, there's going to be a variation in the patterns. Think of it as a visual tape recorder. Rather than hearing things, it's recording other indicators.

Armstrong: *How many years of training does it take to become an expert?*

McCord: We learn constantly. There's a basic training, even today, after thirty-four years I'm still learning. We certainly can learn the basics in a couple years. We learn the basics in polygraph schools.

Then it takes years. Sometimes it takes years to achieve the objectivity.

Armstrong: *Do you think there'll ever be a time when polygraphs are widely accepted in courts?*

McCord: Personally I don't think it should be accepted in court. As a polygraph examiner, if I tell you someone passed or failed a test, you're going to believe me. To accept it in court gives too much power to the polygraph. The polygraph would have too much influence on society. It would be very easy to go to court if a polygraph said he was "guilty" and then the jury would say, "The polygraph examiner said he's guilty, so he's guilty." It shouldn't be that easy. It has its place. But I don't think it has its place in a court of law. But we certainly have a functional place in investigation.

Armstrong: *Did you go into this session with any preconceived notions as to what sort of results you were going to get?*

McCord: Absolutely not. That's one thing I pride myself on. I was first called by Joel Brodsky, and he asked "do you know who my client is?" and I said, "I have no idea." But, of course, once I heard the name, I knew who he was. Anyone in Chicago knows about this case, but no, I've never drawn a conclusion about him. To be honest, I don't know enough about the case. I take pride in my ability to be totally objective. I guess he was shorter than I thought he was. I thought he was much bigger for some reason. If you can't be objective in giving a polygraph, you're in the wrong business. One thing I know is that things are not always as they appear. And on a high profile case like this, I'm putting my reputation on the line. You better be certain that at least the process is right.

Armstrong: *Did you feel any different about Drew afterwards?*

McCord: No. My opinion of Drew hasn't changed from the first moment I saw him. If someone asked me about the case, I'd be inclined to say, "I don't think he did any wrong here, just based on the polygraph test." And that's the only thing I can base an opinion on because I'm not privy to any other investigative information in the case. My opinion is that he is being truthful. That's my professional opinion.

"They cannot put Drew in that house"

Face to face time with Joel Brodsky is very precious, and we end up meeting late at night most times, either in his office, or one block down at a hundred-year-old private club. I've been in Chicago for some time, so wrapped up in Peterson's world I missed all the events leading up to Independence Day, including the street food festival.

Tonight is fireworks night, and I'm going to miss this too. My stomach rumbles alarmingly, in spite of wolfing down some quick room service (my first meal of the day) after Peterson left our all-day interview in my hotel room down Michigan from Brodsky's office.

There are a lot of things on my mind, all things Joel Brodsky would have insight into, so I have to grab whatever time he'll offer me. We're alone in his corner office, at about nine PM, with a view of Chicago's waterfront at night. The park below us is festive with Independence Day festivities, including many kids' events and a concert. But I'm not here on holiday.

"So, what would you like to talk about?" he asks me.

"I'd like to hear your perspective, as defense lawyer. Legal points you've analyzed. Things you feel comfortable talking about. Beyond the polygraphs."

"Which case?"

"Let's start with Kathy Savio."

He has his sleeves rolled up, revealing hairy freckled arms, his tie and coat tossed off. I know he has been in court on an important new case—I overheard bits of the case (and realized this might be another great book), but it's all very confidential, so I stay focused on Peterson. I don't know if the Peterson notoriety has brought him the new case, but I know it's another high profile one.

"All right, well, with Kathleen Savio, we have, quote unquote, a body." Although he's sitting at his desk, even in his chair, he appears animated. "Now, if anyone wants to prove a homicide, you have to prove two things. One, that there was in fact a homicide. That it wasn't an accident. In this case, when you look at the autopsy

Peterson's veteran criminal trial attorney Joel Brodsky during an author interview, here explaining case law. In this session Brodsky went through the status of the Peterson gun charges and the "motion to dismiss," several Illinois case studies of relevance, and Kathy Savio's autopsy.

report—" He pulls out his copy of the autopsy report. (Refer to the previous section, "The subject is received in a body bag." p 171) "What does Nancy Grace always say—oh, by the way, off camera, one of the sweetest people—the 'dry bathtub drowning.' What a crock." He laughs. "No offense to Nancy. I love her.

"What the state police did, when she was found in the bathtub without water, afterwards they filled up the bathtub, during their investigation, and they timed how long it took to drain. It took six to eight hours with the drain plug in. So, forgive me Nancy, but that whole dry bathtub thing is a bunch of—well, I'm sure you can't write that." He smiles, and he's just getting warmed up. "And the other thing they say over and over is that she was beaten mercilessly. That there are bruises all over her body, from head to toe. What a bunch of garbage." He's so animated in his presentation, I'm actually waking up again, after my long day of interviews. Brodsky is never boring.

"I showed this autopsy to a prominent pathologist, Dr. Cyril Wecht. Have you heard of him?"

"No."

"He's eminent. He consulted on very high profile cases. Well—this was not a professional consultation—but he believes that the attribution of accidental cause of death by drowning was certainly supported by the evidence and by what the coroner's—what the pathologist found and what the coroner's jury heard."

Now he's demonstrating the autopsy with his own body—clothes on, of course.

"First, we have the laceration on the back of her head, which clearly was enough to make her unconscious, and led to her drowning. But contrary to the sensational reports, then we have a small handful of contusions and bruises, none more than the size of a quarter." He launches out of his chair and stabs a precise location in his abdomen. "We have three purple contusions—now purple means they were of some age—one to two inches in greatest dimension." He digs through his drawer and finds a quarter and a dime. "So—we're talking three contusions about this size."

He tosses the coins on his desk, and paces the room rapidly, as if presenting to a jury. "Kathy used to work out. She was very fit. She worked out regularly. These kinds of bruises, first of all, are consistent with minor bruising from a gym, or from anything. They're pretty minor. You're running on the treadmill, and you hit your abdomen, you do some aerobics, anything. By the way, with someone like Kathy, you don't hit her in the abdomen. She wouldn't be incapacitated. On the contrary, she'd be mad. She'd really fight back. And she was known as a real fighter."

He goes on to point out the thigh bruising is described as "faint" so "this is very old. Now, the most important are the bruises on the wrist." Again he demonstrates with his body. "Look at the size. Those aren't defensive wounds! Defensive wounds are like this, or like this …" I feel like I'm watching an old Matlock episode, when attorney Matlock excitedly demonstrates for the jury every movement. He shows me exactly how defensive wounds look, where they'd be. "Remember, we're talking Kathy Savio, here. Not a helpless victim. She was more than able to take care of herself. There'd be defensive wounds." He shakes his head. "These are normal marks that come from active living, not from a severe beating." He goes on to show in the autopsy, the notation on "Mild mitral valve thickening." He throws down the autopsy report. "If you check, mild mitral valve thickening has been known to cause unconsciousness."

I did, in fact, check after our meeting, referring to two renowned MDs from the Cleveland Clinic of Medicine, Department of Cardiology, Dr. Brian Griffen and Doctor Emil Hayek: "Common manifestations of mitral stenosis . . . exertional dyspnea, atrial fibrillation, hypothyroidism . . . pulmonary venous hypertension," and the list goes on.[105] I'm not convinced this happened, but dizziness causing a slip and fall is not inconceivable.

"So, you can't even prove beyond a reasonable doubt that there was a homicide. You can't even get to square one." He laughs. "You hungry? I'm hungry. I haven't eaten all day."

Next thing you know, we're marching up Michigan to his private club. It's literally right next door, a massive architecturally beautiful building that overlooks the Chicago shoreline. As we walk, he continues his case: "Even if there's a homicide, you have to connect a suspect to the scene. There's no direct physical evidence that Drew was anywhere near the house, and he's pretty much accounted for that whole weekend. Circumstantial evidence?" He's quite jovial as he walks, and I think I see people's heads turning, either because they recognize him or because he's so energetic. "There's no forced entry. There is no sign of a struggle. They have nothing that shows Drew was in that house during the window of time for time of death calculations. Because she was in water, they aren't precise, but there's a window." He holds the door to the club open for me. "They cannot put Drew in that house in that eight-hour window."

He checks his briefcase with a very friendly girl at an old oak desk, and takes me for a tour of his club. It's an elegant old place. We head straight for the rooftop restaurant garden, and before Brodsky continues, he orders a burger with blue cheese.

The evening is memorable for two light shows, an approaching storm and the Independence Day fireworks over the lake. We sit at the farthest table from the door, to prevent casual eavesdropping, but this is outside of the canopy area. It's a beautiful night over our location, but barely a mile away, a mass of ominous clouds gather, just past the old skyline of Chicago. Lightning dances across a dark sky, illuminating boiling storm clouds. Straight above us is clear sky and stars.

Against this dramatic backdrop of clouds, Brodsky continues his animated description of the case, his face softly lit, but occasionally dramatically illuminated by approaching lightning.

"There was no physical evidence," Brodsky continues, sipping on bubbling San Pellegrino water. "There was no sign of a struggle. Investigators can always find a sign of a struggle if there was one. Even if I'm a careful attacker, and I try to straighten up after my attack, I can never put it back where it was, not perfectly. They can always see from dust and trace, whether there was a struggle, even if there's a subsequent cleanup."

"Oh, look at that!" The magnificent fireworks show has begun. I'm not sure what the juxtaposition of approaching thunderstorm to the north of us, and fireworks to the west means, but it is dramatic. Symphonic music plays, not particularly loud twenty-six stories up, but obviously a spectacular show below. From our height, the fireworks look amazing.

"You mentioned forced entry," I say, pouring myself some water. "Couldn't an attacker have picked the lock?"

"Good question. We brought in an expert. He told us that even an experienced break-in artist, with a lock pick kit, would take thirty-seventy minutes to open that lock. An untrained person would never get past that lock."

"Drew have a key?"

"No, Kathy changed the locks. Alarm codes were changed, too. Her ex-boyfriend might have had a key, but not Drew."

His burger and fries come, and right away he dives into his fries with a ravenous hunger. We watch bright flashes of red and searing cascades of blue and dazzling arcs of shooting stars from the fireworks show below us. Still eating, unable to rest for a moment, Brodsky continues his explanations. He delves into Illinois Case law, focusing on cases involving divorces and circumstantial evidence. He quickly runs through the People of the State of Illinois VS. Nathaniel Davis, where the state tried to prove a case based on a murder weapon and the motive of $1.5 million dollars from a pending divorce. The weapon was conclusively his, but he had reported it missing a few days before. On appeal, the appellate court reversed the conviction—making it current law—based on the fact that the state had not proven he had possession of the weapon. "They also specifically mentioned that going through a divorce is not sufficient motivation for murder in and of itself. If it were, over 50 percent of

Americans would have a motive to kill. So, there's no question, in the State of Illinois, they'll never have enough to even charge Drew Peterson."

"What about Reverend Schori?"

As Brodsky munches on fries, I ask, "Okay, but what about Reverend Schori? Didn't he say that Stacy told him that Drew killed Kathy?"

"I knew you'd ask that!" He finishes off his burger. "I would love to have Reverend Schori on the stand! Schori wants us to believe that this young woman comes in and says, 'I want to leave my husband. He's controlling and abusive. I'm afraid of him. He's watching me. Oh, and by the way, he killed his last wife and I gave him his alibi.' We don't know his full story, because in the media he kept saying he can't reveal it all." He shakes his head, appearing almost mischievous. "And what's Schori's response? Oh, go home. See if you can patch it up with him? And pray. That's what he wants us to believe. Baloney. It's ridiculous to ask us to believe he allowed her to go home after that kind of a story. Any reasonable person would say, 'Sit right there, I'm calling the cops. You're not safe! Is your husband home right now? No? Let's go get your kids and get you to a shelter.' But no, he lets her go home. Right."

Of course, it's also hearsay, generally not admissible. Hearsay from someone who can't vouch for it. Not particularly credible. "Is this good counseling? Even Reverend Schori's senior said, 'If this happened, that's not good counseling.' And, of course, like everyone else in Illinois, Schori's grabbed face time on national TV. Is that appropriate for a pastor?"

After my interview with Brodsky I decided to replay Schori's interview on FOX's *On the Record with Greta Van Susteren*. A very young Pastor Schori, looking every inch the all-American young man with trendy haircut and handsome features, says, "I got to know her at the church … we met at a coffee shop in Bolingbrook … and she said 'He did it.' And I said, 'He did what?' and she said 'He killed his last wife, Kathleen.' " At this point in the interview Schori is smiling at Greta Van Susteren. "I was blown away." Big smile. "I was reeling inside."

Greta, for her part, seems almost not to believe him, her lip trembling, turned down in a frown, but as if trying not to smile, her eyes darting to one side back and forth. "So what did you do?"

Schori goes on to matter-of-factly explain he asked her for specific details that "I can't share."

Can't share? You might be reasonably thinking at this point, you've shared more than you were supposed to as a counselor, young Pastor Schori.

Almost grinning. "This is a crazy amount of information to get. So I asked her 'What can I do with this? Why did you tell me?' I asked her if she'd ever told anyone else." Either because he's nervous or happy, he shakes his head and smiles at the same time. "I hope she felt I was a safe person, someone she could share with."

Greta closes her eyes. "How do you know that it wasn't just speculation on her part?" Her lips are quite obviously pursed.

"She had specific information" He nods, hands clasped in front of him.

"Like?"

When he is evasive, she later asks, "Did he admit it to her, or did she put two and two together?"

Nodding again. "It was more than just putting two and two together … She shared details I'm just not comfortable getting into."

Okay, Pastor. It crossed my mind that he was not a particularly good counselor to go to for confidential conversations.

Greta asked the question that I would have been burning to ask: "Why'd she stay with him after that?"

"It's a really good question. My guess, it'd be out of fear."

A really, really good question. The pastor seemed content to let her go home to a husband she just indicated was a wife-killer. Hmm. Score 1 out of 10 for credibility.

Putting aside Schori's peculiar actions—not reporting the conversation to police (but later reporting it to the media), letting her go home, not getting her and the children moved to a safe house—how does a smart girl like Stacy end up going back home to Peterson if he's this kind of monster? How do people like Schori—or her family—allow it? It doesn't ring true to my ears. At the very least, Schori would be calling every day to make sure she's all right, maybe going to a superior to talk it out, perhaps even going to the police?

"A more bogus case I have not seen."

The only actual charge brought against Drew Peterson, at time of this writing, is the much derided "gun" charge, which has raised the ire of NRA members all across the nation.

"A more bogus case I have not seen," Joel Brodsky said in my third meeting with Peterson's lead attorney. He is referring to the belated charge by Illinois State Police, against Drew Peterson for possession of an illegal weapon. The immediate "motion to dismiss" went mostly in their favor, with the judge agreeing to key points, but not able to dismiss the last point on a point of law.

In laymen's terms, Drew Peterson, while a SWAT team member, had a personal second weapon, approved by Bolingbrook Police in writing, with a barrel that is technically a fraction of an inch too short. As an officer, he is allowed this weapon, and at the time the weapon was seized in a search, he was still active with the force. In a memorandum dated May 14, 2005 from the Police Chief, all the approved weapons for REACT (Bolingbrook's SWAT team) are listed with the names:

"959—Peterson MP5 5 Primary (ISSUED TO OFFICER)/ Personal AR 15 Secondary"

In addition, there are various photos of him on duty, including a famous one with Peterson carrying the weapon on guard duty with John Travolta.

The charge does give the Illinois State Police some wider latitude in terms of investigative leeway, and as a felony charge prevents Peterson from leaving the country, but few people—including the so-called "Drew-haters"—believe the charge is an end in itself.

"It was likely a mistake," Peterson's lawyer Brodsky affirms. "There are certain rules that come into play when a charge is preferred, among them guidelines on reporting to defense attorneys the results of wire taps within specified periods. It was probably a big mistake."

When the story first broke, many people, excited by the headlines that boldly proclaimed, "Drew Peterson arrested," imagined that the gun was in some way related to the cases of Stacy Peterson's disappearance or Kathy Savio's death. The case is entirely unrelated

Photo courtesy of Brodsky & Odeh

So far, Peterson has been arrested only relating to a gun charge. One of his official guns had a barrel a fraction of an inch too short (see opposite). In a move to have the charge dismissed, Peterson's team presented a letter of permission from the Bolingbrook Police Chief and this photo of Peterson with actor John Travolta (showing Peterson on duty as a SWAT member with his gun).

Drew Peterson's SWAT rifle.

The notorious gun, once approved for Peterson's use but now the basis of a charge for possession of an illegal weapon. The barrel was shortened a fraction of an inch, which in theory could earn him a state vacation in the penitentiary for up to five years.

however, with no one implying or stating that the gun was a weapon of interest in either case. It just happens to be a convenient charge. Only time will tell if the hasty charge was a tactical coup or gaffe on the part of the police.

"Who the hell charges a cop with a weapon's violation?" Brodsky continued. "He was an on-duty police officer at the time. A member of their SWAT team. The weapon in question he had with him all the time, either in the police car, or at home, because as part of SWAT you're on call twenty-four hours a day. For years he did this. So now they're trying to tell me, that one week before he resigned it was illegal?" He sounds genuinely incredulous.

"I guess the real question that has to be asked is, What's their real motivation? These are not stupid people. I think the prosecutor—pretty much they've told me—that the state police have come to him several times with a request to indict Drew, and they keep saying no. And I think they brought the prosecution a case where he couldn't say no. I think they misled him about the facts of the case and Drew's qualification with the weapon, because they needed to charge Drew. I think they made a mistake in the bigger picture, and on this charge they simply don't have a case."

Subsequently, the judge ruled in favor of the defense on three points of the motion to dismiss, but still moved the case to trial to argue the fourth point.

Documentary Proof The State Police Weapon Arrest Of Drew Peterson Is Bogus.

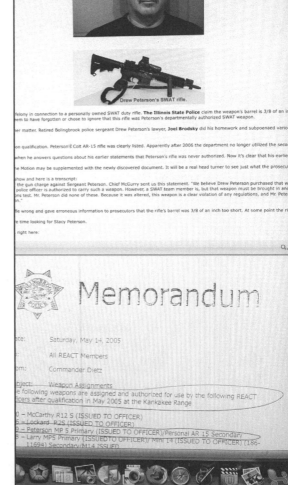

During the author's research, he found hundreds of blog posts and dozens of newspaper articles on Peterson's gun. Contrary to other media coverage of Peterson, which is mostly negative, most blogs and media coverage support Peterson's contention that the gun charge is "trumped up" as a method of putting pressure on the legal team and Peterson in the "other cases." Here, a photo of the author's screen shows the blog of famous private investigator Paul Huebl in California. It reveals a memorandum clearly indicating that as of May 14, 2005, the SWAT weapon in question was approved for Peterson—in writing. This contradicts the Police Chief's statement that the gun was never approved.

Author's photo

Gun Charge Poll
GretaWire Blog, FOX TV, May 21, 2008

Do you think the gun charge is a legitimate charge or just the police harassing former Sgt. Drew Peterson?

54 percent (2923 votes)—the gun charge is a legitimate charge
22 percent (1206 votes)—this is police harassment
24 percent (1305 votes)—this is both legitimate and harassment.

"You have the right to remain silent."

On other matters of hearsay and "listening in" I later spoke with Brodsky about the breaking news of supposed wiretaps by Lenny Wawczak and Paula Stark. Like most experts, he put down the notion that the wiretaps would be in any way admissible. My own research of Illinois law indicated:

- Drew Peterson has invoked his right to counsel and to remain silent. Law enforcement cannot question him about these alleged crimes without first speaking with his attorney. Case law—if a private individual questions someone at the behest of law enforcement, and that person has previously invoked his rights, it is as if law enforcement themselves questioned the person in violation of his rights, and thus the statements are not admissible.
- Illinois is a two-party consent state. Of course a warrant makes a difference, but recording someone who has invoked his right to silence is problematic.

It's somewhat doubtful there are any tapes, for various reasons, including:

- The state police would never sanction going public with the story of wiretaps

- There are more sophisticated methods of recording suspects
- In a follow-up interview on *Good Morning America*, Paula Stark slipped up by saying,[106] "I could prove it. It's not with the state police, but I could prove it." This either means the taping was not sanctioned, didn't happen, or they privately recorded without a warrant, which would not be admissible.

For similar reasons, hearsay evidence from Ric Mims (with so-called hearsay confessions of Kris Peterson, denied by Kris in my interviews) would not be admissible as hearsay.

All in all, together with a bundle of other case law and evidence Brodsky presented that spectacular Independence Day evening, I find it hard to believe anyone thinks there's a case against ex-Sergeant Drew Peterson. Even if they do, it seems he's in good hands with his advocates Brodsky and Odeh.

It all seems to come back to conviction by moral standards (Peterson likes younger women and his life is one string of infidelities) and bad luck (one wife died and one disappeared).

Now it was time to examine the morals. I had to admit that a forty-seven-year-old man marrying a seventeen-year-old girl might draw thumbs up from the club of guys everywhere (secretly, of course), but it does strike most of us as morally questionable.

"Do you mind that
I'm forty-seven?"

"No, not at all," Stacy answered with a quick smile. "Do you mind that I'm seventeen?"

Oh my God! Peterson thought. That's terrible. "I originally thought she was in her early twenties, anyway," he'd later tell friends, with a laugh. "So I'm real quick, looking into the Criminal Code, and seventeen is good. Age of consent." He laughs, nervously. "I was pushing the envelope, but I was in the envelope." Age of consent in Illinois was seventeen. Technically, Peterson wasn't single, either, so that was strike two against him. "Our marriage was over, we were separated, but there was no divorce." Stacy didn't mind.

Photo courtesy of Drew Peterson

The happy couple in their first year.

What did she see in him? She loved his sense of humor, his masculinity, she loved that he was a cop and successful. She didn't see an older man. She just didn't care about things like that.

Peterson, remained in shock over her age for a week or two. He always felt Stacy was drop-dead gorgeous, but he also thought she was older. She worked in a hotel, hung out with older guys, most of her friends were older, and she dressed and acted like a twenty-five-year-old.

The big issue for Peterson, who found Stacy irresistible, was the hotel where she worked. She had a fan club. "There was a line of little guys, young guys around mid-twenties to thirties, who flirted and hung out with her constantly. And she loved the attention."

After a few weeks of dating, he realized she thrived on attention. Contrary to the various theories of media and family, she wasn't seeking a "father figure" replacement for her somewhat abusive father—a man roughly the same age as Peterson. She liked all men. She thrived on being center stage, with men at her bidding. He knew she was vivacious, flirty and men loved her. He had to deal with that. "She was always like that, and remained like that."

The only friction between them was the result of her flirtatiousness. "I wasn't one of these little guys, hanging over her counter at the hotel with their tongues hanging out. She loves male attention." Later, when they took various trips to tropical beaches and cruises, she'd wear the tightest, smallest bikinis, sunbathe topless, and she'd always have a school of young men following her around.

This was a constant with Stacy. She wore tight, short dresses, walked provocatively, made sure her cleavage showed—especially after her enhancement surgery. She just loved it.

"That's why, for me," Peterson said, "it was never a stretch to believe her call that night, October 28, when she told me she was running off to a tropical beach with a man. That was her. She'd love that sort of adventure."

Their time together—first as steady daters, then engaged, later as man and wife—was characterized by Stacy's public persona of seductive charm, her flirting, and a train of men following her. "I just learned to deal with it. What else could I do? It was always there."

In the beginning, it was all very funny to him. Peterson himself was a flirt. He had no illusions about himself as being a pretty boy or a handsome dude or anything along those lines, "but I liked the girls." So it was never more than an annoyance for him that Stacy was a younger reflection of his own personality. "On the other hand, it was a big nuisance. It actually got kind of annoying after a couple years. She was a very beautiful woman, so what could I do?"

He gave her everything, too. She loved the trips, the beaches, the cruises, the first car, and later the Harley Davidson motorcycle he bought her, "just to keep her off mine." In the home, away from the lure of leering men, she seemed to settle in to being a great mother and wife, decorating their home with a light feminine touch, thematically creating rooms for each child: the princess room for Lacy, the cars room for Anthony, the music room for Tommy, and the starry night astronomy room for Kris. "She is very talented." Peterson is truly proud of the jungle bathroom, a room they wallpapered together with artificial plastic vines hanging from the ceiling like a jungle canopy.

One time in a Meijer's, Stacy complained of a guy following her in the aisles. "This guy's looking at me funny."

Peterson snickered. "Well look how you're dressed!" She wore her lowest, lowest cut top.

"But he's looking at me like a pervert."

"You dress like this, your going to get the leering guys. It's human nature."

"No."

"Yeah." He felt like rolling his eyes. He knew she loved the attention, but she just wanted to be sure he noticed the guys were following her. He would later describe Stacy as "the most flirtatious girl I've ever known."

To get Stacy out of the less-than-wholesome hotel crowd of "leering boys" Peterson got her a job with the village of Bolingbrook.

This time in their relationship was very romantic. Every day, Peterson would leave her little notes. She'd leave him cards with hearts. A few times Stacy sent him flowers, which was mildly embarrassing, but also "kinda nice. No one ever sent me flowers before."

They took several trips together. Stacy had never traveled much. Their first trip to Puerto Vallarta was very special. She was like a kid, drinking down the tropical drinks with the paper umbrellas, bathing topless, parasailing, walking up and down the sand beaches in her bikini and making sure the boys were watching. His favorite memories of her are sunbathing on the white sand, him rubbing sun block on her dark skin, kabobs of seafood cooked on fires on the beach. She drank it all in like someone who'd never experienced such warm luxury before. The sunsets were spectacular as they walked through the sand barefoot, holding hands. Seeing her happy made him very happy.

Above: Stacy during their first trip as a couple to Puerto Vallarta.

Top right: sunbathing topless.

Bottom right: Mrs. Stacy Peterson, out for dinner with Drew Peterson.

Photos courtesy of Drew Peterson

Above: Stacy in high school, long before she
met Drew Peterson.

The many, many
looks of Stacy.

Stacy as a young girl.

Left: Stacy in her freshman year in high school.

Above: Stacy tried on wedding dresses, although they ended up deciding on an outdoor ceremony.

Top: Drew Peterson could deny Stacy nothing. One of his first gifts was a new Grand Am.

Left: A high-flying Stacy Peterson parasailing in Puerto Vallarta.

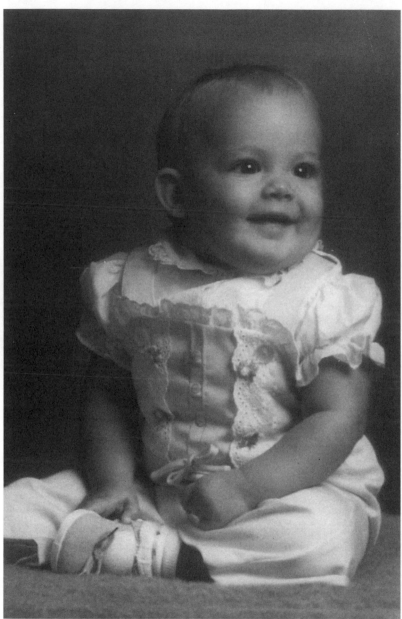

Baby Stacy Cales (future Stacy Peterson).

"I want to be a stripper."

Stacy was seventeen, in love with this man who took her away from a life she so hated. They sat in their favorite restaurant, ignoring the winks and "thumbs up" from waiters who saw Drew Peterson as a sugar daddy.

Sure, there would be problems. Her family lived nearby, so she would still see them often. Drew Peterson, her fiancé, was still married; the marriage was over, but the battles were ongoing. Stacy worked at the front desk of a hotel then, a magnet for young men, but she found security in more mature, stable men.

This night, over dinner, Drew told her he would take her away from "all that."

"What do you mean?" she said, smiling her pixy smile. She had crooked teeth, then—this was before a run of small cosmetic operations on teeth and tummy—but she was a beautiful woman in the blush of full life.

"I mean your family. We'll make our own life together."

"I wish I hadn't told you all that," she said, pushing away her half-eaten dinner.

"But you did."

"I love them."

"Even after all that?"

She nodded.

He leaned across the table, trying to glare, to appear stern. It was impossible against her sparkling eyes and ready smile.

"I'm going to be an exotic dancer."

"You're not stripping," Peterson said, for the tenth time that month.

"Yes, I am. I can make a lot of money being a dancer."

"You're not going to do that."

"Yes, I am."

"We're engaged. You're going to married."

"So?"

"So, you're not."

"I am."

"Not." He ignored the hovering waiter. "This is part of your male attention thing."

"Stop it."

The Peterson wedding, an outdoor ceremony. Baby Anthony was held in Peterson's arms throughout the happy day.

Photo courtesy of Drew Peterson

"No, I mean it. You always have these guys hangin' around."

"I can't help that." She smiled wider.

"Yes, you can. You like the attention."

"So what."

"So, we're getting married."

"I'm going to be a dancer."

Peterson smiled. He knew how to handle this. "The first day you get a job as a dancer somewhere, I'm going to be in the audience with your dad."

Stacy's smile faded for the first time.

"Is Stacy's mother missing or murdered?"

Peterson sighs, staring at a picture of Christie Marie Toutges, Stacy's mom. "This is a good photo of her. I never met her, but this is the best shot of her I've seen." We are going through boxes of photos of Stacy and her family. "No one knows if Christie, Stacy's mom, disappeared or what. Is Stacy's mother missing or murdered? I don't know. I didn't know Stacy for several more years, but Stacy talked about her mom a lot. It bothered her."

I have asked about the negative things in the marriage. He had spoken glowingly of the good times, of the Carnival cruise, of the kids falling in love with her, of how she lovingly decorated the house each Halloween and Christmas.

Peterson came to realize over time, that Stacy craved a normal family life. Part of him knew that he was her rock, that he was her island of normalcy in a blasted stormy ocean of family grief.

Peterson shook his head, rubbed his whiskered chin. "I liked Anthony, I really did. That's Stacy's dad. But that family—well, they're unusual. You know? Two pedophiles in one family, an uncle and her brother? One of Stacy's sisters killed in a house fire, another under mysterious circumstances? A grandfather of eighty-five with a thirty-year-old girlfriend? More than one alcoholic? Half the time on the dole. Mom disappears—just her Bible and purse in hand?"

"History repeats itself, you're thinking?" I ask, because that's what I'm wondering. That and, is there a soap opera in the Cales family? We've been at this seven hours today. I haven't eaten and I'm dying to break and go to the bathroom, but this stuff is just so compelling I can't bear to stop. I keep listening.

"I don't know. I guess her mom could have run off. Then Stacy's sister died of cancer. It's really traumatic, you know? People keep saying, how can a mom run off and leave two children, but Stacy's mom did it. Stacy never got over Tina. I never really thought it so strange, but I know the Cales."

"Do you think her mom influenced her a lot?"

"Yeah. For sure, yeah. A lot. Her mom Christie was seventeen when she gave birth to Tina, and these are the two Stacy was close to."

I made some notes: *"Christie seventeen when Tina born. Stacy seventeen when she met Drew."* I started to build a Christie Marie Toutges timeline,[107] and later verified it with research of birth, marriage, media and police records from multiple sources. I also wrote in my notes: *"Cales family explains Christie's disappearance as a mom distraught over loss of two children— CREDIBILITY ISSUE with this notion: She ran away ten years later?"* I wrote this because according to the timeline, Christie disappeared in 1998, but daughter Jessica died mysteriously before Stacy was even born and Stacy's young sister Lacy died in 1987.

And the entire Cales history is a stunning timeline of an unbelievable (but verified) jumble of arrests, abuse, pedophilia, alcoholism, psychiatric treatment, child neglect, assault, and runaway moms.

Christie Toutges and Cales Family Timeline

01-25-1958: Birth of Christie Marie Toutges.

11-12-1975: At the age of seventeen, Christie gives birth to Christina (Tina) Michelle Toutges.

05-26-1979: Christie, now aged twenty-one, marries Anthony McKenzie Cales, becoming his second wife.

08-07-1979: Christie and Anthony (Stacy's father) give birth to son Yelton, Stacy's brother.

1981: Daughter Jessica Cales born.

1983: The Cales buy a house in Downers Grove, Illinois, not far from Bolingbrook.

12-1983 Daughter Jessica Cales at age two dies in Downers Grove house fire.

1983: Christie Cales files protection order against Anthony (Stacy's father) for aggravated assault with a .357-caliber pistol. Later the charges are dropped.

01-20-1984: Stacy Ann Cales born, daughter of Christie and Anthony.

01-17-1984: The Cales buy a house in DuPont, IL.

1985: Cassandra Cales born to Anthony and Christie.

1986: Christie Cales admitted to psychiatric hospital for alcoholism and child neglect relating to Yelton, now age seven.

1987: Lacy Ann Cales born to Anthony and Christie. Lacy is Lacy Peterson's namesake.

10-17-1987: Mysteriously, Stacy's sister Lacy Ann Cales dies, attributed to SIDS, but not confirmed.

11-1989: Christie Cales is arrested for shoplifting vodka and cigarettes from Osco in Woodridge.

12-26-1989: On Boxing Day, Christie Cales is again charged with shoplifting, this time Old Style beer and Baily's Irish Cream plus cigarettes from Cub Food in Downers Grove.

1990: Christie Cales charged with Driving Under the Influence and once more hospitalized for alcoholism and depression.

1990: Anthony Cales files an order of protection after claiming Christie neglected the children, broke his car windshield and even torched his clothes.

1990: Anthony Cales files for divorce and full custody of fourteen-year-old Tina, ten-year-old Yelton, six-year-old Stacy, and five-year-old Cassandra.

1990: *Unverified by other sources*—According to Stacy, Yelton sexually touches her several times (Yelton is later convicted as a pedophile for abusing a fifteen-year-old).

1990: Christie Cales challenges custody papers of her children but later fails to appear for divorce hearing.

1990: Stacy's sister Tina (Christina) put in Illinois State foster care.

12-03-1990: Divorce final and Anthony given full custody of the three children.

1991: Christie Cales treated with Prozac for depression.

06-16-1993: Property is transferred from Christie Cales to Anthony Cales.

1993: Anthony Cales sells house.

11-12-1993: Tina (Christina), Stacy's favorite sister, turns eighteen and is released from foster care.

1994: Anthony Cales moves to Fort Myers in Florida with Yelton (now age fourteen), Stacy (now age ten) and Cassandra (now age nine).

03-26-1995: Anthony Cales marries Linda June Olson in Fort Myers, Florida. Anthony is Linda's sixth husband.

11-25-1995: The first year of the marriage, Anthony and Linda Cales file protection orders against each other, and she is charged with domestic violence, spending twenty-one days in custody.

1996: Anthony and Linda Cales, Yelton (now age sixteen), Stacy (now age twelve) and Cassandra (now age eleven) move to Morgan City, Louisiana.

1997: Anthony and Linda Cales separate and the Cales family, less Linda, move back to Illinois.

02-11-1998: Christie Cales disappears at age forty in Blue Island. This is recorded under Blue Island Police Agency Case Number: **98-14519:** "Christie Marie Cales was last seen at approximately 4:30 p.m. on March 11, 1998, in the vicinity of the 2300 block of West 199th Street in Blue Island, Illinois. She was carrying a Bible and her purse at the time. She indicated she was going to walk to a friend's house but never arrived."

08-21-2002: Stacy's brother Yelton Cales is arrested for domestic battery and sentenced to fifteen months in DuPage, Illinois.

2002: Anthony and Linda Cales divorced.

02-14-2004: Stacy's brother Yelton Cales is again arrested, this time for aiding and possession of a stolen vehicle; he is sentenced to three years in Will County.

01-20-2005: Stacy's brother Yelton arrested for Aggravated Criminal Sex with a Victim Aged 13 to 16 (AGG CRIM SEX AB/VIC 13-16, DuPage Co), placing him on the Permanent Sex Offenders list as a pedophile.

09-17-2006: The major traumatic event in Stacy's life—besides her mother's running away—is the tragic early death of pregnant sister Tina (Christina Michelle Toutges Ryan) at age thirty. During pregnancy, a tumor is discovered. She dies of cancer in spite of religious vigils attended by a devout Stacy Peterson and her Aunt Candice.

10-28-2007: Stacy Ann [Cales] Peterson disappears.

Above: Two of the most important people in Stacy's life, both tragically taken from her. Christie, her mom, apparently ran away in 1998. Here, Chrstie holds Lacy, Stacy's sister, born 2-10-87, in heaven 10-18-87, apparently a victim of SIDS. Drew and Stacy named their own Lacy after sister Lacy.

Stacy with dad Anthony at Tina's wedding.

Stacy's dad Anthony. His previous wife went on the record stating he was abusive and had an order of protection.

"They're a wacky cast of characters."

Peterson seems agitated as his left hand shoots up the sleeve of his sport shirt's right arm and aggressively scratches his shoulder. Unlike tight television appearances, where Peterson remains immovable and implacable, legs spread wide and hands placed carefully on his lap, in my grueling interview sessions, usually proceeding without meals or breaks for entire days, I've come to notice a different sort of body language. The shoulder scratch indicates frustration.

He sighs again, waving a family Christmas photo in his hand. "This is my Christmas dinner with my four gorgeous kids. With the Cales family. They're a wacky cast of characters." He goes on to describe the dinner with Cassandra and her girlfriend, eighty-something grandpa and his thirty-something girlfriend (kettle black?), one-directional gift giving (Stacy was very generous with the gifts to her family), and several riotous anecdotes.

The wacky world of Peterson's ex-friends and family divides into unique camps resembling a sideshow. Drew sinks lower in the chair, shakes his head, and sighs. "We have the ex-friends who sell their stories to the *National Enquirer*, the friends who claim they wear wiretaps, and the wild and wacky world of the Cales family."

"Ex-friends who sell their stories ..."

The wacky world of witnesses in the Peterson case reads like a Springer episode. "We have ex-friends who sell their stories," explained Joel Brodsky, Peterson's attorney. "We have family members with extensive criminal records who give conflicted timeline accounts."

Peterson's legal team has been widely criticized for their regular release of "damning" background information on various members of the families of both victims, and the friends and neighbors who have offered witness accounts. "But just look at what's happened," Brodsky said. "They're all attacking Drew's character and motives. Some of the early witnesses are already discredited, like the truck driver who claimed to have been hired by Drew to carry a barrel. The police already proved the truck driver lied.

"Since we are in a trial by media, and since the entire case revolves around these people's accounts, the credibility of these witnesses is an important consideration," Brodsky said. "Drew's already taken a polygraph. I wonder of some of these other characters would?"

Stacy Peterson

Stacy's character is used by family members and neighbors to explain, in negative affirmation style, why she would never just "run off." The main reasons given for "she would never run off" are the children. However, given that she knew Peterson was a good father (never disputed by anyone), it is legitimate for Brodsky's team to point out some background that goes to "state of mind" and why the argument that "she wouldn't just run off" isn't a credible one:

- "Stacy had several boyfriends."[108]
- Stacy's mother Christie Marie Cales, disappeared in nearly

identical fashion on March 11, 1998, carrying with her only her purse and Bible. She had several children besides Stacy.

- Stacy had undergone some traumatic recent events that were emotionally draining, including the death of her sister Tina of cancer at a young age in 2007, and the resultant loss of faith.[109]
- Stacy might have had plans to run off. (Refer to the last chapter, "Postscript: Stacy's Plan?")

Thomas Morphey

Thomas Morphey provided the first real soap opera incident, with his spectacular suicide attempt following his public revelations that he "helped Peterson carry a blue barrel" out of the house the night Stacy disappeared. No forensic evidence of the barrel was found, and Morphey became the first of the four ex-friend "discredited" witnesses.[110]

The legal team for Peterson were quick to point out (from various media sources, summarized):

- Morphey's history with drugs and alcohol abuse, which casts doubt on his ability to provide lucid, detailed witness accounts.
- Morphey's own wife ran away shortly after they married.
- Morphey's suicide attempt or drug overdose the day after his claim about the barrel calls into question his soundness of mind.
- The Peterson team's tests of barrel surfaces (plastic, metal, insulated containers) make Morphey's account of a barrel "warm to the touch" unlikely.

"He's in therapy."

Morphey, 40, was identified by police sources Tuesday as the man who said he helped Drew Peterson load a large barrel into Peterson's SUV on Oct. 28, the day Peterson's 23-year-old wife, Stacy, disappeared. About 11:20 p.m. Oct. 29, Bolingbrook police responded to a 911 call for an attempted suicide from Morphey's home. Since then, he hasn't been home in "several" weeks, his girlfriend, Sheryl Alcox, said Wednesday. "He's in therapy," she said. *Chicago Tribune[111]*

Ric Mims

Ric Mims was the second ex-friend to "sell out" with his not very popular decision to sell his story to the *National Enquirer*. Although he occasionally volunteers with the "Search for Stacy" groups, he came under fire for his sale of his story to the *Enquirer*. He quickly promised to donate the proceeds to the Search for Stacy efforts. The main issue is the credibility of a paid-for story in a magazine more known for both gossip and news:

- Mims sold his story, according to Brodsky, for $35,000.
- The hearsay account of an argument between Drew and Stacy attributed to Kris Peterson is denied by him.
- Mims' timeline account contradicts itself and contradicts other timelines (notably Sharon Bychowski's account of when cars were in the driveway).
- The dialogue attributed to Kris Peterson sounds entirely fictional (one moment a toddler tone, the next very adult). Thirteen-year-old Kris does not refer to stepmom Stacy as "Mommy" and Drew as "Daddy."
- Mims claims to be a close friend of Peterson's, but was never a close friend before Stacy disappeared, only an acquaintance.

National Enquirer, December 17, 2007
The secret notes and the paper shredder

Mims told the *Enquirer*: "We all walked into Drew's office, and the first thing Drew does is mouth the words: 'Don't talk, there's bugs.'

"The guy throws down a cell phone and a charger and writes on a piece of paper; 'This is a cell phone for you to use.' And he writes that Drew has to answer it by saying he's from some heating and cooling company. Then they put the note in a shredder."

Pal Fears he Unknowingly Helped Get Rid of Evidence

On the afternoon of November 2, Drew asked his pal Richard Mims for a favor. He wanted Mims to take to his son Steve, a police officer, a suitcase of teenage son Thomas' clothes and a trumpet case. Thomas plays in his high school band. Drew said his younger kids were going to be staying at Steve's home ... Mims got a bad feeling. He was wondering if he had unwittingly removed items from the Peterson home that Drew was nervous about.

The Cales Family

Since Stacy's family are the main spokespeople for Stacy's state of mind—the claim she was divorcing Peterson, her fear for her life, and the characterization that she is a mother who would never leave her children—their background falls under the scrutiny of Peterson's defense team, since he has been named an official "person of interest."

Whether you believe Peterson's account of the Cales family (see "They're a wacky cast of characters") or not, there are a few elements of character which can be determined through standard background checks:

- Stacy's sister Cassandra Cales, who reported Stacy missing, has several arrests, including a violent arrest involving a Tazer.
- Stacy's brother Yelton Cales is a convicted pedophile, just recently re-arrested after drunkenly plowing his car backwards into a house and fighting with three people, including a minor.
- Anthony Cales, Stacy's father, was described as abusive by his ex-wife and by Stacy herself. Linda Cales (ex-wife) filed an order of protection 11/25/1995.
- Some mysterious Cales family elements: Christie Marie Cales disappeared 03/11/1998, in a way strikingly similar to Stacy's disappearance (see "Is Stacy's mother missing or murdered"); Stacy's sister died in a fire at the age of two; Lacy Cales died as an infant, possibly of SIDS.

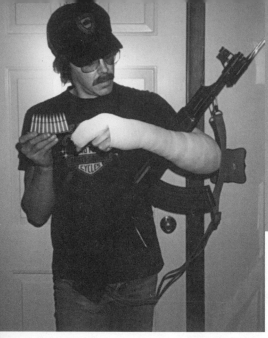

Left: Anthony Cales (Stacy's father) posing with his gun. Above: Stacy with her court-appointed guardian James Maves prior to her marriage to Drew Peterson.

According to Peterson's hearsay accounts of the Cales family, "Stacy spent a lot of time trying to get away from her family. She wanted to move to California. She claims she was abused by family members."

While no one will find an investigation of the Cales family to be an appealing defense tactic, it's a legitimate strategy, given they provide witness testimony regarding timelines and Stacy's state of mind which does not agree with Drew Peterson's accounts.

Reported in *The Herald News*
"Abuse, alcoholism and instability…"

"Abuse, alcoholism and instability were key characteristics of the household in which the Cales children were raised," a family member said …

In the same feature, dated November 7, 2007, Stacy's ex-step-mom Linda Cales said, "The abuse was there. He would want to discipline the kids and spank them when he was drunk. He would say things to the girls like, 'You better be nothing like your slut mom.'"

Top: Anthony after he "abducted the kids from his wife Christie" (according to Drew Peterson). They stayed in Florida for years to avoid Christie, who later "ran away." Bottom left: Stacy found out late in life she had a half-sister, here shown with brother Yelton. Bottom right: Stacy with her favorite sister Christina, performing magic trick as a child. Christina is the magician.

Photos courtesy of Drew Peterson

Peterson goes one step further, telling how Stacy told him many times of sexual abuse at the hands of both sex-offender Yelton, her brother, and "Anthony's drunken friends. She claimed Anthony's friends groped her when she was a child. And she later lost her virginity to one of Tina's friends."[112]

Reported in *Chicago Sun-Times*
Michael Sneed, 8-8-08

The story gets messier and messier: **Yelton Cales**, 28, the brother of missing mom **Stacy Peterson**, was arrested July 24 in Logansport, Ind., for drunken driving, plowing his car backward into a house, and initiating fights with three people. Cales, who was permitted to visit his sister's children in June under the watchful eye of **Drew Peterson** … was released from prison in June where he served time for aggravated criminal sexual abuse to a 15-year-old girl. Classified as a predatory sex offender, Cales is required to register with the state for the rest of his life.

Lenny Wawczak and Paula Stark One-upped Everyone

Not to be outdone, Lenny Wawczak and Paula Stark one-upped all Peterson's other ex-friends by claiming to a newspaper reporter at the *Chicago Tribune* that they had worn a wiretap on behalf of the Illinois State Police for seven months. "He's going down," Wawczak said of Peterson.

Like Peterson's other ex-friends, Wawczak and Stark came under media fire immediately, discredited by their past records of criminal and financial woes. FOX News Chicago, following on the lead from Peterson's outspoken attorney Joel Brodsky, revealed Wawczak was found guilty of hit-and-run, lost a subsequent lawsuit from the victim, and was in dire straights due to the judgment and a pending eviction. He had filed for Bankruptcy Chapter 7.

Top: Yelton, Stacy and Cassandra. Bottom: Stacy's brother Yelton is on the permanent Illinois Sex Offender registry as a sexual predator of minors.

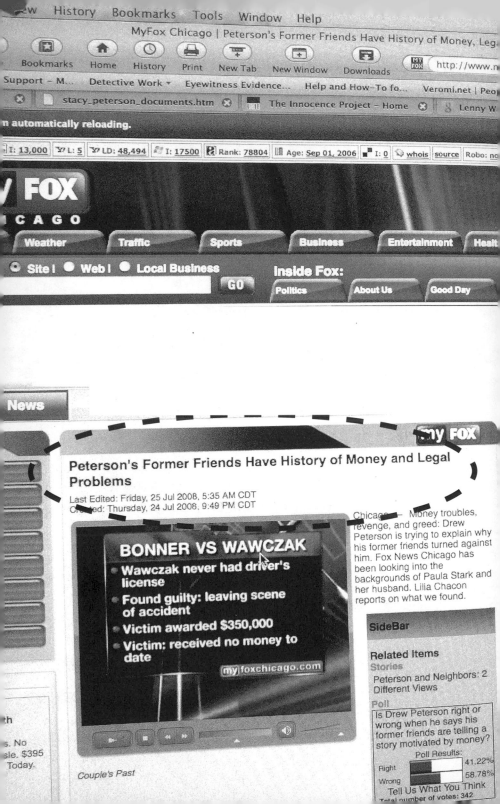

History   Bookmarks   Tools   Window   Help

MyFox Chicago | Peterson's Former Friends Have History of Money, Leg...

Bookmarks   Home   History   Print   New Tab   New Window   Downloads   http://www.n

Support – M...   Detective Work ▾   Eyewitness Evidence...   Help and How–To fo...   Veromi.net | Peo

stacy_peterson_documents.htm ⊗   The Innocence Project – Home ⊗   Lenny W

I: 13,000   L: 5   LD: 48,494   I: 17500   Rank: 78804   Age: Sep 01, 2006   I: 0   whois   source   Robo: no

FOX
CHICAGO

Weather   Traffic   Sports   Business   Entertainment   Health

○ Site | ● Web | ● Local Business   **Inside Fox:**

GO   Politics   About Us   Good Day

News

Peterson's Former Friends Have History of Money and Legal Problems

Last Edited: Friday, 25 Jul 2008, 5:35 AM CDT
Created: Thursday, 24 Jul 2008, 9:49 PM CDT

BONNER VS WAWCZAK
- Wawczak never had driver's license
- Found guilty: leaving scene of accident
- Victim awarded $350,000
- Victim: received no money to date

myfoxchicago.com

Chicago — Money troubles, revenge, and greed: Drew Peterson is trying to explain why his former friends turned against him. Fox News Chicago has been looking into the backgrounds of Paula Stark and her husband. Lilia Chacon reports on what we found.

SideBar

Related Items
Stories
Peterson and Neighbors: 2 Different Views

Poll
Is Drew Peterson right or wrong when he says his former friends are telling a story motivated by money?
Poll Results:
Right   41.22%
Wrong   58.78%
Tell Us What You Think
Total number of votes: 342

Couple's Past

Photo of author's computer during research as story broke of Wawczak's claimed wiretap, their subsequent shoving match in Bolingbrook (right) and FOX News breaking story that Wawczak, contrary to his own claims, did file bankruptcy, was sued for $350,000 (and lost) and had a criminal record. Note sidebar poll from FOX News where 41.22% apparently agreed with Drew Peterson that Wawczak was motivated by money.

Author's photo

EN

TER TO DO, COMMENTS WELCOME

onted the
day,
nine

Wawczak ambushed him in the parking lot, hurling

king lot of a strip mall on the 300 block of North Schmidt
e were called to the scene.

ain't nothing but a murderer. Say something!"

Wawczak pushed him in the back. Peterson later said his

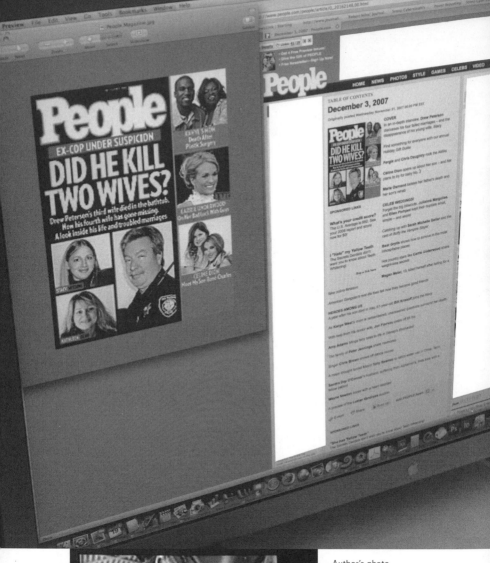

Photo courtesy of Brodsky & Odeh

Author's photo

Above: Media provokes with "Did He Kill?" headlines, even in national media such as *People*.

Left: ABC, NBC, FOX, CNN and all major networks continued to cover the story.

"Drew Peterson Speaks Out" on *Today* with Matt Lauer (right), Peterson (center) and attorney Joel Brodsky (left).

"The media has convicted him with good reason."

The immortal words of Geraldo Rivera of FOX News: "The media has convicted him with good reason."

This seemed an unusual admission for an impartial journalist to make, given the lengths various reporting correspondents go to distance themselves from the notion of "trial by media."

A somewhat more impartial Mike Barz challenged Rivera on a FOX broadcast[113] by asking, "I hate to put you on the spot here—this guy seems to have been already convicted in the media—but ah, your take on this whole thing. Do you think that he was involved in her disappearance?"

Geraldo fumbles a bit on his answer: "Well, if he wasn't he's the most unlucky—the unluckiest guy on earth. Ah, Kathleen Savio—clearly, they had a tumultuous relationship that was marred by violence, ah—he, ah— How that coroner found an accidental drowning in the blithe ignorance of those eighteen domestic violence complaints and the fact that this woman drowned in this ridiculous little tub with no alcohol or drugs in her body is beyond me … this bitterness, this smoldering anger, ah, you know a kind of 'woe is me' attitude, but it was, ah, ah, the media has convicted him for good reason."

The US Department of Justice's Office for Victims of Crime, which advocates for less exploitive media coverage, produced a video designed to coach media in sensitivity in reporting crime.[114] "It's been called a swarm," the video says, referring to the media.

"Oh my God, what's going to happen to me?"

"Why do you think your wacky sense of humor doesn't play well with the media?" I asked this question abruptly, in the middle of one of my interviews about Peterson's past as a cop. "The humor worked for you as a cop, helped you defuse situations, helped you get ahead. Why didn't it work in front of the camera?"

Peterson leaned forward in his chair, eyes unblinking, and focused on me. "See, the public has a certain image of what they expect me to be," Peterson said with some enthusiasm. "They don't like this glib jokester. I work with the camera guys. They're laughing all the time. They're loving it. When I came out with my handycam and filmed them, they thought it was hilarious. They're all laughing behind the camera." He sighs.

The media attention seems to agitate Peterson, who until now has been rolling through the interview with a congenial story-teller's tone. Now, his voice becomes louder, booming, but also higher in pitch, and his hands make sharp gestures.

"Initially, my humor was because of nervousness. It's not so much—it's working with the camera guys. The camera guys are loving it! Cause they're all laughing and having a good time." He shakes his head. "But because I'm not what they want me to be— this crazy killer—it's not working for the editors I guess, and the on-camera personalities. They don't want to see that. They want to keep me sinister. And I go in, and I'm joking with them, and they interpret this as an unfeeling monster."

He's on the edge of his seat now. "I was scared to death, in the beginning, you know. I walk outside, I got forty cameras on me! Forty cameras on me! And, you know, I'm Drew Peterson from Bolingbrook. Holy! I'm accused of all this shit by the media. And I got the police questioning me. Oh my God, what's going to happen to me?" His voice is about an octave higher now: "I'm scared to death!" Then, quieter, "So the humor came out like a nervous tension. Now, it's kinda expected of me."

A psychologist friend, Dr. Dan Dudenz—who Peterson asked to help develop a proper strategy for handling his kids with the media—suggested Peterson start making public service announcements whenever the media show up. "Mention a charity or a cause, talk about what they don't care about, and they'll go away." It didn't quite work out that way, but Peterson did manage to plug a few favorite causes. Soon, though, the camera teams learned to shut down the cameras.

"I thought about renting out space on my lawn for billboards, because for a while there I had the most photographed lawn in America." Peterson's humor came back as he thought about the last few months. "I thought about Hillary Clinton. I'm not too fond of her. So I thought maybe I'd put up pro-Clinton signs, knowing it would turn everyone against her. That's the degree of spite I deal with out there. If Drew likes it, it's a bad thing!"

Then the real fun began. "The media'd be camped out on the street. So I'd go out there first thing in the morning and stick my nose against their glass and scare the shit out of them." He rolls with laughter again.

The degree of coverage approached the absurd, with every moment of Peterson's life caught on camera. Peterson's brother Paul was out walking the dog one. day, standing just behind the camera crews, when Peterson came out of the house. As a lark, Paul started narrating for the cameras, his voice booming out: "Okay folks, and here comes Drew Peterson. Oh, look, he's leaving the house. Now he's putting the key in the lock. He's locking the door. He's giving us a smirk. Now he's getting in his car. He's turning the ignition. He's put the car in reverse ..."

The camera crews were in fits of laughter long after Peterson had disappeared around the corner.

Above: A "forest of lightstands" appears regularly in front of Peterson's house whenever there is news, gossip or scandal to report.

Right: A "fun event"— hopefully not for neighborhood kids—where the "find Stacy" crowd hosted a street party that featured a piñata of Drew Peterson with "I did it" written on the hand. Everyone had a chance to beat the Drew.

Photos courtesy of Brodsky & Odeh

Author's photo

Bordering on Peterson's yard, with the billboard facing the frontyard where Lacy, Anthony, Kris and Tommy play, is a memorial to Stacy asking "*Where is Stacy???*" with a garden of potted plants and angels. Hopefully Lacy and Anthony understand.

Peterson being "wired" up for the *Today* show for his second appearance, this time with lawyer Joel Brodsky. They are interviewed by Matt Lauer.

Author's photo

After the shows, both Matt Lauer of the *Today* show and Dan Abrams of MSNBC sent signed photos. Abrams signs the photo to Joel Brodsky "To a worthy adversary."

"I go on TV because they're trying me on TV"

Peterson is quick to point at the media as the main reason he's willing to speak out on shows such as *Today* and *Larry King Live*. "If they're going to try and convict me, assume I'm guilty, I have to be able to present my story."

Peterson gives a similar rationale for speaking with me in this book format. Having spoken with him for days, I now tend to agree this is his main motivation. In personal one-on-one interviews, with the cameras turned off, he is much more relaxed, he comes across as genuine and sincere. On TV interviews, he tends to be portrayed as arrogant, cynical, even conceited. On You Tube, comments under his *Today* appearance, were quick to assume the worst:

- "He just loves the media. He should shut up."
- "He may be innocent until proven guilty, but all this talking on the media is going to convict him."

His media appearances might, in fact, be working against him.

Do the experts agree with this approach?

Joel Brodsky and the legal team don't disagree, because they hired publicist Glenn Selig to help manage the media message. "He hasn't been charged, but his reputation is being attacked," Brodsky explains.

Yet another high-profile lawyer disagrees. Mark Geragos, famous as the defense lawyer for another Peterson, Scott Peterson, had this to say: "You should be very careful (because) the next time you watch, you could be sitting in the defendant's chair." He represented Scott Peterson, the California man convicted of killing his pregnant wife, Laci. Three of the interviews Scott Peterson gave before he retained Geragos were later played at his trial.

Speaking specifically of Drew Peterson and Stacy, Geragos said media interviews pose another hazard. "If they find Stacy Peterson and she's dead and she was dead at the time the interview was done … those things look awful. Whether (Drew Peterson) had anything to do with it, it looks awful," Geragos said.[115]

Is it playing the way the Peterson team hopes?

Not really. In a MediaCurves viewer tracking study, often used in political debates to measure the results of candidates, Peterson's public rating took a hit after his appearance on *Today*. MediaCurves data revealed that on the question "Do you think Drew Peterson is involved in the disappearance of his fourth wife?":

- 68 percent of responders said Yes after watching the video versus only 56 percent before.
- 42 percent didn't know before the broadcast, versus only 23 percent undecided after.[116]

Of course this study was conducted before either Peterson's lawyer Joel Brodsky or publicist Glenn Selig were engaged, but it does indicate that Peterson's assertive manner and personality in TV appearances isn't helping his public persona.

"Are they nuts, hiring a publicist?"

This is one of the polite comments in the blogosphere, this one on Gretawire. The comment was in response to the move by Joel

Brodsky to engage a publicist to "mitigate the issues related to the rampant trial by media" issue.

I interviewed publicist Glenn Selig of Selig Multimedia to gain a little perspective on this unusual move. Hiring a publicist is not an entirely unheard of defense strategy, but it does tend to provide new material for media attacks. Mr. Selig, a veteran broadcast journalist, helped clarify his important role.

Armstrong: *Tell me how you were originally contacted?*
Selig: I was actually on holiday, on a Disney cruise with my family, when I got a voice mail saying, "My name is Joel Brodsky. I represent Drew Peterson. Can you give me a call?" I remember giving him a call back. It was just so interesting, almost surreal.
Armstrong: *How did he find you?*
Selig: I think it was my background in news and news media that made the difference. They had received an extraordinary amount of publicity. They wanted some

Glenn Selig of Selig Multimedia Inc.

help navigating their way through the media. Initially, I wanted to meet him. I wanted to meet Drew, and see what my impressions were, and see if he was someone I could feel comfortable representing. I met him when he was in Florida in the third week or so of December. I spent a good deal of time getting to know him. He was quite different than they portrayed him to be. I felt quite comfortable working with him.
Armstrong: *You're in Florida. Before you met Drew, how much of the news did you see?*
Selig: It certainly dominated the news, but not like it did in Chicago. And it really had been progressing very rapidly. I had heard about the case, just like everybody else did. I don't think at that point I'd formed any impressions one way or the other.

Armstrong: *How was he being portrayed in the news at that time?*

Selig: He was being portrayed very negatively. It was a very big story, and public sentiment was most definitely against him. I began to research the coverage. It was universally negative, negative, negative. Everybody seemed to believe he did it. It was only a matter of time before he was arrested. I had to give a lot of thought to whether or not this was a case I should be involved in. I had to believe, on a certain level, that he's innocent until proven guilty.

Armstrong: *So now that you've taken the case, what is your role?*

Selig: My role in the court of public opinion is to make sure we uphold the notion that people are innocent until proven guilty. He might, or might not, have his day in court, but my role right now is to make sure he is treated fairly, and it was very clear to me that he was not being treated fairly.

Armstrong: *You believe he was being tried in the media?*

Selig: Oh yeah. Without a doubt. He is definitely being tried in the media. And not only tried, he was being convicted in the media. No one was being careful about what they said or how they said it. The media was judge and jury and they were just waiting for him to be locked up. A lot of times they weren't even using the word allegedly.

Armstrong: *You saw this as a challenge?*

Selig: I didn't take him on because it was a challenge, but I definitely saw it as a challenge. Part of the problem was the unfair accusations. The other problem was his own behavior. It was very apparent to me that what needed to change was his behavior. Some of the antics just couldn't continue.

Armstrong: *Where do you think this trial by media concept evolved from? O.J. Simpson?*

Selig: It probably started there. But I think it really took on a life of its own with these twenty-four-hour news cycles. When you're reporting twenty-four hours, you need a lot of material.

Armstrong: *What's the rationale behind having Drew continue to appear on national TV? You know Larry King and the Today show?*

Selig: I think there are two schools of thought. There are the legal issues, and the public perception issues. I think a lot of damage had already been done to his public persona in the very beginning of this case. It was important for us to show more of what he's like, outside of that goofy guy. When things still come up, where Drew does this or that, people ask me "Well, aren't you trying to improve his image?" I tell them "I'm not trying to change Drew. Drew is Drew. Love him or hate him or whatever. He is what he is." But he's more than a goofy guy who stands outside his house trying to play tricks on the media. There's more to him than that. There is a very serious side to him. He is an excellent father.

Armstrong: *Do you try to manipulate the media?*

Selig: No. I don't expect the media to softball, just to get him on a show. We try to have an understanding of what we'll discuss, and what we won't, but we don't tell them what to do at all. That would serve no purpose at all. I do try to avoid attack-only interviews, where all they're interested in is convicting Drew. As long as they do allow him to speak, and give his side, that's all we can ask for. We never stipulate you can't be tough. We only insist they be fair.

Armstrong: *Is the Drew we see on television the real Drew? For example, when he boasts about his celebrity?*

Selig: Sometimes the opposite of what you see is true. Sometimes when someone is nervous they have to act tougher. Or if they're vilified, they try to show they don't care. We all tend to over-compensate. People aren't usually as they appear in live interviews. I think some people view Drew as cocky, like "Come and get me." Sometimes, though it's good to be humble. And in some interviews he's been very humble. I just tell him to be himself, and I think that's starting to come across.

Armstrong: *What has been your game plan in the court of public opinion given the fact that most people believe that Drew is guilty?*

Selig: People have shaped their opinions based only on what they've heard. They don't know everything I know about Drew. They don't have the full story because they have been fed only the side that implies his guilt. That, for the most part, is the story the media has wanted to tell. But it's important for me to do everything I can to set the record straight because that will be important if charges are ever brought.

Armstrong: *What were your feelings about the polygraph?*

Selig: I urged the taking of the polygraph even though Joel Brodsky, as an attorney, did not initially want Drew to take one. I knew the polygraph would be big news. Drew wanted to take one and my job, frankly, is to change public opinion. And let's face it, with the vast majority of the country believing Drew had something to do with Stacy's disappearance and Kathleen Savio's death, something dramatic was needed to shake up the public's awareness.

Trial by Media

Trial by media fascinates me. Ever since O.J. Simpson's very public trial, I have hunted for a "live" unsolved case—something currently being tried in the court of public opinion—to explore the dynamics of media spin as it relates to criminal investigations. Like most people, I am entertained and horrified by the power of the media to lift criminals to celebrity status, and thrust innocents into the hot furnace of public rage. National media love both innocent men such as Ron Peterson, who lived for years on death row largely due to "trial by media"—so eloquently explored in John Grisham's *The Innocent Man*—and the scandalously guilty, such as Scott Peterson. Major media buzz not only discloses details of current investigations, but impacts public opinion and pollutes jury pools.

Crime stories of the wrongfully convicted also intrigue me, cases such as Gary Gauger and Kevin Fox, both sentenced to death and later found innocent: over 88 Death Row prisoners had been exonerated through DNA by the year 2000.[117]

The allure of this theme really took hold for me when I heard F. Lee Bailey, former defense attorney for O.J. Simpson, on *Larry King Live* in 2000: "When you get thirteen people on death row in one state by mistake, you have a lousy system."[118] In Illinois in 2002, past governor George Ryan commuted 156 death sentences after it was found that "of 263 death sentences, about 60 percent were reversed due to police or prosecutorial misconduct, inadequate counsel or mistaken identity."[119]

This blending of three interests—taking on the trial-by-media theme, the dismal record of wrongful convictions, and the idea of tackling an "unsolved" case—led me in a roundabout way to Drew Peterson. I knew a few Drew Peterson books were in the works, but I assumed they would wait until the entire story was revealed. I wanted to move the story along with an investigation.

Some time after I began my investigation into the Drew Peterson story as a current affairs exposé/unsolved true crime book, I heard a blog radio interview on Crime Rant[120] with prolific true-crime writer M. William Phelps, relating how Drew Peterson's legal and publicity team had approached him to write a book about the now nationally infamous Drew Peterson. M. William Phelps revealed he'd been approached on a "Drew book" and proclaimed, "I felt sick ... I had to have a shower" after the phone conference, but later said, "I wanted to see if I could get involved, because I'm a journalist." And in the same interview, his co-blogger and fellow true-crime author Gregg Olsen said, "It's absolutely disgusting ..."

Since I admire both of these writers, their reactions should have turned me away from my partially drafted Drew Peterson book. However, since I had now met Drew Peterson, this interview actually made me more determined than ever to finish the project.

As I studied the media headlines and coverage, it seemed every journalist had already decided Peterson's guilt based on body language and "lack of apparent remorse." I was struck by these two commonly repeated phrases. FOX News coverage and Internet polls and forums were strewn with comments like, "he must be guilty because he doesn't look upset."

So, now I was more hooked than ever on this story. Peterson would be an interesting story, regardless of what I discovered. The book might even help move along the investigation, and at the very least it would be stimulating. Drew Peterson, an ex-police officer with thirty years on the force, who comes across on television as arrogant, sarcastic, witty, sometimes disturbingly unfeeling, would at the very least be a worthy adversary. Or, I might find that the media had it all wrong, and he was entirely misunderstood. Either way, a great story.

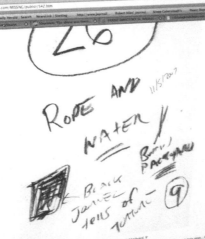

This RV is still open, and your help is requested

Possible related information: RVS42 RVS45 DD5624 DD6254 DD6277 DD6249 DD6536

WHOLE HOUSE
FILTER HAS HER
BLOOD IN IT

HE WILL TRY
AND CHANG FILTER

BLEACH

.15/20.

"whole house filter has her blood in it, he will try and change filter -- bleach"

Even the psychics get in on the Drew Peterson case. In this blog, the dream psychic speaks of bleach and filters and rope and water. Photos of Derek Armstrong's computer screen by author.

Author's photos

Bookmarks   Tools   Window   Help

lansprediction.com & BriansPrediction.com :: Stacey Peterson World's most popular dreaming site's :: I'm not psychic, we all have our own dream, all I did was find a way out of my own mind into what many are now calling The Universal Consciousness...where time does not exist, and

http://www.briansprediction.com/MISSING/public/542.htm

ROPE AND   11/5/2007
WATER

BLACK   BURY
JAMEL   BACKYARD
TELLS OF
TORTUR — 9

"I saw Stacy"

What seems difficult for the media and American public to accept is the notion that a young woman, in her early twenties, with two of her own children, and two more adopted, could run away.

Conveniently forgotten are recent major headlines of false kidnappings, statistics about grown-up runaways, and the currently bizarre case of young Caylee Anthony, who's mother may or may not have harmed her own child. Mothers don't always focus solely on the wellbeing of their children or loved ones when emotionally distraught. Jennifer Carol Wilbanks, also known as the "Runaway Bride," tried to avoid her wedding by disappearing and then later claiming she was kidnapped and sexually assaulted, to avoid the consequences of her action.

"She was found alive but wished to remain a runaway"

In a scholarly treatment on this issue, published by the National Council on Family Relations, Rubin Todres interviewed a total of thirty-eight runaway wives in Toronto alone. That's one city.[121]

The same report reveals there were 971,000 motherless families in the USA and 106,680 in Canada, an increase of 40 percent from 1966 to 1975. Many of these are runaway mothers (or the cynics might say, victims of foul play by husbands). A typical example was given, that of a thirty-four-year-old woman, upper middle-class, who ran away from her marriage and children. She was found alive, but wished to remain a "runaway."

A Scripps Survey Research study at Ohio University found that slightly more than 12 percent of the 1016 adults interviewed reported they ran away from home. Numerically extrapolated, this would amount to 27 million Americans. They don't always stay as runaways. They sometimes do.[122]

The US Justice Department does not report on missing and runaway cases at this time, even though Congress ordered an annual accounting in an Act dated 1990. The FBI won't report on these records since they classify them as the property of local police departments and confidential.

Dear Drew Peterson,

Hello, I am writing to you and I am taking a wild chance communicating with you but I do not care. I just want you to know that i believe I saw your wife Stacy. I saw her at a local grocery store in Peoria. I ran into her on Monday night Nov.12,2007.She is alive!!! She was wearing a black coat,black pants and wearing white athletic shoes. I did not speak to her. I do not want to be identified. I saw her though,she did not even have a grocery cart. She just stood in the aisle and stared at me with those big beautiful brown eyes. Drew,is there any chance that she could be pregnant???She has a little pudge. Maybe that is why she dressed in black.

I am very upset with Dr. Michael baden. I hope that your lawyers will be able to get rid of him. I do not believe in anything he says. He needs to retire. He got paid pretty well for that. I am not fooled.

Please take care of yourself. I know that your boys love you. And just make sure you spoil them. Make them happy!!! Just make sure they all get alot of hugs. Your little girl Lacy is very cute. She will feel the loss of her mother.I pray for your whole family. God bless you.

I hope that no one will think that I am obstructing justice. I did not call the police when I saw her. That will be up to her if she decides to go back. I saw this guy outside the grocery store and he was pacing real bad right in front of me. I could tell he wanted to talk to me. He made me quite upset and uncomfortable. He was all dressed in black. He had dark olice skin and straight black hair. I feel that he is connected to her.He looked like his nationality was from India. She was in the dairy section of the store and all she did was stare at me. She wanted me to see her. She was up at Kroger's on Harmon Highway. I doubt that they will have a surveillance tape of her. Please take care of yourself. You really have a

Author photo of the famous "Stacy sighting" letter from Peoria.

"It is 83.36 times more likely she is a runaway"

Stacy's own family, the Cales family, put forward the notion that Stacy would never run away from "those children." This conveniently sidesteps the fact that Stacy's own mother, Christie Marie Toutges, ran away when Stacy and the other siblings were young. When Peterson brings this up, the family shoots back with comments such as "It's not the same."

In fact, it might very well be more than a case of history repeating itself. Daughters are often influenced by the actions of their parents. Statistically we know that adult runaways, including mothers running away from family, are widespread.

It is 83.36 times more likely she is a runaway than a victim, based on the number of known adult runaways annually, versus the number of spouses charged with homicide, based on 2004 data. This is based on my own calculations, and is not statistically perfect, but it is reasonable to assume the ratio is on this order:

- In 2004, homicide by intimates (female victims only) declined to a low of 1102 according to Bureau of Justice Statistics.
- Allowing for a margin of error, the National Runaway Switchboard data shows 88,550 runaway women in the same year.[123]
- As a ratio, 88,550 / 1102 = 83.36.

"I believe I saw your wife Stacy"

"Stacy sightings" we call them now. So far, various media, letters, phone calls, emails, blogs and forums have reported Stacy in Peoria, Florida, Puerto Vallarta, and various places in Asia. While these may indeed be hoaxes, they are still an interesting aspect of the "celebrity" scenario that has become a disturbing side effect of this case.

One letter, postmarked Peoria, IL, November 19, 2007:

"Dear Drew Peterson,
… I want you to know that I believe I saw your wife Stacy.
I saw her at a local grocery store in Peoria. I ran into her on

Monday night Nov. 12, 2007. She is alive!!! She was wearing a black coat, black pants ..."

A comment on GretaWire blog November 14th, 2007 at 3:15 pm (name Marcy):

"Is Stacy's hair still a blonde color? I swear I saw a young woman down here in the 309 area code. (Note: Area code 309 is Peoria, Illinois.) She was at a local grocery store. She hauntingly looked like Stacy. Her hair was shoulder length. But it was completely medium dark brown. She was wearing a black coat. And all she did was stand there and stare at me. I did not do anything. I looked at her though ..."

And also in Kentucky—

Mr. Drew Peterson
6 Pheasant Chase Court
Bolingbrook, Illinois 60490

Mr. Peterson,

I was in the parking lot at the mall in Florence Kentucky, on the Macy's side entrance on November 18, 2007 and saw your wife with another man. I so happened to have a news article on the front seat of my car and it had a picture of your wife on the front of one of the sections. When I saw your wife as I parked I grabbed the article and looked at her and then the picture several times and was stunned. She was standing between cars in the parking lot about half way out from the mall entrance. I saw a man with her and it looked like they were scoping out cars in the parking lot ..."

And in February 2008, in *Thailand Sun Times*, 01-02-2008

"Drew Peterson's attorney says new photos may show Stacy alive and well and in Thailand. The attorney released the photos to Fox News, saying he got them from a retired police officer who said he saw Stacy Peterson in Thailand. Peterson says he can't be sure that the photos are of his missing wife, who disappeared in October."

Please Help Us Find Stacy!

Find Stacy Peterson - $35,000 Reward

Home

News

Searches

Events

Photos

Stacy's Garden

Map

Donations

Videos

Links

Contact

Site Map

Light a candle for Stacy!

Donations received will be used to pay the expenses of the search efforts to find Stacy. Your donation will cover the cost of the equipment that is used, fuel for the equipment used, lodging and meals as needed for the search teams. Every donation no matter how large or how small is appreciated and will be used in the efforts to find Stacy Peterson. Thank you for your support!

Mailing Address:
Friends of Stacy Peterson
PO Box 1112
Bolingbrook, IL 60440

Paypal Donations:

Donate

VISA

Who We Are

We are the friends and family of Stacy Peterson who went missing October 28th, 2007 from Bolingbrook, IL. We are looking for our lost loved one, and we will not stop looking until we find her!

Contact Information

If you have any information on the whereabouts of Stacy or wish to send us a message, please use this following information:

Illinois State Police Tip Line:
815-740-0678
Family Tip Line:
866-847-5143
Postal address:
Friends of Stacy Peterson
PO Box 1112
Bolingbrook, IL 60440
Electronic mail:
findstacypeterson@gmail.com

Above: $35,000 reward offered from the findstacypeterson.com volunteers.

Below:
The findstacypeterson.com speed boat and flat-bottom boat permanently located at neighbor Sharon Bychowski's home, together with a semi-permanent shrine.

Polygraph

Regarding the Disappearance of his Wife Stacy

Polygraph Subject: Drew Peterson
Session: Stacy Peterson disappearance
Polygraph Examiner: Lee McCord, over thirty years' experience
Result: Conclusive Results.

Lee McCord refers to the chart and his notes as he gives them the results. A patient Drew Peterson and a less-patient Joel Brodsky sit opposite him, waiting for the results.

"To the question 'On Sunday October 28, 2007, did you last see your wife Stacy in your home before going to bed after coming home from work?' you answered Yes. This is a deceptive answer."

He waits for a reaction. He sees none.

"To the question 'Did you have any involvement in the physical removal of your wife Stacy from your home on Sunday October 28, 2007?' you answered No. There is No deception."

Still no reaction.

"To the question 'Did you in any way physically harm your wife Stacy during the time that she disappeared?' you answered No. There is no deception."

Peterson stares at the chart.

"To the question 'Do you know the whereabouts of your wife Stacy?' you answered No. This was a deceptive answer."

"To the question 'Did you receive a phone call from your wife Stacy on the evening of October 28, 2007, telling you that she was leaving you?' You answered Yes. This was a deceptive answer."

"To the question 'Did your wife Stacy call you on Sunday, October 28, 2007, and tell you that if you wanted the car it was parked at the Clow Airport?' you answered Yes. There was no deception."

Peterson nods. "Thank you."

Three out of the ten relevant questions, regarding Kathleen Savio and Stacy Peterson were deceptive, on relatively minor matters of details. On the key questions of whether he harmed either wife, the answer seems to be conclusively no, he did not harm them. Assuming we accept the researched statistics on polygraph reliability, the likelihood is between 86 percent and 98 percent that Drew Peterson is telling the truth.

His ordeal of "trial by media" was perhaps unnecessary.

The matter of the three deceptive answers remains. He may not have harmed either wife, but why is he being deceptive regarding the less important questions regarding seeing Stacy after he went to bed the morning of October 28, 2007 and whether she called to tell him she was leaving? My theory is a personal one. There is some ego involved here. He has given his timeline and explanations of events as he remembers them. The polygraph might point to errors or deliberate oversights on two key points, but his pride or ego won't allow him to clarify.

I propose this theory after having spent a lot of time with this enigmatic man. He strikes me as a misunderstood man, a good father, a moral enigma, but not a killer. Is he a liar? Perhaps in areas that might affect the opinion of his children.

In Peterson's world, his children are everything.

Did Peterson distort the truth on these two key points of seeing Stacy and her calling to say she was leaving him because the truthful answer would be less appetizing to his children? I think this might be the case, but it's only my opinion. A plausible one, but not definitive.

McCord and Associates

On May 18, 2008, Drew Peterson voluntarily submitted to a polygraph examination at the request of his Attorney Joel Brodsky of Brodsky and Odeh. The examination was administered by McCord and Associates regarding the disappearance of his wife Stacy Peterson.

Prior to the examination the subject signed a form releasing Brodsky & Odeh of any liability which may results from the polygraph examination. The polygraph release form signed by the subject is on file in our office.

During the polygraph examination the subject was asked the following relevant questions:

1. On Sunday, October 28, 2007, did you last see your wife Stacy in your home before going to Bed after coming home from work?

ANSWER - YES
RESULTS - DECEPTIVE

2. Did you have any involvement in the physical removal of your wife Stacy from your home on Sunday, October 28, 2007?

ANSWER - NO
RESULTS - NO DECEPTION

3. Did you in any way physically harm your wife Stacy during the time that she disappeared?

ANSWER - NO
RESULTS - NO DECEPTION

4. Do you know the whereabouts of your wife Stacy?

ANSWER - NO
RESULTS - DECEPTIVE

The subject was further questioned about receiving a telephone call from his wife Stacy on the evening of Sunday, October 28, 2007.

Page - 2
Drew Peterson

1. Did you receive a phone call from your wife Stacy on the evening of October 28, 2007, telling you that she was leaving you?

ANSWER - YES
RESULTS - DECEPTIVE

2. Did your wife Stacy call you on Sunday, October 28, 2007, and tell you that if you wanted the car it was parked at the Clow Airport?

ANSWER - YES
RESULTS - NO DECEPTION

Lee McCord

Lee McCord
Polygraph Examiner

Polygraph results from the session on May 18, 2008, focused on the disappearance of Stacy Peterson. The results were conclusive. See analysis in the text. The test was conducted by Lee McCord, an expert polygraph examiner with over thirty years' experience.

Friends of Stacy Peterson

www.FindStacyPeterson.com

FRIENDS OF STACY PETERSON

DIRECTORS

SHARON BYCHOWSKI
KERRY SIMMONS
DEBBY FORGUE
ANTHONY LAATZ

COMMITTEE

CAROL PENNING
AMY ALDWORTH
ROY TAYLOR
CARRIE TAYLOR
STEPHANIE KREIDLER
JACQUE TIEGS

Friends of Stacy Peterson
P.O. Box 1112
Bolingbrook, IL 60440

www.FindStacyPeterson.com

TIN #: 51-0661911

Searching for Stacy

We are the Friends and Family of Stacy Peterson, a mother of four who has been missing from her home in Bolingbrook, Illinois, since October 28, 2007. We are hosting a fundraiser on **March 2, 2008**, at **115 Bourbon Street** in Merrionette Park, Illinois, to raise funds to continue our search for Stacy. Funds will help pay for the expenses incurred by volunteers that come from across the nation to help. They specialize in land, water, and aerial searches. Funds are needed to continue to pay for their transportation, lodging, gas, food, and numerous supplies. It is necessary that we continue our search for Stacy so that we may bring her home, and bring whomever it is that took her from us to justice. Donations of products and services for the silent auctions and raffles are greatly appreciated.

Friends of Stacy Peterson Benefit Concert
115 Bourbon Street
3359 West 115th Street , Merrionette Park, IL 60803
708-388-8881
Sunday, March 2, 2008 ~ Doors open at 1 pm
Purchase tickets at GROOVETICKETS.com Or 1-877-71GROOVE
$25.00 pre-sale or $30.00 at the door
Live Web Cast of the Event - $25.00
Price includes Water, Pop, and Buffet
We Will Have Live Music, Raffles, and Silent Auctions

Information on this event can also be found at www.FindStacyPeterson.com
Donations accepted via PayPal at our website
Or mail to:
Friends of Stacy Peterson, P.O. Box 1112, Bolingbrook, IL 60440

Items for raffle or silent auction may be sent to:
Friends of Stacy Peterson
c/o Kerry Simmons
304 E. Quincy Street, Riverside, IL 60546

One of several fund-raising ventures designed to raise funds for the search. A search of tax records does not turn up the TIN # indicated, although this is an active group who arrange regular searches and parties. Drew Peterson has also offered a $25,000 reward for information leading to Stacy Peterson.

"Here's the case for Peterson's guilt in a nutshell"

The main case against Peterson can be summed up fairly simply:

- Stacy disappeared October 28. Mothers don't run away from their children, even if they're unhappy.
- Peterson's previous wife died in a bathtub. It could have been a homicide or an accident, but nothing connects Peterson to her death.
- Motive: impending divorce, the potential for child custody and monetary issues could be a motive.
- The Blue Barrel. The infamous blue barrel, "warm to the touch," that Peterson's ex-employee Thomas Morphey claims he helped Peterson carry out of the Peterson house to Peterson's GMC Yukon. The credibility of the witness is in doubt because of an ongoing problem involving depression, suicide and alcohol.
- The "wiretap" buddies, Lenny Wawczak and Paula Stark, who claim they recorded incriminating statements secretly for Illinois State Police. Their credibility is in doubt due to past arrests for assault (Wawczak), theft (Stark), an unpaid judgment against Wawczak for $350,000 after Wawczak ran down a man in a vehicle (while driving without a license), and several bankruptcy filings that challenge their motivation.[124] Peterson claims they want to "sell" their story.

In order of reliability, evidence tends to break down into two broad categories with sub-categories in each:

- Forensic evidence
- Witness evidence

The Case for Stacy

Forensic Evidence

Forensic Evidence is fairly non-existent in the case of Stacy Peterson's disappearance:

- No victim. Stacy disappeared but there is no evidence of a homicide.
- No signs of struggle: no blood splatter, DNA evidence, minimal trace evidence, even after several searches.

Witness Evidence

Witness Evidence is far more complicated in this case, as illustrated in the dramatized reconstructions in this book and the timeline critique. Because several conflicting accounts and timelines have been presented to the media, Peterson's legal team have spent considerable time and resources examining the reliability of the sources:

- Richard Mims, whose extensive conflicted account is entirely hearsay, presents a story apparently relayed to him by Kris Peterson. Kris Peterson denies this. Mims' story was paid for, making it "enticed" testimony.
- Thomas Morphey, who gave the most conflicted report to police and media, is very unreliable in the context of his ongoing drug and alcohol use. He had a drug overdose the day after Stacy disappeared. His account fluctuates and doesn't mesh with other witness accounts
- Cassandra Cales, who initially reported Stacy missing, has changed her story in the media on some details (particularly relating to phone calls, and her conversation with Kris Peterson). A background check revealed that she has been arrested several times, once turning herself in to Drew Peterson. One of her arrests involved a high-speed chase in excess of 100 miles per hour. At the end of the pursuit, the Woodbridge Police Department had to Tazer her due to her temper. Many of her arrests involve theft, including shoplifting at a Meijer's Store.

Circumstantial Evidence

- No indications of foul play beyond the circumstances of "a mother wouldn't run off and leave her children."
- The first two evidentiary elements of the case cannot be connected to Peterson, except by innuendo—in other words, there are no witnesses, there's no forensic evidence and, in the case of Stacy's disappearance, not even evidence of foul play. There is no body.

The Case for Kathleen

In the case of Kathleen Savio, there is raging debate over whether there is sufficient merit to re-rule her death a homicide, but in this case there's no evidence linking Peterson to the crime. Without such a ruling, it's a no-starter.

Motive is probably the only provable element of the case.

To this we should add the standard police and media practice of immediately suspecting intimates in any homicide. This became apparent again in an unrelated case breaking just as I write these words, the story of a Carolina mom, Nancy Cooper, who disappeared when she went jogging. Following instantly on the trends created by media coverage of O.J. Simpson and Scott Peterson—and indeed, Drew Peterson—FOX and other networks were quick to write stories hinting at the implication of Brad Cooper, the husband. "Lawyers for the widower of the slain North Carolina mother said Friday that his client did not kill his wife," FOX reported under the headline: "Attorney for Dead North Carolina Mom's Husband: 'He Did Not Kill His Wife'" dated July 21, 2008. This case is developing, but so far Mr. Cooper isn't a suspect, even though national news stories have already started reporting on the possibility he will be, based on family members stating: "Garry and Donna Rentz, and her twin sister, Khrista Lister, alleged that Brad Cooper was having an affair, had threatened suicide and posed a threat 'to the physical safety of the children.'"[125]

w Peterson Heroes!

rson-heroes.html

M.   Detective Work ▾   Eyewitness Evidence.   Help and How-To fo.   Veromi.net | People ...   stacy_peterson_chri.   Databa:

erson Heroes!: Help   Ⓔ

o Density Links: 17 | 23(6) ◀ ⊠

Creat

SON HEROES!

BLOG ARCHIVE

▼ 2008 (1)

　▼ August (1)

　　Help the Drew Peterson Heroes!

ABOUT ME

STEVEN

I am a family friend of Paula Stark
and Len Wawczak. I decided to start
this site because I know Paula and
Len are looking to relocate and are
getting no help from the Illinois State
Police. Their house was just
vandalized last week when someone
smashed beer bottles all over their
driveway, so they hope to get out of
the neighborhood before something
worse happens.

One of the many scam/
fraud charities that arose
around the new "Peterson"
industry, this one purporting
to raise funds via Paypal
for the "Peterson heroes"
Lenny Wawzcak and Paula
Stark. The site suggests
they are in "danger" from
Drew Peterson and must
move "before something
worse happens." They ask
for money to help the heroic
couple. In a separate blog,
this is condemned as a
scam, and not associated
with the couple. Photo
of the author's computer,
during research.

Author's photo

Christie Marie Toutges, mother of Stacy Peterson. A tragic chapter in Stacy's life included the oddly similar disappearance of her mother at forty years of age (March 11, 1998) when she apparently ran away from her ex-husband and her children. This is put forward by Peterson's legal team to refute the statement by various family members that "Mothers don't leave their children." She disappeared before Drew knew Stacy. Christie is also known as Christina, Christy, Chris and also she goes by Cales as well as Toutges.

5 Author's photo

Even the psychics want in on the story. Here, a popular online psychic at www.briansdreams.com, with over 600 "open cases" of missing persons, performs a "remote viewing." His reading indicates: "DP killed her, was going to talk about affair when Christine was 16." Not every psychic is 100% correct, one has to suppose, since Drew Peterson never met Stacy's Mom, who disappeared years before in 1998.

"Here's the case for Peterson's innocence."

"They have no body for Stacy, and as far as we know she's a runaway," Peterson's evangelical lawyer Joel Brodsky says, pacing back and forth in front of his window in a burst of energy. "Without a body, there really hasn't been a successful case for homicide in the United States unless there's convincing forensic evidence such as DNA, blood or signs of struggle."

Here's the case in synopsis for Peterson's innocence:

- No body
- Stacy had affairs and was young, making a runaway scenario statistically probable, and by my calculations this is 83.36 times

more likely than a homicide.

- No evidence of struggle
- No forensic evidence supporting the "blue barrel" theory
- No credible witnesses: the only two witnesses to have stepped forward appear to be Tom Morphey, discredited with lack of supporting evidence, and his own checkered past, and Len Wawczak and Paula Stark, both with criminal records and numerous bankruptcy filings, who claim to have worn a wire and tape-recorded incriminating statements. It is doubtful the state police would allow Wawczak and Stark to speak out on the tapes due to admissibility issues, and the bankruptcy filings seem to give economic motives for a manufactured story.
- Peterson has not run and in fact is active in publicly presenting his view of events. He has remained a stable father of four dependent children.
- He passed a polygraph on key questions pertaining to Kathy Savio's death and Stacy's disappearance.
- The search warrant statement of Stacy's friend indicating there was in fact a plan to run away (see the last chapter "Postscript—Stacy's Plan?")
- In the case of Kathleen, the death was originally ruled an accident.
- Even if it was a homicide, there is no physical or circumstantial evidence linking Kathleen's death to Peterson.
- Motive doesn't stand up to a reasonable degree of scrutiny. Some have stated the divorce and custody were the motivations in both cases, however Peterson as a police officer due a pension would have more to lose than gain by homicide(s).

"No body homicide charges are impossible in Illinois."

Joel Brodsky is no doubt correct. In fact, in the entire United States, in the last one hundred years, I was able to compile records of only 259 trials in "no body homicides."

- Nearly all were based on a confession, DNA evidence, or a preponderance of forensic evidence.
- Twenty-four of the charges resulted in acquittals or reversals on appeal.

Author's photo

Peterson keeps Stacy's motorcycle gleaming, hoping she'll return.

Left: Stacy and Drew in happier times.

Joel A. Brodsky

From: Joel A. Brodsky [█████████████]
Sent: Wednesday, December 19, 2007 11:40 AM
To: █████████████████
Subject: Joel Brodsky

Dear Det. Callaghan,

Pursuant to our discussion, this is the text message that I have been informed was received on Stacy's old cell number: "You my love are the hottest little bitch in the world. Thanks for ridding me like a bucking bronco last night". The message was a text message from █████████████████ to telephone# ████████████ at 9:47 a.m. on 9/20/07.

If you are able to trace the source I would hope that you would provide me, in the strictest confidence, with the identity of that person. Obviously, this e-mail is strictly confidential, and not for release to anyone outside the Illinois state police or the cooperating police agencies. Thanks.

Joel A. Brodsky
Brodsky & Odeh
8 S. Michigan Ave.
Suite 3200
Chicago Illinois 60603
████████████████
www.brodskyodeh.com

> Report from one of the private investigators to Joel Brodsky of a text message recovered from Stacy's phone, indicating a boyfriend.

"No one's rushing this investigation."

There are a lot of good reasons to go slow in investigating a homicide. Yes, the intimates are quite rightly the first to be investigated, but increasingly the statistics show intimates are less likely to be culpable than non-intimates.

The Innocence Project reports on an alarming trend in law-enforcement that has "slowed" the progress in many investigations. Without compelling DNA or a strong bundle of circumstantial evidence, it's unlikely most jurisdictions—stung by major lawsuits for wrongful convictions—will rush to an arrest, regardless of increasing media and public pressure. With more than half of the victims of wrongful conviction successful in obtaining substantial compensation, authorities tend to take a more cautious approach to investigations.

SPECIALIZED INVESTIGATIVE CONSULTANTS, INC.

TINA CHURCH

ATTN: JOEL BRODSKY,

The undersigned investigator has discovered the following:

On January 11, 2007 at 9:56 p.m. the undersigned investigator placed a telephone call from my home number ▮▮▮▮▮▮▮ to the cellular telephone number of 630-803-5005 which is the cell phone number assigned to Stacy Peterson. The recorded message came on which a message stating that it was Stacy, and she had to have her telephone number changed and to jot down the new number which was ▮▮▮▮▮▮, and to give her a call. The undersigned investigator subsequently called again on 01/11/08 at 9:22 p.m., 01/11/08 at 10:56 p.m.. 01/11/06 at 11:39 p.m, 01/12/08 at 12:14 a.m., 01/12/08 at 2:13 p..m., and all calls had the same message. On 01.12.08 at 7:23 p.m. the undersigned investigator placed another call to ▮▮▮▮▮▮▮, and again on 01/13/08 at 7:13 p.m. and the telephone answered with a message stating to please hold while the Nextel subscriber is located, and this message was repeated again, and went to the recorded greeting stated earlier in this message. This was disturbing to the undersigned investigator, so I concated Sprint/Nextel, and was told by customer service that this meant that the telephone was searching for a signal.

On 01/15/08 at 5:32 p.m. the undersigned investigator called ▮▮▮▮▮▮▮, and the recorded message was no longer on the telephone, the telephone did ring and just the name Stacy was said, and a person could leave a message. The same recording was on the telephone during subsequent calls until 01/17/08 where the phone message states that the telephone is temporarily not in service. The unusual activity from messages prompted me to contact Spring/Nextel again, and according to their customer service a person has to manually change to recorded greeting to just the name being said, and this could also mean that a person can have what they referred to as a "network", and the telephone subscriber could prevent those not in their network to go to voice mail.

Signed: _Tina Church_   dated: 2-6-08

> A written report from the private investigators
> reporting on Stacy's cell phone use
> after she disappeared.

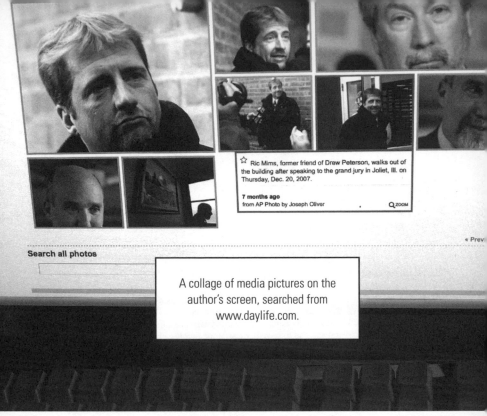

☆ Ric Mims, former friend of Drew Peterson, walks out of the building after speaking to the grand jury in Joliet, Ill. on Thursday, Dec. 20, 2007.

7 months ago
from AP Photo by Joseph Oliver   Q ZOOM

« Prev

Search all photos

A collage of media pictures on the author's screen, searched from www.daylife.com.

Author's photo

The Innocence Project, a large non-profit undertaking established in 1992 at the Benjamin N. Cardozo School of Law by well-known civil rights attorneys Barry Scheck and Peter Neufeld, reports[126]:

- There have been 218 post-conviction DNA exonerations in the United States.
- The first DNA exoneration took place in 1989. Exonerations have been won in thirty-two states; since 2000, there have been 154 exonerations.
- Sixteen of the 218 people exonerated through DNA served time on death row.
- The average length of time served by exonerees is twelve years. The total number of years served is approximately 2,694.
- The average age of exonerees at the time of their wrongful convictions was twenty-six.
- The true suspects and/or perpetrators have been identified in eighty-four of the DNA exoneration cases.

In absence of DNA evidence, or a solid bundle of conclusive forensic and circumstantial evidence and eyewitnesses—the latter being the leading cause of wrongful convictions—law enforcers and prosecutors are less and less likely to rush to charge suspects. Increasingly, it is left to the journalists to propose suspects and people of interest, with relative impunity in their opinions, due to constitutional protection.

The Innocence Project also reports that "eyewitness misidentification is a factor in 77 percent of post-conviction DNA exoneration cases in the US," and that "unreliable or fraudulent forensic science has played a role in 65 percent of wrongful convictions."

"What could they be doing?"

I asked this question early on of Joel Brodsky and ex-police officer Drew Peterson, who is not only an experienced undercover officer, he was licensed for surveillance operations.

"There are many avenues of investigation open to them," Brodsky said. "But the frustrating fact is that we're fairly sure they're not pursuing any other theories of these cases. They're very focused on Drew. We're fairly sure they're electronically monitoring Drew's cell, his house phones, and they're listening in at his house. They're not supposed to monitor privileged attorney communications."

Peterson, who used to supervise an electronic surveillance room, knows how it works, right down to the dramatic planting of "actors" to get people talking. "That's why I was on to Lenny and Paula pretty much from the beginning. Mostly, I was playin' with them."

Of course we know about the Lenny Wawczak and Paula Stark claims that they were working wiretaps for Illinois State Police.

"It's a bit unlikely, given the ready access with warrants to cell phone taps," Brodsky said. "All they need is a warrant, and the cell phone company clones the phone. From that point on, they not only get all the calls, they get the text messages, emails, address book, everything. They can GPS track. Why bother with old-fashioned wires? They could have just given Lenny and Paula phones with the software installed. It's that simple. So their story doesn't ring true, no."

I investigated the state of technology to see if it was really this simple, that cell phones could simply act in place of old-fashioned wiretaps and tapes. I found extensive references to their use, dating back some time, and some famous cases—including a famous high-end drug bust involving gangs and thirty-four defendants in 2006. In a feature article "Is Someone Eavesdropping on Your Attorney-Client Conversations?" by Louis Akin,[127] in *The Champion*, the magazine of The National Association of Criminal Defense Lawyers, he writes:

"A lawyer and his client are sitting in a café having coffee while on recess in a major case ... Unknown to them, a third-party—miles away—remotely turns on the lawyer's cell phone and records every word of the conversation. When the conversation ends the lawyer turns on his phone, calls his investigator, and gets the latest on statements taken from key witnesses. The third-party records that conversation too, and while she is at it, downloads all the text messages and e-mails the lawyer has on his cell phone."

Clearly it's not only possible, it's actually quite simple. Later in the same feature, Louis Akin writes: "When law enforcement officers get your cell phone number ... They obtain a search warrant, call the service provider, and have the provider clone the phone on which they want to eavesdrop..."

Of course savvy lawyer Brodsky has formally requested notification of any taps. "They have fourteen days to let me know" after an operation is closed down. He points out they probably made a tactical error in arresting Peterson on the "trumped up" gun charge. "On one hand they gain fast access to warrants. On the other, they have to now report all their activities to the defense team within guided parameters. We now must know what they know."

"Peterson's computer was hacked, we know that," Brodsky said. "Whether it was Lenny Wawczak planting keystroke software on one of his visits, or a Trojan from a journalist via email—or more likely similar software from the state police—we don't know, but the computers are definitely showing lag and strange behavior." In other words, anything being recorded or typed by Peterson is with full knowledge of the taps and software.

On the first day of interviews, when I visited Drew Peterson's home, he casually mentioned the wire taps "in most rooms of my house." He also pointed to the web cameras set up by neighbor

Sharon Bychowski to spy on his outdoor activities, both front and backyard.

Apparently, he's used to the idea that Big Brother is watching every movement, and listening to every word.

All of this, of course, points to a single-theory investigation. In absence of concrete evidence, most investigators pursue all theories. At this stage in the state police investigation, all indications point to a single-theory investigation, whether because they have eliminated other theories, or because they only suspect intimates, or because they have no other leads.

James Bond or Good Old-Fashioned Police Tools?

These tools aren't just police tools anymore. Software from FlexiSpy Pro, at only $49.95, can be dropped on to any cell phone as a Trojan. Or any VOIP phone or computer. Sophisticated software can actually turn on the microphone in a cell phone, even when the phone is manually turned off, and act as a wire tap. Keystroke software is now old-fashioned, although still reliable, and it, too, can be planted by email Trojan. Accept the attachment, and it's installed. This software does not show in registries of computers.

Are they legal? Law enforcement must be held to the highest standard, and almost always needs probable cause to obtain a search warrant. For anyone else, no warrant is needed. FlexiSpy Pro is inexpensive and easy to use. Even the top line versions are only $150. FlexiSpy Pro tap software is a Trojan, but gets around the law by positioning as software that must be installed. Keylogging software, another way of monitoring activities, is even less expensive, and the better software, such as WebWatcher, is almost good enough to be used by the FBI. They can even "sift" for keywords.

"Homicides cleared by arrest have been declining"

At the same time as prosecutors and law enforcers attempt to rein in near epidemic wrongful convictions, the homicide and clearance rates are under siege. While homicides are dropping as a trend, clearance rates—defined as charges in a homicide rather than conviction—continue to drop, down from 79 percent clearance in 1975 to a very low 62 percent in 2005.[128]

Clearly, this is not ineffective law enforcement, but more careful prosecution, an attempt to ensure fewer wrongful convictions. Few would argue with a drop in the murder clearance rate (charges laid), if it results in fewer wrongful convictions. In 1975, 16,744 homicides were reported, and 13,228 cleared as suspects were charged. In 2005, 14,772 homicides were reported, but only 9,159 cleared. Still, the drop in homicides, is reassuring.

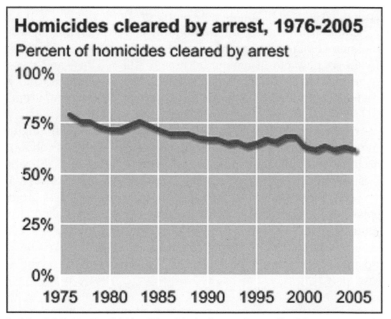

Homicides cleared by arrest, 1976-2005
Percent of homicides cleared by arrest

Statistics: U.S. Department of Justice, Office of Justice Programs Bureau of Statistics.

Intimate Homicides

Putting aside the original autopsy findings of an accidental drowning in the case of Kathleen Savio's death, statistics from the US Department of Justice don't seem to support the intimate homicide suspect assumption.

Only 10.9 percent of 64,520 homicide victims between 1976 and 2005, were "killed by an intimate" versus 53.9 percent killed by a non-intimate, and the numbers are declining rapidly.[129] As a practical matter, however, investigators still consider intimates as prime suspects (and often sole investigated suspects) as espoused in somewhat dated classics such as *Practical Homicide Investigation*,[130] long recognized as the definitive resource for homicide detectives. In this book, investigators are coached based on 1992 FBI data: "Statistics indicate that most women who are murdered in the United States are killed by former husbands, lovers and friends." Current data indicates that less that 30 percent of female murder victims are killed by an intimate.[131]

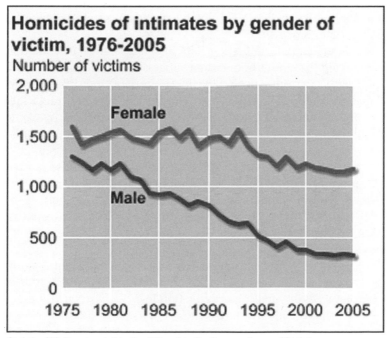

Homicides of intimates by gender of victim, 1976-2005
Number of victims

Statistics: U.S. Department of Justice, Office of Justice Programs Bureau of Statistics.

Robert Snow wrote in his popular text *Murder 101: Homicide and its Investigation*: "When I first became a police officer more than thirty-six years ago, a large percentage of the murders we saw then were intimate partner murders. This type of murder is relatively easy to solve. Unfortunately for the homicide clearance rate, though, this type of murder is no longer prevalent."[132]

Recently, the JonBenet Ramsey case made it clear that even where authorities automatically suspect intimates—in JonBenet's case, her parents—this line of thinking can become exclusive, preventing investigation of other viable suspects. In 1998, DNA evidence should have cleared the intimates, but they remained under suspicion. Twelve years after her death in 1996, the Boulder County District Attorney wrote a letter to John Ramsey re-affirming that DNA evidence cleared them and apologizing.

Boulder County District Attorney Mary Lacy blamed "evidence reported by the media" rather than "evidence that had been tested in court" for suspicions cast on the Ramseys as the case was investigated, suspicions that she said "created an ongoing living hell for the Ramsey family and their friends."

John Ramsey added, "It became an entertainment event for a lot of the media, sadly ... It boosted ratings, attracted viewers, to develop that controversy."[133]

The Department of Justice data also suggests that women are just as likely to commit homicide against their male partners. Some of this data is currently buried in the category of "multiple offender" killing because statistically women are more likely to contract a killer than men. In addition, many homicides of men intimates by women are through poisons, which often go undetected. Department of Justice statistics also show that women are "nine times as likely as men to be acquitted in the trial for the murder of a spouse, and ten times more likely to receive probation instead of prison time."[134]

In a Harvard School of Public Health study in 2008, it was found that, "among men who killed their female intimate partner with a firearm, 59 percent also took their own life" making it "the norm."[135]

Extrapolating the mathematical odds from these data—in the event Stacy Peterson's disappearance is later linked to a homicide, or Kathleen Savio's death is ruled a homicide—there's a 70 percent likelihood that the homicide was the act of a non-intimate, especially given the norm that 59 percent of intimate homicide perpetrators commit suicide. In the event that either of these incidents is later linked to an "intimate," there are several intimates in the peculiar world of the Petersons who could equally be considered suspects.

In other words, by way of mathematical modeling, although the intimates should be pursued in any investigation, at least 70 percent of any allocation of investigative resources should be applied to alternative theories, and of the 30 percent of resources allocated to "intimates" theories, sizable resources should be allocated to investigating alternative intimates.

"Why aren't there alternative theories?"

A quick survey of the appalling statistics of "wrongful convictions" of intimates is reason enough for a more thorough investigation of alternative theories, especially if combined with the declining statistics in intimate-related homicides.

Stacy Peterson is not the first woman to mysteriously disappear in Will County. Lisa Stebic also disappeared similarly, and likewise her husband became the prime suspect, although the case is now cold at more than a year old. Is there a link between the two cases?

The disappearance of women in similar circumstances in the same area, within a year of each other seems to suggest at least one alternative theory could exist. Could there be a random stalker? The probability is not as remote as investigators and media seem to believe, considering the proximity in time and region of two possible victims, Stacy Peterson and Lisa Stebic.

Alternative theories that should likewise be explored might include:

- Runaway: young, attractive people can feel the lure of freedom from responsibility, even when they have children. There are over 115,000 runaways each year.[136]
- One of her boyfriends (flings) might have done her harm.
- Random assault or victimization, as seen in dozens of cases each year where intimates were first suspected.
- Other intimates, such as brothers, sisters, cousins, friends could be involved.

- Revenge runaway scenario, while quite rare and improbable, is not unknown. The "victim" runs away, knowing an intimate will be in trouble for it.
- A remote possibility can include a serial assaulter.
- A very remote possibility put forward in a "Police" Blog: "And it is my opinion that Stacy Peterson killed Drew's third wife. Stacy knew that Drew would collect $1,000,000.00 in life insurance money plus another $600,000.00 in assets if the third wife was out of the picture ... Her brother is a convicted child molester and the rest of the family is just as *****."[137]

Note: Drew Peterson states this theory is "improbable" since Stacy was "no match for Kathy physically." It is presented only to round out the possibilities. There are inevitably more.

Typically, detectives with long caseloads and low clearance rates do not pursue a long shopping list of alternative theories. With polygraph results in hand, however, this seems to be a case that requires a more elaborate investigation into the alternatives.

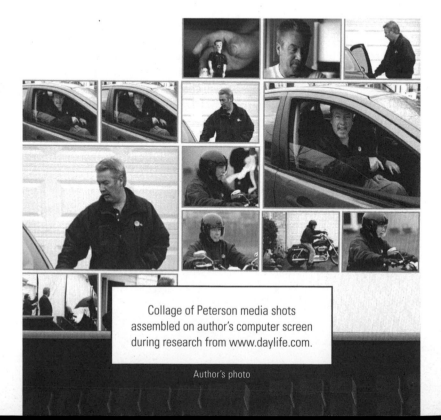

Collage of Peterson media shots assembled on author's computer screen during research from www.daylife.com.

Author's photo

Drew Peterson's weekly
fan mail

His notoriety in the national media has brought both fan mail and hate mail, often with phone numbers, contact information, scented envelopes and lipstick impressions. The hate mail is more often unsigned and tends to be out-numbered by the fan mail about four to one. The most common request in fan mail is for an autographed item, which will often appear later on eBay. Various samples of hate and love mail on next spreads.

Author's photo

Mr. Peterson

for the followi...

this. We are all in...
which you are Mr...

you something. Where...
weeks ago in Peru, th...
pumping fuel next to...
wondering. Please answer...

Thank you very much Mr. Pe...
not bothering you in anywa...
meant to do so.

Also can you a...
enclosed photo, and book plate...
for that is I collect autographs...
collection. I never sell them or m...
out for public viewing. Mainly collect...

04304513

for my letter to you is

I would like to tell you

t until proven guilty.

son

And I have to ask

t a Shell a few

ght you were

Just was

f you can.

n. Hope I am

se I never

ph the

cason

my

hem

II

C036

APR.20.08
I JUST WANTE
TO KNOW THAT
LOOKED
The "LADY KING"
"STEW" IT was nice
who did for
you on "FOX". That
WAS good. Please
TAKE CARE
A FRIEND"

March 26th 2008

ife of a retired police

r the auto

A Celebrity "Post" Script.

Almost certainly the most disturbing factor in this case is the awkward reverse-celebrity national headlines can bring. Let's call this a cool celebrity post-script.

The Constitution protects freedom of the press, including the right of this author to his reporting freedom, and this is the way it should be. The flaw with this system is the tendency, in our twenty-four-hour-a-day news environment, to yield to reporting on "persons of interest" and "suspicious circumstances" sometimes with dire results. If we are too quick to report, we can hamper investigations, allow perpetrators to escape, even cause harm. In a free-press world it is more than fine to "presume guilt." If it means a few destroyed lives, anxious children and the odd suicide, then that's the cost of freedom of information.

On the flipside of this is the right to be presumed innocent until proven guilty in a court of law. An anxious American public, more worried about perpetrators escaping justice, seems somewhat more willing today to allow a few innocents to go to death row. A small price to pay, it seems. Fortunately, our system is supposed to prevent this, and often does, especially with the help of wonderful groups such as The Innocence Project, a group that has already been responsible for exonerating over two hundred innocents through DNA evidence.

As long as we have freedom of the press and freedom of information (including this book) we will have the occasional miscarriage of justice. This is the price we must pay for this high concept in a free society.

The other outcome of this aggressive coverage, largely a phenomenon of superstars such as Larry King, Nancy Grace and even Oprah Winfrey, is that notorious suspects become celebrities.

I may have come around to the notion that Peterson is innocent—I'm at least 80 percent convinced of this, based on the polygraphs and my other investigations. But this is my opinion.

What is interesting, though, is the celebrity that comes along with notoriety.

HaTe

11/16/0?

Dear Mr. Peterson,

I ask only that you would read this entirely before discarding. Thank you.

The Lord Jesus has been watching you ALL your life. He has seen every decision, action, & choice you've ever made. He has heard every word you've ever spoken.

Mr. Peterson, if you have committed these two barbaric and cowardly acts of murder, I strongly urge you to confess these sins before the Holy LORD God, and REPENT. If your words have been untruthful, I strongly urge you to confess these lies also.

Mr. Peterson, God loves you. He is HOLY, and you & I cannot come into or be in His presence with sin. I IMPLORE you, Mr. Peterson to receive the Lord Jesus by faith as your Savior TODAY. He came to earth to die for your sins and mine.

We have a choice: heaven as a free gift and being totally forgiven. The other option in ETERNAL damnation & punishment in HELL — FOREVER.

Mr. Peterson, now YOU have a choice to make today. If you are guilty of committing these deaths, you will be held accountable on Judgement Day. Judgement is coming to us all. Count on it.

Mr. Peterson, if you have killed these two women you may get away with it here on earth. BUT NOT ON JUDGEMENT DAY. Eternal torment and punishment is something no one here can fully comprehend. Plus, it is FOREVER, for ETERNITY.

If you are innocent, then you have nothing to fear. If the LORD Jesus is your savior, you will have no shame or guilt.

Mr. Peterson, again if you've never been reconciled to God thru His Son, I urge to come to him TODAY. If you have never experienced His love and forgiveness, come to HIM by faith today.

Mr. Peterson, your own very soul is at stake here for ETERNITY. Where you spend eternity is ALL that matters now.

People are praying for you, Mr. Peterson. Experience God's love and forgiveness today. Or you will experience HIS eternal wrath + anger.

REMEMBER, Mr. Peterson, the Lord Jesus has seen all we have done, and all the words we've spoken — WHETHER true or untrue.

Please, PONDER these four verses from the Bible — God's INERRANT words to you and me.

HATE

HaTe

Dear Sline bag murderer—

You are one of the lowest
life forms on planet Earth. The
country and you both know that
you killed both Kathleen and Stacy.
It's just a matter of time before
they haul your pathetic ass into
jail. You won't get away with this.
You think that you're smarter than
everyone else. You're not. It's going
to be great to watch the news the
day that they cuff you and lead
you off.

What a miserable human being
you are. You have murdered the
mothers of 4 of your children. Once
these kids realize that it was you
who took their mom's away, they'll
view you as the piece of shit that
you are. I'm sure that there is a
special place in hell with a
reserved sign on it waiting for you.

It's just a matter of time, Drewey!

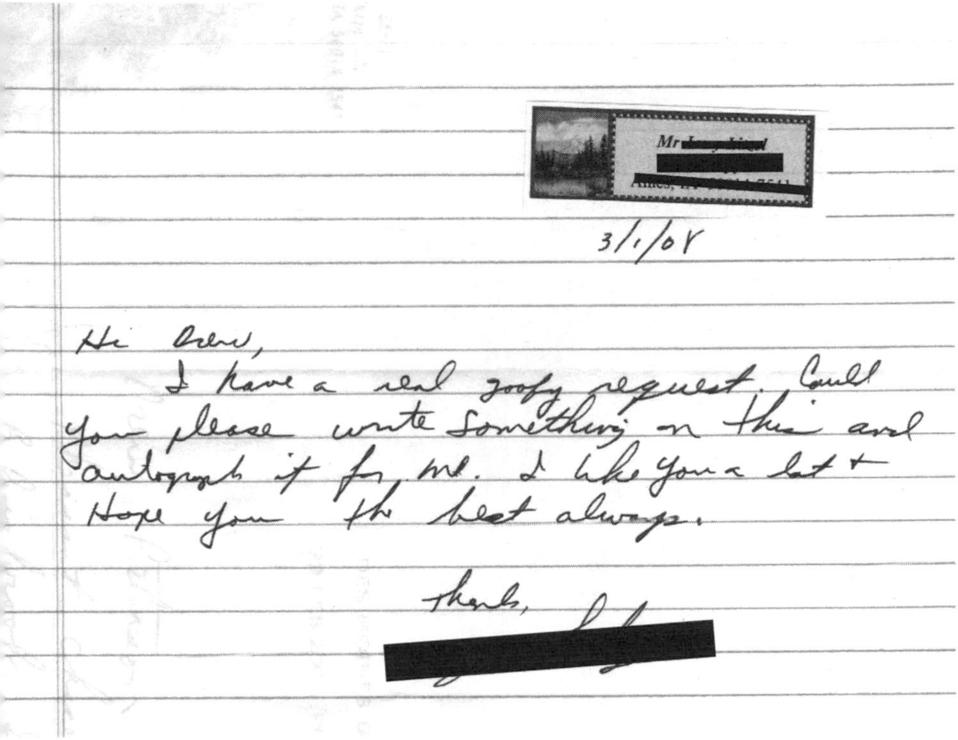

3/1/08

Hi Drew,
   I have a real goofy request. Could you please write something on this and autograph it for me. I like you a lot & Hope you the best always.

            thanks,
[redacted]

LoVe

Happy Mr. Mom Mother's Day!
You are one of the most dedicated
Parents I have ever had the pleasure
to know. I hope by the time this
reaches you my scent will not have
evaporated. I absolutely believe you and
in you! My intention was to let you know
I believed in you. The connection we made
from day one has been an unexpected and
wonderful joy Drew. I
look forward to the day   Just a little
I can please & spoil you   tease babe, my
in a way you have never   lips desire to open
known.   wide ↓ For you!
              ME xo

Drew,

I am a former Illinois State Trooper and can totally sympathize with your situation. Last weekend I was in the Chicago area for Army reserve drill and decided to drive by your house. I was appalled at the radio circus surrounding your house. I told my sons that this is a prime example of an innocent person being tried and convicted in the public opinion of something that a person is totally innocent of. I personally know how quickly your "friends" and co-workers can turn against you when sensational accusations are made. I just want you to know that you and your children are in my thoughts and prayers. I believe in you and hope everything turns out OK for you and your family.

Sincerely,

LoVe

Most famous of all in these types of scenarios, would be The Night Stalker, Ramirez, who married one of his avid fans on death row.

Peterson, too, who I now believe to be innocent, has fans who:

- believe he is innocent, or
- believe he is guilty, but don't care because he's famous.

Letters to a Killer?

I use the term "killer" lightly here, since I intend to leave this book on a somewhat light note. No, I'm not making light of the tragedies:

- Kathy Savio is dead, by homicide or accident, a real tragedy.
- Stacy is a mystery, although I'm now convinced the mystery has nothing to do with Peterson.
- Peterson's life was ruined: he was forced to resign, vilified in public, crucified in the media.

But the upside for Peterson, tragedy and all, is that over the course of the last couple of months he received hundreds of fan letters, and dozens of hate mail. I suppose it's an interesting analysis, as a "post" script to this book, to look at these interesting letters.

One letter stands out as very special. Covered in real lipstick kisses, and still smelling of fragrance, it is a love letter to Peterson. There are dozens of these, including several penned by the same woman. There is also some very colorful hate mail, some very ominous threats, and a few offers to help Peterson find religion. I'll quote some of the more fun one-liners here (un-edited), and I hope some of the letters make it into our elaborate picture gallery:

- Believe in yourself … I am the former wife of a retired police officer. As you well know, the public does not and cannot understand what goes on in our towns … I cannot understand why the public is reacting the way they are, making you out to be a monster. The crime being committed is against you and your family …
- You won't have trouble finding a woman … I wish it was me.

- Keep you head held high … I'll say a prayer for you and your family.
- You looked great on the "Larry King" show.
- Drew, You will be alright.
- Mr. Peterson, I stand by you all the way. Even my girlfriend of three years. We both are with you in this. Your kids have a great dad.
- Please don't think I'm a nutcase for writing to you. I'm an attractive blond who is very intelligent, married twice to military guys. Please keep me in mind if you want to meet someone new. Oh, and by the way, the motorcycle is definitely 'hot!'
- I am sorry about your lovely wife. I am disgusted that more effort is put into watching you than looking for her. I don't know how you deal with this … you seem like a good guy.
- My prayers are with you always. I quit watching the media coverage. It's awful and makes me cry when I see it.
- I just want you to know I believe you! Sorry you have to go through this!
- Here's my number. Call me anytime.
- You are in my thoughts everday. Take care of yourself and the kids.
- I'm sorry for what you are enduring. Call me anytime. I'm a good listener.
- You seem like a decent enough guy and I don't think you did any of these things they're saying you did. Be strong for your family.
- And just over a hundred phone numbers and love notes.

And now the fun stuff, the HATE mail (as if the media isn't enough)—

- Dear vile and disgusting murderer …
- Don't forget judgment day …
- Just what are you doing? … Since you were the murderer of your wife, the insurance policy is null and void … Your minor children will be taken away and mostly likely put into foster care … Maybe you will find the love of your life behind bars. Don't drop the soap Drew! Prepare to be abused daily. All your pitiful life you have abused people … Drew, this media circus

has gone on long enough. End it … now. Step up to the plate …
Call the police and confess. Peace.

- (All in caps, etc): The authorities are going to put you in a box
and throw away the key. There are no words to describe what
a monster you are!! People like you don't deserve to live. Your
poor misinformed mother and friends have been hurt by you
too. Not to mention how unfortunate your children are. May
God Bless all of them. You are going to hell!!!! Good riddance!!!!
These are the printable ones. There are many more.

Ah, the Internet

Ah, the Internet. A place where one can put up a website and
ask for donations without a charitable license, just by setting up a
PayPal account. There are several Find Stacy fundraising initiatives,
and even discredited fund-raising for the "Drew Peterson Heroes"
Lenny Wawczak and Paul Stark. Early on, raising funds for Peterson's
defense, a site was shut down almost immediately with nearly a
million hits and more than enough funds to support the fees.

The Internet, where anything goes and where commenters to
blogs can never be sued for slander, according to a recent Superior
Court judgment: "federal law immunizes interactive internet services
from liability."[138] Oh, and juiciest of all, a place where moderators
can ban commenters if they post the wrong opinions[139]:

- That Cassandra Cales website findstacy.com is truly scary. They
are calling for death threats to be made against Drew …
- You bitter hateful crazy bitch … you uneducated uninformed
bag of wind … Stacy Peterson was no innocent girl … Stacy had
a right to live …
- I think Cassandra and Drew are in the sack together and she is
playing the grieving sister—something is wrong with that site!
- Cassandra is openly gay … don't think so!
- Anyone who suggests anything diff than DREW DID IT is
instantly called DP or drewpies …
- Go ahead and start a thread that states … he is innocent until
proven guilty. You will be banned … Gestapo comes to mind.
- Greta has one up Drew Peterson blog today … They pimped out
Stacy name pushing their website on the first blog. Awful! This
people are scary!

LOVE

12-9-07

Dear Drew,

Hi Drew,

This is Pamela

██████████████ ♡

Do you remember me?

Love Ya!

P.S. Wanna see you!

Love — Pamela ♡

Drew

In the past few weeks you have been painted guilty to many people. As you said this morning, based on the media's portrayal of you, you are guilty. There is no way as you know that they will get off your back, this simply is too big of a story. The only one who can help you now is GOD. He is the final judge. I have been and, will continue to pray that justice will be served in this case, as well as Kathy's case.

However I also want you to know that I have been praying for you. regardless of where you stand in either case God Loves You. Jesus Hung On The Cross For You, Drew Peterson. Jesus died for all of our sins. I think its only fair to tell you what the Bible says

Romans 3:23 "For all have sinned and fallen short of the glory of God"

There is no greater or lesser sin, sin is sin

Romans 6:23 "For the wages of sin is death, but the gift of God is eternal life in Christ Jesus

How do I receive this gift? The bible says.

Romans 10:9-10 "That if you **confess** with your mouth Jesus is Lord, and **believe** in your heart that God has raised Him from the dead, you will be saved. For with the heart one believes unto righteousness, and with the mouth confession is made unto salvation."

Romans 10:13 "For whoever calls on the name of the LORD shall be saved."

Saved from what?

Eternal punishment, Hell, Separation From God.

Drew

God has impressed it upon my heart to share with you at this time, he wants you to trust him, Regardless of your involvement he Loves you and is willing to forgive you, for any unrighteous acts you have been involved in. All you have to do is pray to him and receive his gift. Guilty or not I hope to see you in Heaven someday.

Your Brother In-law

Jamie

Here is an example of what your prayer could be.

> *"Father, I know that I have broken your laws and my sins have separated me from you. I am truly sorry, and now I want to turn away from my past sinful life toward you. Please forgive me, and help me avoid sinning again. I believe that your son, Jesus Christ died for my sins, was resurrected from the dead, is alive, and hears my prayer. I invite Jesus to become the Lord of my life, to rule and reign in my heart from this day forward. Please send your Holy Spirit to help me obey You, and to do Your will for the rest of my life. In Jesus' name I pray, Amen."*

HaTe

"It's all about Ashley"

An infamous installment in the Springer-like publicity antics that seem to orbit Drew Peterson involves his online sex-capades.

"I'm a prisoner in my home, anyway," Peterson said in our last face-to-face interview. "I'm Mr. Mom, surrounded by media, with no job and no one who likes me. People ask for autographs, but that doesn't stop them from hating Drew. So, I fool around online."

On any given night, Peterson receives no fewer than fifteen to twenty instant messages from women—he hopes—who want to get together, or as Peterson puts it, "Who want to get with me."

Of course I point out the obvious. "This just makes you more notorious, you know. And, of course they could be guys, journalists, chubby truck drivers, or eighty-two-year-old voyeurs for all you know."

"I know." He giggles like a school kid. "But it's so fun." I remembered, just then, pictures Peterson had shown me of himself dressed in drag for Halloween. When I asked him about that, he said, "I don't give a shit what people think. Life is for having fun, isn't it?" With Peterson, it seemed, these aren't just words. They amount to a manifesto.

Just the previous day, Peterson chatted with fifteen women—and one guy—by instant messaging.

Inevitably, any talk of online chatting comes around to the notorious, and now legendary Ashley. When I first started interviewing Peterson, I was quick to ask about the online blogger Ashley who claims to have enticed Peterson with talk of sex and get-togethers. Of course, I immediately pointed out my theory that it was likely a journalist or a police officer. Again, he laughed. "I'm bored, so who cares?" Later, it would turn out to be probably worse than either journalist or police officer on the "spy."

By the time of my interviews, Ashley had already disclosed her relationship with Peterson online, posting their very personal and private "sexually charged" conversation online, with spicy chats such as:

DP: Ok so how much broken glass do I need to crawl through to get a date with you?
Ashley: I wouldn't want you to crawl thru broken glass... a date?

Hmm? Where & when?

DP: … hot dogs and a video at my house

Ashley: let's fly to maine for lobster & then come back home for a late movie

DP: don't laugh I'll do it name the terms your that important to me…

The chats would go on like this, back and forth, with subtle humor about cheat dates and boxes of wine and movies on ipods, day after day:

Ashley: why because your Drew Peterson?

DP: I can't even post a photo on my profile…

Ashley: … and let me tell you most bitches are not like me… once they hear Drew or see Drew their gonna be running…

At one point the rumor mill on the "anti-Drew" sites had Ashley selling her story to the *National Enquirer*. But, as it turned out, my prediction was a little too close for comfort.

Ashley turned out to be one notorious Lenny Wawczak, the wiretap "friend." He tried to grab headlines both for wearing the wiretap for the state police, and for posing as Ashley and revealing Peterson as a guy who chats with girls online about lobsters in Maine.

A very "Jerry Springer moment," as they phrased it in Jerry Springer The Opera.

"I don't know if I'll be arrested."

So, where does this take us, at the end of a long investigation? Will Peterson be arrested or not? Very telling, in my interviews, Peterson repeatedly said, "I don't know if I'll be arrested." Does that mean he's guilty? "No, I just don't know if they'll arrest me. They seem to want to."

The media seems to lead the investigation, reporting on truck drivers with blue barrels who turn out to be liars, and plotting out timelines that wildly contradict from witness to witness and relying on hearsay and "paid" testimony.

The Illinois State Police investigators are more hampered than helped by media theories, pronouncements of suspicion and story breaking. Wire-tapping friends appear to break the law in claiming cooperation with the state police, at this point either a story deliberately planted by the police to shake up Peterson, or an incorrectly leaked proper wiretap. Blue barrels come and go, supported by suicidal witnesses. Ex-friend Mims, who was, by all accounts, not a close friend, first steps forward in exaggerated defense of Peterson, then denounces him when the *National Enquirer* pays for the story. His story doesn't ring particularly true against his hearsay witnesses' denial, nor does the story itself sound particularly genuine with wild tales of "suicide pacts" and "hostages" and "snapped necks." To a casual observer, this appears to be a bad melodrama. To an intense follower of the story, it feels more like a profit-making venture, with Peterson as the source of big bucks for as many people as can line up to tell stories.

Peterson comes across as convincing, and his story is somewhat more credible than those of his ex-friends, but still there is enough in the way of disturbing circumstances to concern any investigator, myself included. Polygraphs go a long way to reassuring myself and other investigators, but not to the point where we'd want to stop pursuing the truth.

I asked lawyer Brodsky "Will there be an arrest?"

As usual, he launched from his chair and paced the room with boundless energy. "Possibly. Not likely, but possibly. If they do, we're ready, because we know he's innocent. But there could be an arrest. I really do doubt it though."

At this point, I tend to agree. In the absence of more convincing evidence than I've been able to turn up, I think this case may remain open for some time to come.

Can I make a call on his guilt or innocence?

No, I cannot. I do believe in "innocent until proven guilty." I've presented findings, some evidence, new interviews, polygraphs, challenged the time flows, picked apart the public testimonies—but it is for a court to judge, if charges are ever preferred.

Breaking News—A Clean Break Stacy's Plan?

Shortly before the publisher's deadline to go to press with this book, the state's attorney finally delivered the response to the defense motion of discovery.

The discovery is over five-hundred pages long, and already the media has leaked an interesting, and very telling gem of information that indicates Stacy Peterson might indeed have planned and executed a runaway plan and a clean break from Drew Peterson. As reported in the *Chicago Tribune*:

> *"According to (name deleted to protect identity) a fellow student from Joliet Junior College with Stacy Peterson, Stacy had complained to (name deleted) over drinks after class on October 27th, 2007 at approximately 4:30 PM that she wanted out of her marriage. (Name deleted) suggested to her at that time that she should take the cash money and not use her credit cards to preclude being found. She responded that if she was to leave, she would leave in the morning when Drew was asleep."*

Analysis: This is direct witness evidence that corroborates Peterson's story almost exactly, and was obtained by police not by the defense team. According to this evidence, Stacy clearly developed the plan to leave Peterson the day before she disappeared. Peterson always maintained Stacy disappeared when he was sleeping and took substantial cash. Combined with the polygraph results, this is a compelling piece of evidence that supports Peterson's claim: Stacy ran away.

From noted private investigator Paul Huebl, on his CrimeFileNews.com:

Either *(name deleted)* is telling the truth or not. The way to find out is to begin by asking him to take a polygraph examination. If *(name deleted)* is telling the truth Stacy Peterson made it clear she was going to run away and hide. If *(name deleted)* is lying he just became a suspect in a very big way.

Another disturbing fact is that *(name deleted)* claims that Stacy Peterson never mentions her children in her run away plans. I find that beyond incredible.

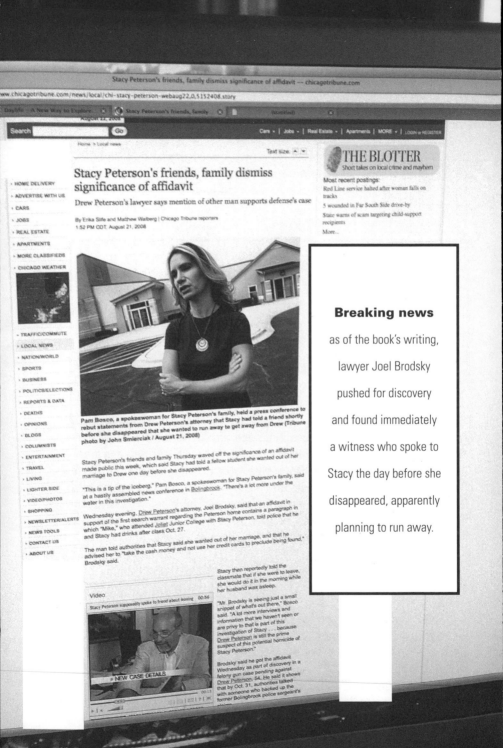

Breaking news

as of the book's writing, lawyer Joel Brodsky pushed for discovery and found immediately a witness who spoke to Stacy the day before she disappeared, apparently planning to run away.

For More—Stay tuned

Since the case remains open, and to encourage a dialogue, as well as report on new findings, news, and future interviews with the notorious Drew Peterson, please visit this new website:

www.drewpetersonexposed.com

I will keep the latest news, pro-Drew (Drewpie news) and anti-Drew, provide a forum/blog for all opinions, report on insider information from the notorious man himself, continue to report on new evidence, and hopefully we'll some day soon, have an ending to this soap opera—I mean—story.

I also plan on uploading podcasts of my exclusive Peterson interviews. You can hear much of this story from his own mouth. I will add pictures we couldn't fit in this book.

www.drewpetersonexposed.com will be the place to go for all things Drew Peterson, Stacy Peterson and Kathleen Savio in one place.

Until then, I hope the polygraphs will at least help Peterson's children find normalcy. I really enjoyed my time with Lacy, Anthony, Kris and Tommy, and hope this book will move the case forward to a conclusion. In life, there are no endings, only journeys. I hope their journey will be eventful, interesting and satisfying.

I hope one day to close this case with finality.

"Polygraphs don't lie?"

Polygraphs don't lie? From all the research, and in my talks with experts, the consensus is that polygraphs don't lie. Based on the lack of evidence against Peterson, the low credibility of the ex-friend witnesses, the conflicted time flows, and Peterson's polygraphs, and the new information discovered in the excerpt from the search warrant, I think a reasonable person—short of any conclusive forensic evidence—must at least give him the benefit of the doubt, inherent in our system of "innocent until proven guilty." Perhaps it is time to stop assuming guilt, and pursue evidence. Until then, the polygraphs are the most convincing and conclusive evidence available.

Based on this, my conclusion as an investigator: case—not quite closed.

The Peterson family fridge and
insets of the family.

CHICAGO

DREW'S PALS WORE WIRE

Two of Drew Peterson's closest friends say they cooperated with State Police by wearing a wire and recording seven months of intimate conversations with the former police sergeant

TODAY EXCLUSIVE
DREW PETERSON SPEAKS OUT

OLD. HIGH AROUND 30. TONIGHT: MOSTLY CLEA

Program Guide   Send Us Email

Southwest

People

EX-COP UNDER SUSPICION
DID HE KILL
TWO WIVES?

Appendix

Secondary Cast of Characters Alphabetical

Aikin, Shanda—Stacy Peterson's Cousin. El Monte, California

Akins, Mike—Aunt Candice's husband.

Alcox, Sheryl—Girlfriend of the suicidal Thomas Morphey who claimed to have helped Drew Peterson load a blue barrel in an SUV on the night after Stacy disappeared.

Allen, James Jeffrey (Judge)—Allen presided over Savio's famous 14 Day Emergency Order of Protection (Case 2002 OP 000460) on 11 March, 2002

Baden, Michael M.D.—Forensic Pathologist and Medical examiner formerly the New York City chief medical examiner, now a "for hire" pathologist hired in the Savio exhumation for a second opinion. He is also famous in high profile cases such as O.J. Simpson.

Beck, Alexander H.—Drew Peterson's lawyer for the March 11, 2002 Petition for 14 Day Emergency Order of Protection from Savio

Belcher, Bill Jr—A witness on Kathleen Savio's Autopsy, March 1, 2004.

Blum, Larry Dr.—Forensic Pathologist, worked on the Savio autopsy.

Bolden, Raymond—Special prosecutor who dropped charges against Drew Peterson allowing his reinstatement with Bolingbrook Police after Peterson was terminated in 1985 for disobedience and misconduct while working in undercover narcotics.

Bolger, Don—Drew Peterson's neighbor, who characterized Peterson as "a jokester."

Bosco, Pamela Kay—Apparently the "spokesperson" of the Cales family (Stacy's family).

Brenczewski, Bob—Will Co Chief Deputy Coroner.

Brown, Carol L.—Peterson's first wife, and now the wife of David Brown, who described accusations against Drew as "very unbelievable."[140]

Brown, David—Husband of Peterson's first wife Carol Brown.

Cales, Gary—Uncle of Stacy Peterson, lives in Hemet, California.

Cales, Jessica—Christie's daughter, who died at two years of age in bed in a house fire, when Christie was eight months pregnant with Stacy. This event precipitated Stacy's mom's depression.

Cales, Lacy Ann—Another sister of Stacy's who died under mysterious circumstances which were later ruled SIDS. (Deceased, Oct. 17, 1987, Downers Grove, Il.)

Cales, Linda June—Stacy's stepmother, also known as Linda Olson.

Carcerano, Marge and Steve—Friends and neighbors of Drew and

Kathleen who describe the Petersons as "awesome parents."[141] Steve found Kathleen Savio's body March 1, 2004.

Carroll, James B.—Drew Peterson's uncle and executor of estate of Kathleen Savio.

Carroll, John Paul—On the legal team for Drew Peterson.

Carstens, Tom—Deputy director of Bolingbrook Park District, Illinois.

Cepuran, Mike—A friend of Stacy who helped search for the "mysterious blue barrel." In his kayak search he found a barrel, although it was empty.

Cesare, Steve—Claims Stacy wrote him an email saying Peterson was "somewhat abusive" although came under fire when the email was analyzed as not written in Stacy's style of writing.

Charnisky, William—Earlier Bolingbrook Police Chief who "fired" Peterson when the then-narcotics officer refused to name a source, then was forced to re-instate him.

Chira, Ralph—Stacy Cales' high school sweetheart for three years.

Claar, Roger C—Bolingbrook mayor.

Conner, John—Head of computer crimes unit Illinois State Police. Computers were seized and then returned from the Peterson household, including the children's computers.

Connolly, Victoria L.—Second wife of Drew Peterson. In media interviews she talks of a 'controlling' Peterson.[142]

Daniels, Rob—Pastor at Westbrook Christian Church, who first floated controversial hearsay statements to another pastor, allegedly from Stacy, that "she feared for herself because of her husband." Pastor Daniels would not reveals details or the name of the Pastor involved.

Dastych, Charles—DuPage County's Chief Deputy Coroner who reviewed Savio's autopsy at the request of CBS 2 and proposed "evidence of a possible struggle."[143]

DePaulo, Joe—Clow International Airport Manager, who authorized searches of the airport pond for the body of Stacy.

Diehl, Bob—A witness on autopsy of Kathleen Savio March 1, 2004, Illinois State Police.

Dobrich, Carl—Commander of investigations and captain of Illinois State Police, who publicly announced Drew Peterson went from person of interest to a suspect, "in his fourth wife's disappearance." [144]

Doman, Anna Marie—Sister of Kathleen Savio.

Doman, Charles H—Nephew of Kathleen Savio.

Doman, Melissa—Niece of Kathleen Savio, who first spoke to media about the Savio's suspicions of Drew Peterson.[145]

Doman, Susan— Sister of Kathleen Savio.

Dorencz, Mark—Illinois State Trooper, District 5.

Elliot, Kathleen—Bolingbrook Fire and Police Commission attorney, witness on Peterson grand jury.[146]

Fico, Dawn—Neighbor of Tom Morphey, the man who attempted suicide after claiming he helped Peterson move a suspicious blue barrel. [147]

Forgue, Debby—Half-sister of Stacy Peterson.[148]

Giovenco, Josh—Ex-classmate of Stacy Peterson who made news as a "searcher."[149]

Glasgow, James—The state's attorney for Will County, Illinois.

Glass, Lillian—Self-proclaimed body language expert and "communication psychologist" who went on NBC *Today* as an expert denouncing Peterson's body language.[150]

Grabiec, Edwin—Judge, 12th Judicial Circuit, State of Illinois, who ruled police and fire commissioners should not have fired Peterson in 1985 from Bolingbrook Police.[151]

Grady, Scott—Attorney for Kathleen Savio's lawyer in Order of Protection petition.

Gutierrez, Luis—Master Sergeant, Illinois State Police, who disclosed on NBC that Peterson was not under arrest and free to do as he wished.[152]

Grace, Nancy—The master Crime-TV hostess on CNN has had Joel Brodsky and publicist Glenn Selig on several shows. Their producers have asked for Drew Peterson, but so far he has not appeared on her show. "I'm not afraid of her," he jokes. "I respect her. But you know me. I'm a talker."

Hamilton, Carol—Drew Peterson's first wife, currently married to David Brown.

Hardy, Herbert—Special Agent who testified in the coroner's 2004 inquest into Kathleen Savio's death that the death was "anything but fishy."[153]

Hogan, Kevin—So-called body language expert who pointed to Peterson's blinking eyes as deceptive on NBC broadcasts.[154]

Holt, Jamie—Family friend of Stacy, who said, "There's no possible way she would have left without those babies" on national television.[155]

Holt, Kaitlyn—One of Peterson's babysitters.[156]

Hudetz, Michael—Owner of A&M Sports who sells ultralights and who was questioned by state police about Peterson's ultralight airplane and its flight capabilities.[157]

Janota, Ronald—Retired state police who claimed Peterson sabotaged a drug sting, although no evidence was ever presented and Peterson was re-instated.[158]

Johnson, Gary—Early lawyer for Peterson, claims he left the team when Peterson appeared on television.[159]

Kaupas, Kenneth—Captain, Illinois State Police.

Kaupas, Paul—Will County Illinois Sheriff.

Kavanagh, Dick—Governor-appointed public administrator of Will County, had concerns over Kathleen Savio's executor after her death.

Klitzke, Dawna—Linda Cales' daughter.

Knobbe, Sharon—Peterson neighbor.[160]

Koslowski, Mark—Spokesperson for Oak Brook Police Officer where Drew Peterson's son Steve Peterson serves as a police officer. Koslowski denied Steve Peterson was a suspect in the disappearance of Stacy.[161]

Laatz, Anthony—Stacy's friend.[162]

Lee, Alyssia—Bolingbrook Police Pension board trustee who voted no on Peterson's pension.[163]

Leiberman, Jon—*America's Most Wanted* correspondent.

Lepper, Jim—Drew Peterson neighbor.[164]

Lisy, Cheryl—Illinois State Police Master Sergeant.

Litman, Ross—St. Louis, MN County Sheriff, whose teams participated in searches.[165]

McCants, Kevin—Cassandra Cales' Attorney who was retained around the time the FBI became involved. Cassandra "wanted an attorney who would help her because she is young … to insure that the evidence is preserved."[166]

McClennan, Marni—Owner of Saddle Up Stables, helped with an equestrian search group of "close to 60 volunteers."[167]

McGury, Raymond—Bolingbrook Police Chief.

Margliano, Dave—Computer forensics team member who reviewed Peterson's computers.[168]

Martineck, Walter—Neighbor of Tom Morphey, who went to state police with Morphey's story after the attempted suicide of Morphey.[169]

Maves, James—Stacy's guardian prior to her marriage to Drew.[170]

Mitchell, Bryan, M.D.—Examining physician in autopsy report of Kathleen Savio.

Mitchell, Mont Reverend—Pastor of Westbrook Christian Church in Bolingbrook, once attended by Drew and Stacy Peterson.

Morelli, Alex—Bolingbrook police officer who has now testified to the Special Grand Jury "whom sources describe as a close friend of Drew Peterson.[171]

Morphey, Betty—Drew Peterson's mother.

Mucha, Randy—Friend of Steve Peterson.

O'Neil, Patrick K.—Coroner, Will Co., Illinois.

O'Neil, Victoria L.—Drew Peterson's second wife.

Odelson, Burt—Attorney Burt Odelson, who represents numerous towns and civil service commissions, said the Bolingbrook board has no choice but to accept Peterson's resignation letter." [173]

Olson, Linda June—Stacy Peterson's stepmother.

Patterson, Marcus—Harvey police officer and former Bolingbrook Police Officer.

Penning, Carol—"On Tuesday night, friends and family of Stacy Peterson, along with representatives of a domestic-violence awareness group, Take

Back the Night, met with Village Clerk Carol Penning to discuss a possible benefit concert to raise funds for volunteer searches." [174]

Perez, Alex—NBC5 Reporter.

Peterson, Carol L.—"Meanwhile, Carol Brown, Peterson's first wife, appeared on ABC's *Good Morning America*. She said Peterson was attentive during their marriage and a good father to their two sons ... Asked if her ex-husband was capable of murder she replied: "The Drew that I knew, I would never expect that."[175]

Peterson, Gary—Texas EquuSearch Mounted Search and Recovery.

Peterson, Paul—Drew Peterson's brother.

Peterson, Teresa—Wife of Stephen Peterson, Federal Agent: Inspector General's office for the US Housing Department.

Peterson, Victoria—Drew Peterson's second wife (Victoria Rutkieweicz, Victoria Connolly, Victoria O'Neil).

Powers, Michael—"On April 8, 2005, Will County Judge Michael Powers entered a judgment in the financial aspects of the divorce case."[176]

Reimer, Richard—"Peterson also filed for pension benefits Monday, said Richard Reimer, attorney for the pension board. He said the current investigations will not affect his benefits."[177]

Rice, Ross—FBI spokesman.

Robinson, Michael—Drew Peterson friend.

Robison, Suzan—Stacy Peterson's aunt.

Rossetto, Keith—Scott Rossetto's twin brother "(Scott) Rossetto said his brother dated Stacy Peterson for about two months years ago and they broke up when he left for the Army. His brother Keith declined to comment on the case Saturday, saying he would first need to check with prosecutors."[178]

Rossetto, Scott—"A police source said (Scott) Rossetto and (Stacy) Peterson, 23, were romantically involved ... Police tracked down Rossetto through phone and text messages."[179]

Rozak, Daniel—Will County Circuit Court Judge signed exhumation petition 11/09/2007 on Ryan, Christina Michelle—"Christina Michelle Ryan, 30, of Marseilles, formerly of Downers Grove, died Sunday, Sept. 17, 2006. Mrs. Ryan was born Nov. 12, 1975, in Long Beach, Calif., to Christie Toutges. She married James P. Ryan of Downers Grove in 2003. She was a member of Rock Regional Church. She is survived by her husband; two sons, Tyler and Colin at home; six sisters, Kerry (Matt) Simmons of Riverside, Debby (Martin) Forgue of Westchester, Stacy (Drew) Peterson of Bolingbrook, Cassandra Cales of Bartlett, Erin Kokas of Redland, Calif., and Brittany Kokas of Ottawa; and a brother, Yelton Cales of Downers Grove. She was preceded in death by two sisters, Jessica and Lacy Cales."[180]

Savio, Henry M.—Kathleen Savio's brother.

Savio, Henry—Kathleen Savio's father.

Savio, Marcia—Wife of Henry Savio and Kathleen Savio's stepmother.

Savio, Mary—Kathleen Savio's mother, deceased.

Savio, Nick—Kathleen Savio's brother.

Savio, Susan—Kathleen Savio's sister.

Schori, Neil—Pastor at Naperville Christian Church (Since November 18, 2007) heard Stacy Peterson's statement, in August 2007 at Westbrook Christian Church in Bolingbrook, that Drew Peterson murdered his third wife, Kathleen Savio in March 2004."[172]

Shelton, Carol—Stacy Peterson's neighbor.

Siekmann, Peter—DuPage County Coroner.

Simmons, Kerry—Stacy Peterson's half-sister.

Simmons, Mathew—Stacy Peterson's brother-in-law.

Stevenson, Kevin—Deputy coroner, a witness on Kathy's original autopsy.

Taylor, Roy—Stacy Peterson's friend.

Teppel, Ken—Lieutenant, Bolingbrook Police, a sergeant at the time of Kathy Savio's death, and once a partner of Peterson's.

Toutges, Kyle J.—Stacy Peterson's uncle.

Vitiritti, Cynthia—Drew Peterson's neighbor.

Walsh, John—Host America's Most Wanted.

Ward, Lisa—Vicki Connolly's daughter, Drew Peterson's stepdaughter.

Wecht, Cyril Dr.—Forensic pathologist. JOEL BRODSKY: That's correct. At this time, the only other person we've consulted with an additional discipline is Dr. Cyril Wecht on the autopsy issue. VAN SUSTEREN: And what has Cyril Wecht told you about Kathleen Savio? Does he think it's a homicide or an accident? BRODSKY: Well, his unofficial review of the initial autopsy, which is the only thing we've been able to get—we would love to look at Dr. Baden's autopsy report—but looking at the initial autopsy report and the initial testimony before the coroner's jury, he believes that the attribution of accidental cause of death by drowning was certainly supported by the evidence and by what the coroner's—what the pathologist found and what the coroner's jury heard.[181]

Zidarich, Bruce—Cassandra Cales' friend, who claims to be the last person to speak with Stacy.

Endnotes

1   November 14, 2007, by Mike Celezic *TODAY* show contributor.

2   "Cops Love Corruption: Sgt. Drew Peterson Free Despite Two Murders," Brian K. White, Glossy News, Dec 8, 2007, 05:20.

3   "Exclusive Conversation With Drew Peterson," FOX News, Last Edited: Monday, 12 Nov 2007, 12:44 PM CST.

4   The word ALLEGED or ALLEGEDLY (depending on tense and content) should be read in ALL statements throughout this book that pertain to any person's guilt or innocence, act or conduct, reported or otherwise, up until such time as a conclusive legal position is taken in a court of law. In other words, readers understand the sentence, "He climbed the fence and ran to the waiting van" SHOULD BE READ AS: "He allegedly climbed the fence and ran to the waiting van." Also, be aware, the author very much believes all people are innocent until proven guilty in a court of law and makes no judgments regarding any person, regardless of the phrase or sentence construction.

5   From *TODAY* show, November 14, 2007, Drew Peterson's body language says a lot.

6   For example, July 24 on CBS2 Chicago "And Peterson: War of Words."

7   Public Survey, August 7, 2008 on Juror Thirteen, with 1597 voting yes (96%) to the question "Did Drew Peterson have anything to do with Stacy's disappearance" and only 31 voting "no" (2%) and 42 (3%) voting "unsure."

8   Any otherwise unattributed quotes from Drew Peterson are sourced from exclusive interviews conducted by Derek Armstrong for this book. Interviews took place in Peterson's home, his lawyer Joel Brodsky's office, a hotel room in Chicago, or by phone, most during the months of May, June and July 2008.

9   "Mark Fuhrman Shares New Evidence in Peterson Probe," FOX News, December 13, 2007, and other stories.

10   "Geraldo in Bolingbrook," FOX News November 12, 2007.

11   "Stacy Peterson's Pastor Goes 'On the Record,'" FOX News, December 11, 2007.

12   NBC5, November 27, 2007, "Peterson's Family Demands Drew Take Lie-Detector Test".

13   Rumor reported on TMZ and later in *The Huffington Post*, officially denied by lawyer Joel Brodsky.

14   November 20th, 2007 2:50 PM Eastern, "To take or not to take: Drew Peterson and the Lie detector question." by Jamie Colby, FOX News.

15   Larry King Exclusive with Drew Peterson, April, 2008.

16   *Chicago Tribune*, "Drew Peterson: Tapes would clear me," July 23, 2008.

17   Gretawire blog on FOX News website.

18   Blog comment on Blog post "One thing to be a rat...Its another thing to be a loud mouth rat fink who brags - Paula Stark and Len Wawczak - White Trash AwardWinners" on July 24, 2008.

19   Text comments to the video post "Murder suspect Sgt Peterson interview, Part 1" added November 14, 2007, YouTube.

20   Widely reported, this quote from *Geraldo at Large*.

21   Associated Press story, August 1, 2008, "Lawsuit against Nancy Grace, CNN moves ahead."

22   Alban Bane is the sarcastic detective in my tongue-in-cheek crime thrillers, starting with *The Game* (ISBN 9781601640017), where I take stabs at reality TV, described

as a "super sleuth" by *Kirkus* and a "tongue-in-cheek thriller" by Library Journal, and *MADicine*, which landed to starred reviews from *Booklist* and as "top of your summer reading list" by the *Free-Lance Star* newspaper (ISBN 9781601640178).

23 *Daily Herald* Editorial Board, published 12-18-2007 in response to complaints from readers that they weren't "covering" the Drew Peterson story.

24 11-04-2007 Sunday Overnight Update: Search for Clues of Cop's Missing Wife Gets Bigger WBBM 780.

25 "A local ABC television report said records of three Oak Brook officers were subpoenaed in connection with Stacy Peterson's disappearance, and named Steve Peterson as one of the officers. Officer Mark Koslowski, spokesman for the Oak Brook Police Department, said, "As far as I know, that's not true." In late October, Oak Brook police said Steve Peterson was not a "person of interest" in the case and said they were cooperating with state police."— 12-13-2007 "Former cop disputes Peterson link," *Bolingbrook Reporter*.

26 Rick Mims: "Sunday, me and Jon Leiberman from "America`s Most Wanted," we're going up, flying all day. We've got some high-resolution digital cameras we're taking up with us. We're really going to search some areas that me and Drew flew over and some areas that he frequented. And mainly, keep Stacy's picture in the news. Keep the story alive."—11-16-2007 NANCY GRACE "Peterson's Second Wife Tells Similar Tale of Control and Threats" Bloggers on Gretawire.com seem convinced he will not be donating the fee from the National Enquirer to the search for Stacy—http://gretawire. foxnews.com/2007/12/03.

27 Fox News Chicago reports on the past criminal record, suit judgment and bankruptcy filings, "Peterson's Former Friends Have History of Money, Legal Troubles," July 25, 2008, reported by Lilia Chacon.

28 "One of Drew Peterson's relatives overdosed on pills after helping the former Bolingbrook police sergeant load a large barrel into Peterson's SUV the day Stacy Peterson vanished," a police source said Tuesday. Thomas Morphey, a stepbrother, was hospitalized but survived what the source described as a suicide attempt. Morphey's wife called police, saying her husband heard of the disappearance, became distraught and feared he might have unwittingly helped dispose of Drew Peterson's wife's body, the source said." —11-27-2007 "Drew's relative attempted suicide, source says," *Police Link*.

29 Interview with author Derek Armstrong at the Peterson house in June, 2008.

30 Quoted from Crime File News: Crime, Guns and Video Tape (**http://www.crimefilenews.com**) "Drew Peterson Case is Cheap Entertainment."

31 Associated Press, July 24, 2008.

32 A phrase mentioned regularly in the media, most recently on CBS2, July 24, 2008, in an interview with Wawczak about the sensational Peterson wiretaps.

33 This account is a narrative version of an interview with Cassandra Cales on FOX News, in an interview with Greta Van Susteren and Mark Fuhrman, November 1, 2007, "Where is Stacy Peterson?"

34 *People Magazine*, "Did He Kill Two Wives," p 106, 12-03-07 issue.

35 *National Enquirer*, "Stacy murdered in bed. Stacy's final minutes of terror," 12-17-2007.

36 Greta on FOX News, "Greta with Bruce", according to transcription on websleuths.com by poster mssheila on November 2, 2007.

37 Mark Fuhrman was charged with perjury and pled no-contest to the charge, impeaching his testimony on the O.J. Simpson trial. This quote of Fuhrman's timeline from *On the Record wtih Greta Van Susteren Van Susteren*: FOX NEWS, breaking news "Peterson Timeline: Mark Fuhrman pieces together timeline of Stacy Peterson's disappearance"

*   Dec 6, 2007 air date.

38   *Chicago Suburban News* October 30, 2007.

39   *On the Record wtih Greta Van Susteren*, November 1, 2007, FOX News.

40   *Nancy Grace Show*, "Petrson's Second Wife Tells Similar Tale of Control, Threats." 11-16-2007.

41   By Danya Hooker, *Bolingbrook Reporter*, Fri Mar 14, 2008, 01:27 PM CDT.

42   Mark Fuhrman was charged with perjury and pled no-contest to the charge, impeaching his testimony on the O.J. Simpson trial. This quote of Fuhrman's timeline from *On the Record wtih Greta Van Susteren*: FOX NEWS, breaking news "Peterson Timeline: Mark Fuhrman pieces together timeline of Stacy Peterson's disappearance" Dec 6, 2007 air date.

43   Mark Fuhrman was charged with perjury and pled no-contest to the charge, impeaching his testimony on the O.J. Simpson trial. This quote of Fuhrman's timeline from *On the Record wtih Greta Van Susteren*: FOX NEWS, breaking news "Peterson Timeline: Mark Fuhrman picccs together timeline of Stacy Peterson's disappearance" Dec 6, 2007 air date.

44   FOX News, quoting Bolingbrook Police Lieutenant Ken Teppel.

45   See note 34.

46   See note 34.

47   Mark Fuhrman was charged with perjury and pled no-contest to the charge, impeaching his testimony on the O.J. Simpson trial. This quote of Fuhrman's timeline from *On the Record wtih Greta Van Susteren*: FOX NEWS, breaking news "Peterson Timeline: Mark Fuhrman picccs together timeline of Stacy Peterson's disappearance" Dec 6, 2007 air date.

48   *On the Record wtih Greta Van Susteren*, 11-30-2007 "There is new surveillance video from the night Stacy Peterson Missing."

49   Reported by WGN Weather Center Chief Meteorologist Tom Skilling.

50   Peterson's description.

51   Projected by Wise and Safe, according to extrapolation from statistics of Ronald Huff, *Wrongful Conviction: Societal Tolerance of Injustice*, 4 RES. IN SOC. PROBS. & PUB. POLY 99-115 (1987).

52   The Innocence Project, "Eyewitness Misidentification" 2008, also referenced in John Grisham's *The Innocent Man*.

53   Refer to McCord's resume.

54   The actual words of Drew Peterson's own attorney Joel Brodsky on *Larry King Live*

55   Mark Furhman, first detective on the scene of the Nicole Simpson and Ron Goldman murders, later pled no-contest to perjury, and left behind many years as an LAPD detective to become an author, journalist, talk show host. He reported on the Simpson polygraph in his bestselling book *Murder in Brentwood*. On page 88 of the book: "One of the first things Shapiro did was arrange for Simpson to take a polygraph test. But he failed the test so completely that the results were kept secret until well after the trial."

56   (Fuhrman n.d.), 88

57   *Larry King Live*—Can Lie Detector Tests Solve the O.J. Simpson Case? Aired June 7, 2000 - 9:00 p.m. ET 7, 2000 - 9:00 p.m. ET

58   ibid.

59   American Polygraph Association FAQ found at http://www.polygraph.org/faq.

60   According to the American Polygraph Association: "Polygraph results (or psychophysiological detection of deception examinations) are admissible in some federal circuits and some states. More often, such evidence is admissible where the parties have agreed to their admissibility before the examination is given, under terms

of a stipulation… The Supreme Court has also held that a Miranda warning before a polygraph examination is sufficient to allow admissibility of a confession that follows an examination, [Wyrick v. Fields, 103 S. Ct. 394 (1982).] In 1993, the Supreme Court removed the restrictive requirements of the 1923 Frye decision on scientific evidence and said Rule 702 requirements were sufficient, [Daubert v. Mettell Dow Pharmaceuticals, 113 S.ct. 2786.]… The rules followed when polygraph results are admitted over objection of opposing counsel usually cite [State v. Dorsey, 539 P.2d 204 (New Mexico, 1975)]."

61 According to the American Polygraph Association.
62 ibid.
63 ibid.
64 ibid.
65 ibid.
66 ibid.
67 *TV Guide,* Wednesday, Feb 6, 2008 "The Truth About Fox's Controversial Reality Show."
68 ibid.
69 *TV Week,* "Darnell in Defense of the 'Truth', Fox Executive Talks About the Network's Controversial Lie Detector Show" by James Hibberd.
70 ibid.
71 Bound copies of the research available at: American Polygraph Association, National Office 951 Eastgate Loop, Suite 800, Chattanooga, TN 37411-5608, (423)892-3992 or 1-800-272-8037.
72 "More Americans Suspect Drew Peterson in Wife's Disappearance After Viewing *Today* Interview", MediaCurves.com, Flemington, NJ, November 20, 2007.
73 "Standards & Principles of Practice," American Association of Police Polygraphists
74 Foxnews.com, December 14, 2007 Post *"What Do You Think?"* by Greta Van Susteren, with comments from 745 visitors, all universally condemning Peterson.
75 Why it makes sense to suspect Drew Peterson COMMENTARY By Clint Van Zandt, MSNBC, updated 5:56 p.m. ET, Tues., Nov. 13, 2007.
76 Popular and edgy TV show about characters in a trailer park that was created from an indy short film, and later spun off into an immensely popular mainstream release movie *Trailer Park Boys: The Movie.* Stars Rob Wells as Ricky, John Tremblay as Julian, and Mike Smith as Bubbles, developed from a 1998 short by Mike Clattenburg.
77 Greta Wire blog comment.
78 Quick snippets of dialogue from the hit TV show *Trailer Park Boys.*
79 **http://drewpeterson1.blogspot.com/** N.B. Ashley IS Lenny Wawczak, as he later revealed.
80 My Fox Chicago, "Peterson's Former Friends Have History of Money and Legal Problems" Last Edited: Friday, 25 Jul 2008, 5:35 AM CDT.
81 ibid.
82 NBC5, November 27, 2007, "Peterson's Family Demands Drew Take Lie-Detector Test."
83 Excerpt of *Steve Dahl Show* segment with Drew Peterson in January 2008 on 104.3 JACK FM WJMK.
84 FOX News, Studio B, Exclusive with Shepard Smith.
85 As in the movie *American Graffiti* (1973), from George Lucas starring Richard Dreyfuss, Ron Howard, Cindy Williams and others.
86 Jim and Bill are pseudonyms to protect the identities of the actual police officers.
87 Source: Bolingbrook Police.
88 11-04-2007 story. Refers to Romeoville High School.

89   11-17-2007 "The man Stacy went to in trying time," *Herald News*, Joseph Hosey and Janet Lundquist.

90   10-31-2007 Headline: "Man says wife leaving him," *Chicago Tribune*.

91   11-06-2007 Greta: "Bolingbrook Police Chief Goes 'On the Record.'"

92   11-08-2007 "Coroner disagrees with inquest finding," *Chicago Tribune*.

93   11-04-2007 "Search for Clues of Cop's Missing Wife Gets Bigger," WBBM2

94   "A history of failed marriages." *Suburban Chicago News*, 12 Nov 2007.

95   11-08-2007 NBC5 "Neighbor Who Found Savio."

96   *Today*, hosted by Matt Lauer, November 17, 2007.

97   Anna Marie Doman, the sister of Peterson's previous wife, Kathleen Savio.

98   11-01-2007: "Police Seize Evidence from Peterson Home" *Chicago Suburban News*.

99   11-05-2007 "Missing Mom: Is Stacy Peterson Dead?" CNN

100 11-09-2007 "Foul play debated in ex-wife's death," *Bolingbrook Sun*, Joe Hosey.

101 Press release from The Innocence Project dated 01-18-2008.

102 *Murder in Brentwood*, Mark Fuhrman, Zebra Books, New York, 1997, p. 89.

103 "Mysterious Death of Drew Peterson's Third Wife", *On the Record wtih Greta Van Susteren* Van Susteren as host, November 5, 2007, FOX TV.

104 US Consumer Product Safety Commission, 2006 Report.

105 http://www.clevelandclinicmeded.com/medicalpubs/diseasemanagement/cardiology/mitralvalve/mitralvalve.htm.

106 July 24, *Good Morning America*, ABC News.

107 Original timeline built from several separate interviews with Drew Peterson, then later researched extensively to add actual dates of incidents by Derek Armstrong, using incident reports, police reports, missing person reports, birth records, and various media as sources.

108 See "I Saw Stacy."

109 See "Do you mind that I'm forty-seven?"

110 "One of Drew Peterson's relatives overdosed on pills after helping the former Bolingbrook police sergeant load a large barrel into Peterson's SUV the day Stacy Peterson vanished, a police source said Tuesday. Thomas Morphey, a step-brother, was hospitalized but survived what the source described as a suicide attempt. Morphey's wife called police, saying her husband heard of the disappearance, became distraught and feared he might have unwittingly helped dispose of Drew Peterson's wife's body, the source said," *Police Link*.
     —11-27-2007 "Drew's relative attempted suicide, source says."

111 11-29-2007 "Helper's messy history." *Sun-Times*.

112 *The Herald News* (Sun Times News Group) "Stepmom: 'The abuse was there'", November 7, 2007, by Jennifer Golz.

113 "Exclusive Conversation With Drew Peterson", Last Edited: Monday, 12 Nov 2007, 12:44 PM CST.

114 "The News Media's Coverage of Crime and Victimization," United States Department of Justice, OVC, Office for the Victims of Crime video.

115 11-22-2007 "Attorneys: Drew Peterson on TV a Bad Idea", FOX.

116 Media Curves data from HCD Research, study of 300 viewers on November 20, 2007.

117 The Innocence Project.

118 *Larry King Live*, Can Lie Detector Tests Solve the O.J. Simpson Case? Aired June 7, 2000 - 9:00 p.m. ET 7, 2000 - 9:00 p.m. ET.

119 Kate Randall 27 April 2002, WSWS, Published by the International Committee of the Fourth International.

120 *Crime Rant*, hosted by Denny Griffin, air date 6-26-08, with M. William Phelps an author, crime expert, lecturer and investigative journalist and Gregg Olsen, a *New York*

   Times bestselling author.

121 "Runaway Wives: An Increasing North-American Phenomenon," Rubin Todres, *The Family Coordinator*, Vol 27, No. 1 (January 1978), pp. 17.21).

122 "More youths run away than commonly known, poll finds" Thomas Hargrove and Guido H. Stempell III, Aug 11, 2005.

123 "Life on the street" by Nathan Gonzalez, *Farmington Daily Times*, New Mexico, April 25, 2005, reporting on The National Runaway Switchboard. This would not represent the total number of runaways, but given the data from other sources, represents a reasonable conservative number for the hypothetical ratio.

124 Fox News Chicago reports on the past criminal record, suit judgment and bankruptcy filings, "Peterson's Former Friends Have History of Money, Legal Troubles," July 25, 2008, reported by Lilia Chacon.

125 FOX News, "Attorney for Dead North Carolina Mom's Husband: 'He Did Not Kill His Wife,'" July 21, 2008.

126 "Facts on Post-Conviction DNA Exonerations," The Innocence Project (http://www.innocenceproject.org/Content/351.php).

127 Feature March 2007, Page 12 of *The Champion.*

128 Bureau of Justice Statistics, "Homicide trends in the U.S.," "The Percentage of homicides cleared by arrest has been declining." Source FBI, "Supplementary Homicide Reports 1976-2005".

129 U.S. Department of Justice, Bureau of Statistics, 2005 data.

130 *Practical Homicide Investigation* by Vernon Geberth, published 1982 by CRC Press and still recognized as the pre-eminent text in homicide investigation methodologies.

131 U.S. Department of Justice, Bureau of Statistics, 2005 data.

132 *Murder 101: Homicide and Its Investigation*, Robert L. Snow, Greenwood Publishing Group, ISBN 978-0-275-98432-8.

133 Reported on CNN, updated 5:57 a.m. EDT, Thur, July 10, 2008. DNA clears JonBenet's family, points to mystery killer.

134 Department of Justice statistics. Summarized data can be read in the article "Let's not Learn the Same Lessons from Blake That We Learned from OJ," April 30, 2002, by Glenn J. Sacks, columnist in *L.A. Times, The Houston Chronicle* and the *San Francisco Chronicle.*

135 Homicide Studies, Vol. 12, No. 3, 285-297 (2008), DOI: 10.1177/1088767908319597, © 2008 SAGE Publications, "Suicides and Suicide Attempts Following Homicide Victim–Suspect Relationship, Weapon Type, and Presence of Antidepressants" contributed by Catherine W. Barber, Harvard School of Public Health, Boston; Deborah Azrael, Harvard School of Public Health, Boston; David Hemenway, Harvard School of Public Health, Boston; Lenora M. Olson, University of Utah, Salt Lake City; Carrie Nie, Medical College of Wisconsin, Milwaukee; Judy Schaechter, University of Miami, FL; Sabrina Walsh, University of Kentucky, Lexington.

136 National Council of Family Relations data.

137 "One thing to be a rat… its another thing to be a loud mouth rat fink who brags" July 23, 2008 on Detective Shave Longcock blog. (Detective ShavedLongcock is, allegedly, a Chicago Illinois Detective) This blog is a high-ranked Google blog, popular with police officers. Mayor Daley of Chicago, publicly has tried to discover the identity of this detective. From a recent post on August 1, 2008: "Keep trying Mr. Mayor! The elusive Det. Shavedlongcock will always be one step ahead of you…And I am not changing the name of my blog for the Mayor, the media or anyone else! It is Det. Shavedlongcock, like it or not! When in mixed company or kids around. Use SLC instead of Shavedlongcock as others do."

138 *Publishers Weekly*, "Court Dismisses Agent's Lawsuit," p.4, July 7, 2008.

139 Quotes from blog comments on various News blogs, including Gretawire, US News, and Topix.

140 ABC's *Good Morning America* [11-19-2007].

141 11-16-2007 "A Cop Under a Cloud," *Newsweek*.

142 11-16-2007 "Drew Peterson's second wife tells her story," *Sun-Times*

143 11-09-2007 "Body Of Kathleen Savio To Be Exhumed," CBS2

144 11-14-2007 "Cop Denies Involvement in Wife's Death," AP

145 "There's only one person that stood to gain anything from her dying. Her ex-husband, Drew."—11-10-2007, "Family members speak out in Peterson case," ABC

146 "Kathleen Elliot, attorney for the commission said McGury does not have the authority to refuse a resignation, and said the board will acknowledge it at its meeting next week." 11-15-2007 "Witnesses head to Peterson grand jury," *Chicago Tribune*.

147 "Dawn Fico, who has lived next door to Morphey for seven years, said the suicide attempt was "totally out of character." While Fico described him as "very quiet, laid back," others haven't been as generous." —11-29-2007 "Helper's messy history."

148 "Simmons confirmed that, telling Vieira, "It was the end of pretty much every conversation that we had when we were together or when we spoke on the phone, that one day if she never answered her phone or if we ever couldn't get a hold of her, we would need to look for her, that something happened." Debby Forgue, Stacy Peterson's stepsister, told Vieira that the missing woman had said the same things to her." —11-07-2007 "Wife #4's disappearance raises questions about #3," *TODAY*.

149 "Bolingbrook resident Josh Giovenco, an employee with Naperville-based Platinum Care, an ambulance service, said he volunteered because he knew Stacy Peterson when she was a freshman attending Bolingbrook High School."—11-07-2007 "Peterson searchers include group on horseback."

150 Lillian Glas, Ph.D., Author of *I Know What You're Thinking: Using the Four Codes of Reading People to Improve Your Life*, Wiley, 2003. "After watching the interview (NBC Today 07-14-07), Lillian Glass said Peterson's hard swallowing, clenched jaw, rigid posture, shoulder movements and more left her unconvinced about what Peterson told Lauer." - "Glass, also a communication psychologist, took issue with what Peterson said and how he said it, including focusing on himself more than his missing wife. "When you look at all of those, your gut reaction is, something doesn't smell right," Glass said."— 11-15-2007 "Body language experts: 'Something doesn't smell right,'" *TODAY*.

151 "More than 20 years ago, Drew Peterson was fired from the Bolingbrook Police Department after the village board of police and fire commissioners found him guilty of disobedience, conducting a self-assigned investigation, failure to report a bribe immediately and official misconduct. He had been indicted two months earlier on charges of official misconduct and failure to report a bribe. Peterson was working under the auspices of the Metropolitan Area Narcotics Squad at the time. Indictments alleged he solicited drugs in exchange for information about his agency. The charges later were dropped. Special prosecutor Raymond Bolden said at the time the charges were not provable. Drew Peterson won reinstatement with the department in March 1986. Judge Edwin Grabiec ruled police and fire commissioners lacked sufficient evidence to find Peterson guilty of the charges."—10-30-2007 "Bolingbrook Police Sergeant's Wife Disappears," CBS2

152 "State Police Master Sgt. Luis Gutierrez would not comment on investigators' view of the interview, but said Peterson is not under arrest and his travel is not restricted."—11-15-2007 "Witnesses head to Peterson grand jury."

153 "The testimony from Special Agent Herbert Hardy at the May 2004 coroner's inquest of Kathleen Savio's death painted the 40-year-old's demise as anything but fishy... she died from drowning... There was nothing to lead us to believe that anything else

occurred."—11-09-2007 "Foul play debated in ex-wife's death," *Chicago Tribune*.

154   "Another expert, Kevin Hogan, said Peterson's rapid eye blinking could indicate nervousness—or deception... Is he guilty of the disappearance, I don't know... Is he acting out of character for a normal person, very much so."—11-15-2007 "Body language experts: 'Something doesn't smell right.'"

155   11-04-2007 "Friends and family search for missing Bolingbrook woman," NBC.

156   "She wouldn't have let her family suffer like this. She has a really big heart and she wouldn't have been able to stand it," said Kaitlyn Holt, babysitter for Peterson kids.— 11-04-2007 "Friends and family search for missing Bolingbrook woman."

157   "Hudetz said he showed investigators Bolingbrook Police Sgt. Drew Peterson's two-seater Aquilla Trike and the hangar where Peterson keeps it. "They asked a lot of questions," Hudetz said. "They seemed very interested in how it works. They wanted to know where the people sit, where they put their feet. They wanted to know how the [aircraft's] parachute works."—11-03-2007 "Raking the bottom", NBC.

158   "In 1985, Janota was Peterson's boss at the Metropolitan Area Narcotics Squad—working out of a "clandestine" office near Joliet, Janota told the Chicago Sun-Times this week. Peterson, for reasons Janota said he has never been able to explain, allegedly sabotaged one of the squad's drug stings and gave the identity of an undercover narcotics agent to a convicted killer under investigation for dealing drugs, Janota said." "We found out from different sources that the identity of an Illinois State Police officer was revealed to the [killer], by Mr. Peterson," Janota said. " . . . We immediately notified the undercover officer that his life was in jeopardy." — ...Janota said."—11-10-2007 "Cop once fired over claim of betrayal", NBC.

159   "Peterson's TV appeal for legal help, however, has cost him one of the two attorneys who had already agreed to represent him. Lawyer Gary V. Johnson, who had accompanied Peterson to his Nov. 7 grand jury appearance, has dropped Peterson as a client because of the TV appearance, a source close to the case said."—11/16/2007 "Can't deny pension to Peterson: board $72,000 A YEAR", NBC.

160   "Sharon Knobbe said she first saw the trucks and TV crews Wednesday morning, before she had heard about Stacy Peterson's disappearance. "It made me a little uneasy, because you don't know why all these news stations are out here and it's so close to the school," she said. Knobbe and her husband, B.J., still took the kids out trick-or-treating."—11-01-2007 "'Quiet neighborhood' center of media attention," *Bolingbrook Reporter*.

161   See endnote 13.

162   "Anthony Laatz, a close friend of Stacy Peterson and her family, said those looking for the missing mother of two are excited about today's new developments* in the case. "We're definitely excited," Laatz told ABC News from the house of Sharon Bychowski, Drew and Stacy Peterson's neighbor."—2-1-2007 "Peterson Rips 'Package' Claim as Result of 'Crazies'" *Illinois State Police released a statement saying: "On Oct. 29, 2007, at approximately 3:30 a.m., two truck drivers were approached by two men at a truck stop in Bolingbrook, Ill. One of the two men is believed to be Drew Peterson." This turned out to be a non-story.

163   "Earlier Thursday, the Bolingbrook Police Pension Board voted unanimously to give Peterson his pension, saying the law prohibited it from taking any other action, even though one board trustee expressed apprehension... While I understand the pension statutes, I'm not comfortable with the decision we have to make today," Trustee Alyssia Lee said, reading a prepared statement. "I am aware that if I am the only no vote, Sgt. Peterson will receive his pension. Therefore my decision is based solely on the statute."—11-16-2007 "Drew Peterson's second wife tells her story."

164   "It's a young neighborhood. There are a lot of kids who are going to be trick-or-treating,"

Lepper said. "Hopefully it won't disrupt them. As long as the kids aren't nervous, I'm OK with it."—11-01-2007 "'Quiet neighborhood' center of media attention," *Bolingbrook Reporter*.

165 "The St. Louis County search and rescue squad has been called to assist in one of the most talked about cases in the country today. he squad has both a remotely operated underwater vehicle and a sonar scanner and has become proficient in dangerous underwater searches" —11-13-2007 "The Illinois State Patrol Is Asking The St. Louis County Search Squad For Help," NBC3.

166 12-15-2007 "Lawyer hired in Peterson investigation."

167 11-07-2007 "Peterson searchers include group on horseback."

168 Illinois State Police Press Conference 11-09-2007:"John Conner is head of computer crimes unit. Dave Margliano is highly skilled in computer forensics. Computers are now a real issue, everyone has them. There is always valuable info in computers. Can't comment on what evidence is on computers, but computer crimes detectives have been very busy in this case."

169 "Walter Martineck, 40, of Bolingbrook, told the Tribune that on Oct. 29, Drew Peterson's relative tried to get rid of the money he said was payment for helping Drew Peterson remove the plastic tub. Drew Peterson's relative wanted to give it to Martineck, he said. Hours later, the relative allegedly tried to commit suicide, and Martineck said he went to the state police with his friend's story." 11-30-2007 "Peterson relative defended by friend," *Chicago Tribune*.

170 "Peterson's one-time guardian ... James Maves, said he first heard about her disappearance on the news. He hadn't seen her in several months, since the last time he went over to the couple's house. "I was there briefly," he said. "There was no arguing. They seemed happy, but who doesn't have their ups and downs?"—10-31-2007 "Man says wife leaving him," *Greta Wire*.

171 11-15-2007 "Witnesses head to Peterson grand jury"

172 *On the Record with Greta Van Susteren*: 12-10-2007 "Stacy Peterson's Pastor Goes 'On the Record."

173 11-15-2007 "Witnesses head to Peterson grand jury."

174 12-05-2007 "3rd search warrant served on Drew Peterson."

175 11-19-2007 "Another 'Today' appearance."

176 11-06-2007 "Court filings tell story."

177 11-15-2007 "Witnesses head to Peterson grand jury."

178 11-18-2007 "Police check Shorewood area for Stacy Peterson connection."

179 11-18-2007 "Police check Shorewood area for Stacy."

180 Tribune Obituary 09-18-2006 "Christina Michelle Ryan 1975-2006."

181 11-29-2007 "Drew Peterson's Attorney Goes 'On the Record.'"

DREW PETERSON EXPOSED

Derek Armstrong

Best known for mystery thrillers, Derek Armstrong is also a journalist, screenwriter, publisher and well-known marketing guru.  He is the author of the popular Alban Bane thrillers, including *The Game* and *MADicine*.

Derek Armstrong authored two non-fiction titles: *Blogertize—A Leading Expert Shows How Your Blog Can Be A Money-Making Machine* and *The Persona Principle*. Armstrong is a freelance journalist and member of the Canadian Association of Journalists. He was also a private investigator.

Armstrong was described in an American Library Association's *Booklist* starred review as "mesmerizing ... the best of the lot ..."

Provocative. Bold. Controversial.

Hot Titles

By Derek Armstrong

MADicine
■ Derek Armstrong

What happens when an engineered virus, meant to virally lobotomize psychopathic patients, is let loose on the world? Only Bane and his new partner, Doctor Ada Kenner, can stop this virus of rage.

■ "Like Ian Fleming, he somehow combines over-the-top satire with genuinely suspenseful action ... Celebrate the upcoming centenary of Ian Fleming's birth by reading this book." —STARRED REVIEW *Booklist*

■ "Tongue-in-cheek thriller." *The Game* —*Library Journal*

US$ 24.95 | Pages 352, cloth hardcover
ISBN 978-1-60164-017-8 | EAN: 9781601640178

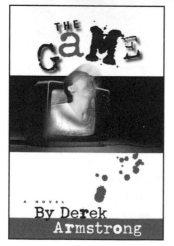

The Game
■ Derek Armstrong

Reality television becomes too real when a killer stalks the cast on America's number one live-broadcast reality show.

■ "A series to watch ... Armstrong injects the trope with new vigor." —*Booklist*

US$ 24.95 | Pages 352, cloth hardcover
ISBN 978-1-60164-001-7 | EAN: 9781601640017
LCCN 2006930183

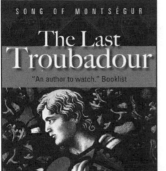

The Last Troubadour
Song of Montségur, Book One
■ **Derek Armstrong**

Against the flames of a rising medieval Inquisition, a
heretic, an atheist and a pagan are the last hope to save
the holiest Christian relic from a sainted king and crusading
pope. Based on true events.
■ "... brilliance in which Armstrong blends comedy,
parody, and adventure in genuinely innovative ways."
—*Booklist*

US$ 24.95 | Pages 384, cloth hardcover
ISBN-13: 978-1-60164-010-9
ISBN-10: 1-60164-010-2
EAN: 9781601640109

The Last Quest
Song of Montségur, Book Two
■ **Derek Armstrong**

Based on the true history of the Albigensians-Cathars,
The Last Quest continues the grand epic begun in *The Last
Troubadour*. Populated with real historical characters and
modeled on Tarot character archetypes, the epic follows
the early history of the famous troubadour Ramon Lull and
his companions as they try to bring the Holy Grail and the
Dame of the Cathars to safety.

US$ 24.95 | Pages 384 | Cloth Hardcover
ISBN 9781601640116

Blogertize
A Leading Expert Shows How Your Blog Can Be a
Money-Making Machine
■ **Derek Armstrong**

- 12 ways to make money online, proven to work
- Generate higher-qualified traffic and sales
- 33 easy how-tos
- Proven to work with rapid results
- Spend time instead of money on your marketing
- Secrets of a twenty-year online marketer
- The ultimate secret—credibility sibling technique

US$ 19.95 | Pages 288 | Paper 7x10"
ISBN 9781601641649